D1691607

STUDIES IN THEORETICAL PHILOSOPHY

Herausgegeben von Tobias Rosefeldt
und Benjamin Schnieder

in Zusammenarbeit mit

Elke Brendel (Bonn)
Tim Henning (Stuttgart)
Max Kölbel (Barcelona)
Hannes Leitgeb (München)
Martine Nida-Rümelin (Fribourg)
Christian Nimtz (Bielefeld)
Thomas Sattig (Tübingen)
Jason Stanley (New Brunswick)
Marcel Weber (Genf)
Barbara Vetter (Berlin)

vol. 6

VITTORIO KLOSTERMANN

ALEXANDRA ZINKE

The Metaphysics of Logical Consequence

VITTORIO KLOSTERMANN

Gedruckt mit freundlicher Unterstützung der
Geschwister Boehringer Ingelheim Stiftung für Geisteswissenschaften
in Ingelheim am Rhein.

Bibliographische Information der Deutschen Nationalbibliothek
Die Deutsche Nationalbibliothek verzeichnet diese Publikation in der Deutschen
Nationalbibliographie; detaillierte bibliographische Daten sind im Internet über
http://dnb.dnb.de abrufbar.

© Vittorio Klostermann GmbH Frankfurt am Main 2018
Alle Rechte vorbehalten, insbesondere die des Nachdrucks und der Übersetzung.
Ohne Genehmigung des Verlages ist es nicht gestattet, dieses Werk oder Teile in einem
photomechanischen oder sonstigen Reproduktionsverfahren oder unter Verwendung
elektronischer Systeme zu verarbeiten, zu vervielfältigen und zu verbreiten.
Gedruckt auf Eos Werkdruck von Salzer,
alterungsbeständig ∞ und PEFC-zertifiziert.
Druck: docupoint GmbH, Magdeburg
Printed in Germany
ISSN 2199-5214
ISBN 978-3-465-04345-4

– to Stromi and Misriy –

Acknowledgment

This book is based on my PhD thesis, which I submitted in 2013 at the University of Konstanz. While working on the thesis – but also before and after – Wolfgang Spohn was a real *Doktorvater* to me, caring and daring. There was never any pressure, but a continuous warm-hearted encouragement to think things through. My gratitude also goes to Holger Sturm, my second supervisor, for sharing his expertise and for invaluable literature suggestions.

Moreover, I wish to thank the editors of *Studies in Theoretical Philosophy*, Tobias Rosefeldt and Benjamin Schnieder, for being so uncomplicated, Anastasia Urban at *Klostermann* for her kind guidance during the publication process, Christopher von Bülow for helping with the typesetting, and Peter Anstee for English proofreading. I am indebted to the *Studienstiftung des deutschen Volkes* for financial support (but please change your name).

Somehow, I always wanted to write this book. And then again, I definitely didn't. I am thankful to my mother and my brother, and to my friends Sandra and Katrin for lending me their ears again and again when I once more doubted my doings.

Then there is this one person where words fail me. Nobody influenced and influences my philosophical thinking nearly as thoroughly and deeply as he did and does. He is the Logic of my Life. And I love the consequences!

Contents

Introduction 1

1 Models of Models: Interpretation and Representation 15
   1.1 Tarski's Definition 18
   1.2 The Model-Theoretic Definition 30

2 Interpretation and Representation: A Systematic Approach . . 37
   2.1 An Alternative Semantic Theory: Form-Logical Semantics 37
   2.2 Definitions of Logical Consequence and Logical Truth . . 44

3 From Structural Truth to Logical Truth 49
   3.1 Grammatical Restrictions 49
   3.2 Structural Restrictions 52

4 From Analytic Truth to Logical Truth 59
   4.1 Identity Restrictions 59
   4.2 Hesperus and Phosphorus 66
   4.3 Semantic Restrictions 71

5 From Necessary Truth to Logical Truth 79
   5.1 Metaphysical Presuppositions 79
   5.2 Etchemendy's Critique 85
   5.3 Modal Restrictions 93

6 Logic and Formality 101
   6.1 Schematic Formality 101
   6.2 Restrictions in Formal Languages 108

7 Representational Definition 117
   7.1 The Problem of Logical Objects 119
   7.2 Restrictions on States 125

8 The Problem of Logical Constants 131
   8.1 The Criterion of Permutation Invariance 135
   8.2 Counter Examples 144

9 Logic, Language and Metalanguage 157
   9.1 Permutation Invariance Reinterpreted 157
   9.2 Metalanguage 165

Concluding Remarks 171

Bibliography 175

Index of Names 185

Introduction

Logic is the art and heart of reasoning. As such it pervades all our theoretical endeavors. It is omnipresent in philosophy, in the sciences and humanities, in everyday life. Logic is not only all-pervasive, but also most general. It is concerned with the structure of reasoning as such. Logic is 'topic-neutral', independent of the specific contents of our reasoning. It determines which arguments are valid and which are invalid. Logic itself is impeccable and thus is beyond any dispute. Where our favorite empirical or metaphysical theories may fail, logic still prevails.

The special status of logic has given rise to high expectations. Many thinkers had the hope that it could play a foundational role and maybe replace metaphysics, the most fundamental, but also contentious field of theoretical research. Where metaphysics even lacks a uniform methodology, logic was meant to provide a firm basis and a neutral, general, and immaculate scheme. Although time has shown these expectations to be exaggerated, logic has had a great influence on philosophy and metaphysics itself. It has purified our thoughts and put those that survived onto secure footing. It has done so, people claim, in an unbiased way, independently of any metaphysical assumptions.

My aim in this book is to challenge this view and to show that logic is by no means independent of metaphysics. Both are deeply intertwined. More specifically, I will argue that a proper definition of logical consequence, the core concept of logic, rests on metaphysical presuppositions. To the extent that logic can replace metaphysics, it is able to do so only because it is imbued with metaphysical considerations. Logic is not as nearly as neutral a frame of thought as has often been assumed.

I expect serious and immediate resistance, based not only on the desire to preserve the purity of logic, but on the following obvious argument. The classical model-theoretic account of logical consequence involves only well-defined set-theoretic concepts. It defines logical consequence as truth-preservation in all models: a formula φ logically follows from a set of formulas $\varGamma$ iff it holds that φ is true in every model in which all elements of Γ are true. No contentious metaphysical notions seem to be involved.[1]

It would, however, be premature to conclude that logic does not have any metaphysical presuppositions. In so far as the model-theoretic notion is to play the role we assign to it, it must capture our pretheoretical concept of logical consequence. Or, if we are skeptic that there is a pretheoretical or intuitive notion of logical consequence, the definition must at least capture some of the essential features we assign to logically valid arguments. Logic has its special status only because we consider logically valid arguments to have certain distinguished modal, epistemic and formal properties. *Prima facie* nothing whatsoever secures that truth-preservation in all models has anything to do with this. As Timothy Williamson (2007: 65) puts it: "[…] the mathematical rigor, elegance, and fertility of model-theoretic definitions of logical consequence depend on their freedom from modal and epistemological accretions. As a result, such definitions provide no automatic guarantee that logical truths express necessary or a priori propositions." In order to establish that only arguments with certain distinguished features are truth-preserving in all models, we have to spell out what truth-preservation in all models amounts to, i.e., we have to lay out what is modeled by the models of model theory. It is here, I claim, that metaphysics enters the stage.

I will plunge right in and draw your attention to some of the central characteristics of the pre-theoretic notion of logical consequence and therefore those desiderata that a formal definition has to meet. I do so by way of example. The argument:

(A1) All humans are mortal. Plato is human. Therefore, Plato is mortal.

is a paradigm case of an argument that is pretheoretically logically valid.[2] The same holds for the two following arguments:

(A2) All humans are male. Plato is human. Therefore, Plato is male.

---

[1] I ignore here that sets themselves are ontologically problematic entities.
[2] Throughout this book, I am concerned solely with arguments that have exactly one conclusion and bracket multiple-conclusion arguments. I allow the set of premises to be empty, however. As I take the totality of premises to be a set, I also do not take into account the order of the premises and that they might have multiple occurrences.

(A3) All humans are female. Plato is human. Therefore, Plato is female.

Valid arguments allow for different combinations of truth values. Importantly, however, we will not find a logically valid argument containing only true premises and a false conclusion. Logically valid arguments are *truth-preserving*. Yet that characteristic seems insufficient for validity, as the following argument shows:

(A4) Plato is human. Therefore, Plato is male.

Both, the premise and the conclusion of (A4) are true. Nevertheless, the argument is invalid. It is truth-preserving, but only – as one might say – accidentally so. In contradistinction to the arguments (A1)-(A3), where the conclusion must be true if the premises are true, the conclusion of (A4) is not guaranteed to be true by the truth of the premise. In a logically valid argument, the premises somehow necessitate the conclusion. Logically valid arguments are not merely truth-preserving, but *necessarily* truth-preserving.

Yet this amendment still does not suffice. Consider (A5):

(A5) Gaia is a mother. Therefore, Gaia is female.

In (A5), the conclusion also follows from the premises by necessity. Nevertheless, according to the standard view, (A5) does not qualify as logically valid. In reaction to cases like (A5), it is usually claimed that logically valid arguments must not only be necessarily truth-preserving, but also *formal*. They are said to be truth-preserving in virtue of their *form*. The notion of form then is evoked in explanations like the following.

The difference between (A1) and (A5) is a difference with respect to formality. (A5) is truth-preserving only in virtue of the particular meaning of the terms "mother" and "female". If we were to substitute "male" for "female", the argument would no longer be truth-preserving. The fact that (A5) is truth-preserving rests on certain semantic facts. The validity of (A1) does not, however, depend on (A1) being about Plato or about humanity or mortality. The argument is necessarily truth-preserving not because of its particular semantic content, but because of its form alone. To illustrate this position, consider a further example:

(A1*) All planets are eternal. Pluto is a planet. Therefore, Pluto is eternal.

The logically valid argument (A1*) is of the same form as (A1). In fact, the arguments (A1) and (A1*) are both instances of the following schema:

(S1)   All F are G. a is F. Therefore, a is G.

To account for the validity of (A1*) and (A1), we need not know anything about the meaning of the particular terms occurring in the respective arguments; it is fully sufficient to know that these arguments are instances of (S1). They are valid in virtue of their being an instance of a valid schema. (A5), on the other hand, is not valid in virtue of it being an instance of a valid schema, but in virtue of its content.

These examples suggest two intuitive desiderata on logical validity. Logically valid arguments must be *necessarily truth-preserving* and they must be *formal*. It is far from obvious that the classical model-theoretic definition of consequence as truth-preservation in all models meets these requirements. Whether it does, will depend on our conception of a model.

There are competing conceptions. John Etchemendy, in his groundbreaking monograph *The Concept of Logical Consequence* (1990) makes two proposals for what the models of model theory might model. According to one conception, we may understand a model as representing a way the world might be. This is known as the *representational* notion of a model. Alternatively, we might conceive of it as representing a possible interpretation of the linguistic items involved. This constitutes the so-called *interpretational* notion. Truth-in-a-model, conceived of representationally, amounts to truth with respect to a way the world might be. Truth-in-a-model, understood interpretationally, amounts to truth with respect to a certain interpretation of the language.

If one understands a model representationally, the definition of logical consequence as truth-preservation in all models seems to obviously fulfill the desideratum of necessary truth-preservation. If models stand for worlds, then, so it seems, only metaphysically necessary arguments are truth-preserving in all models. However, the second criterion, emphasizing formality, appears to be violated. Indeed, the representational conception seems to declare argument (A5) logically valid. For this very reason, there is a wide consensus in the literature that the representational definition of logical consequence is extensionally inadequate and thus fails to capture our intuitive notion of logical consequence. Besides extensional inadequacy, there is a second kind of objection. The representational definition, the argument goes, rests on dubious modal notions: it grounds the notion of logical consequence on the notion of metaphysical necessity, which itself stands in need of analysis. For these reasons, the representational definition is usually considered to present an inadequate definition of our concept of logical consequence.

It is therefore no surprise that the interpretational conception of logical consequence has been dominant in philosophical logic. According to this view, a model provides a specific interpretation of the sentences used in the argument. Truth in a model then is truth under a certain interpretation of these sentences. Given this construal of the model-theoretic definition, logical consequence amounts to truth-preservation under all interpretations.

One major advantage of this conception is that it appears to be 'free of metaphysics'. In contrast to the representational definition, no unexplained modal notion seems to play a role. Furthermore, an interpretational reading clearly enforces the formality condition. Argument (A5), for example, is obviously not truth-preserving under all interpretations: if you reinterpret the predicate "is female" as having the meaning of "is male", the conclusion will be false, while the premise remains true. There is a drawback to this theory, however. The interpretational reading struggles with the criterion of necessary truth-preservation. Etchemendy (1990) famously argues that there is no conceptual reason why truth-preservation in all interpretations should guarantee truth-preservation in all worlds. He actually provides examples that aim at showing that the interpretational definition is not even materially adequate. There seem to be arguments which satisfy the interpretational definition, but fail to be necessary truth-preserving.

Furthermore, there is yet another problem for the interpretational definition: the so-called *problem of the logical constants*. If reinterpretation is unrestricted, the intuitively valid argument (A1) would no longer come out as valid. Not only the terms "human", "mortal" and "Plato" could be given a novel meaning, but also the term "all". In that case, there would be a reinterpretation of the argument such that it is no longer truth-preserving. In fact, if the interpretational definition allows a reinterpretation of the so called "logical constants" ("all", "and", "not", etc.), no argument whatsoever would be declared logically valid by this definition. On pain of trivialization, the interpretational definition must declare such interpretations inadmissible and thereby presuppose a demarcation of the logical from the non-logical terms.

The problem of logical constants is generally held to be the most pressing problem of the interpretational definition of logical consequence. Tarski himself mentioned this problem at the end of his seminal article "On the concept of logical consequence":

> I am not at all of the opinion that in the result of the above discussion the problem of a materially adequate definition of the concept of consequence has been completely solved. On the contrary, I still see several open questions, only one of which – perhaps the most important – I shall point out here. Underlying our whole construction is the division of all terms of the language discussed into logical and extra-logical. This division is certainly not quite arbitrary. [...] On the other hand, no objective grounds are known to me which permit us to draw a sharp boundary between the two groups of terms. [...] Further research will doubtless greatly clarify the problem which interests us. Perhaps it will be possible to find important objective arguments which will enable us to justify the traditional boundary between logical and extra-logical expressions. (Tarski 1936: 420)

Three decades after this remark, in a lecture from 1966, published 1986 as "What are Logical Notions?", Tarski displayed a more optimistic attitude and characterized the logical constants by reference to the mathematical property of permutation invariance. Yet it has ever since been disputed whether permutation invariance yields an adequate criterion for logical constants. It is fair to say that the problem of logical constants has not yet been solved.

Reviewing the situation, we are presented with a dilemma. There are two readings of the model-theoretic definition of logical consequence. Under a representational conception, the definition of logical consequence seems to analyze logical consequence with unexplained modal notions and the definition fails to satisfy the criterion of formality. Using an interpretational reading, it remains questionable whether the criterion of necessary truth-preservation is satisfied, and the definition depends on a solution to the problem of logical constants which so far has been lacking.

The dilemma is serious given the alternatives presented so far. I venture to show, however, that it can be avoided if we adopt a different perspective. Upon closer consideration, it will turn out that the interpretational and the representational definition do not constitute real alternatives. Given certain plausible assumptions they turn out to be extensionally equivalent. Furthermore, they struggle with analogous problems, which I dub the *problem of admissible interpretations* for the interpretational view and, as far as the representational definition is concerned, the *problem of admissible states*. I will argue that both definitions rely on a prior demarcation of the admissible from the inadmissible interpretations and states, respectively. In particular, the problem of logical constants turns out to be merely a special case of this more general and deeper problem type. The demarcation problem is essentially the same for both approaches to logical consequence. The central question of the philosophy of logic is the demarcation of the admissible from the inadmissible models. I will claim that such a demarcation requires substantial semantical and metaphysical considerations.

Before going into the sundry details of the discussion, some preliminary methodological remarks will be helpful. I am primarily interested in definitions of logical consequence, but discussions in terms of logical truth are often less cumbersome. Fortunately, we can treat the notions of logical consequence and logical truths as interdefinable. The standard model-theoretic definition of logical consequence construes logical consequence as truth-preservation in all models. The model-theoretic definition of logical truth understands logical truth as truth in all models. We can thus translate the one definition into the other as follows: a sentence is logically true ("$\vDash \varphi$") iff it is a logical consequence of the empty set. Conversely, a sentence φ follows logically from a set of sentences Γ ("$\Gamma \vDash \varphi$") iff the material conditional containing the conjunction of the members of Γ as antecedent and φ as consequent is a logical truth. In short: $\Gamma \vDash \varphi \Leftrightarrow \vDash \gamma_1 \wedge \ldots \wedge \gamma_n \rightarrow \varphi$

(where $\Gamma = \{\gamma_1, \ldots, \gamma_n\}$).[3] I am confident that this also captures our pretheoretic intuitions about the relation of logical consequence and logical truth. Therefore, I allow myself to switch back and forth between the two notions.

Let me also address a methodological worry having to do with the relation of natural and formal languages. Our pretheoretic intuitions about the concept of logical truth pertain to natural language sentences like (A1)–(A5). Definitions of logical truth, such as our standard model-theoretic definition, are, however, formulated for formal languages. One might thus doubt the legitimacy of discussing these definitions with recourse to natural language examples on the grounds that, in order to test whether or not a certain natural language sentence is declared logically true by a given definition of logical truth, we have to first *formalize* the respective sentence. It is therefore important to say something about formalization.

A formalization is a function[4] f from a class N of natural language sentences on a class F of sentences in our chosen formal language. A formal definition D of logical truth determines for each sentence of the formal language whether or not it is logically true. We can think of this classification as a function g^D from the class F on the set $\{0, 1\}$: the function g^D maps a sentence to 1 just in case it is declared a logical truth according to the definition D, and to 0 otherwise. Our intuitive judgments whether or not a given sentence is logically true apply to sentences in natural language. We can also model this intuitive classification of natural language sentences by a function. Let h be a function mapping a natural language sentence to 0 or 1. We then judge the definition D of logical truth as extensionally adequate iff $g^D(f(p)) = h(p)$ for every sentence $p \in N$.

---

[3] This equivalence only holds if we assume that the set Γ of premises is finite or assume that the language allows infinite conjunctions. This limitation will not play any role in the present discussion.

[4] By calling f a *function*, I make the simplifying assumption that a natural language sentence is mapped on exactly one formula. By letting the domain of f be the class of all natural language sentences, I furthermore presume that there is a formula in the target formal language for every natural language sentence. I do not necessarily want to subscribe to these assumptions, but we can safely disregard these peculiarities in the present context.

Introduction

Trivial as this reconstruction may be, it makes the role of the formalization explicit. It shows that whether or not a natural language sentence is declared logically true by a given definition of logical truth crucially depends on the way this sentence is formalized. If there are no restrictions on formalizations, i.e., if arbitrary functions f are allowed, it holds that for any given functions g^D and h, and arbitrary sentence p, we can provide an f such that $g^D(f(p)) = h(p)$ and an f such that $g^D(f(p)) \neq h(p)$. In other words: for any natural language sentence and any definition of logical truth, we can formalize the sentence such that it comes out logically true (or not logically true). If there are no restrictions on the formalization f, we can yield any arbitrary definition of logical truth extensionally adequate or inadequate, simply by choosing a formalization function f that yields this result.

Which lesson is to be drawn from these considerations? The classification of natural language sentences as logically true does not, by itself, support or undermine a certain formal definition of logical truth. All that we can put to the test is a package consisting of a certain formalization f of the natural language sentence and a formal definition of logical truth D. If the natural language sentence is classified contrary to intuition, the formalization or the formal definition of logical truth (or both) are to be rejected. If, on the other hand, the natural language sentence is classified in agreement with the pretheoretic notion of consequence, this does not speak in favor of either the definition or the formalization: in such case, it may be that both are adequate, or that both inadequate, or that only one of them is correct.

We could break out of this quandary if there were a reliable means to evaluate a given formalization in isolation. However, the conditions for adequate formalizations are themselves highly contentious.[5] Not only are there no generally accepted rules for generating the formalization of a natural language sentence, but there are no strict criteria to evaluate it. We formalize sentences according to our gut feelings and by means of some rules of thumb. Nothing even remotely resembling a consensus on the exact adequacy conditions of formalization has been reached.

---

[5] See especially Brun 2003 for a detailed investigation of the adequacy conditions of formalizations.

A lot would be gained if – at least at this early stage of the debate – questions concerning the adequacy of formalization could be disregarded. Indeed, I think that we can apply the definitions of logical consequence and logical truth to natural language arguments and sentences directly and thereby sidestep the topic of formalization. In this respect, I am a student of Richard Montague, who famously applied the model-theoretic concepts and the rules of formal semantics to natural language sentences. He thought that there is no relevant difference between formal and natural language – at least as long as we only consider a limited fragment of natural language.[6] I agree and use the same method which I will briefly illustrate. To check whether a given sentence turns out to be logically true under the model-theoretic definition, I will skip formalizing it, but apply the formal interpretation function to the original sentence straightaway. Consider exemplarily the sentence "Plato is a philosopher". This sentence could be formalized as "Fa". One could then check whether "Fa" is true in all models, i.e., whether $i(a) \in i(F)$ for all interpretation functions i (and all domains). I will avoid this detour by applying the interpretation function to "Plato" and "is a philosopher" directly, i.e., I examine whether $i(Plato) \in i(is\ a\ philosopher)$ for all interpretation functions i. The sentence "Plato is a philosopher" is a logical truth only if this condition is fulfilled. I sidestep the problem of formalization by eliminating the necessity of formalizations.

Importantly, this procedure is unproblematic only because I restrict the discussion to a small and regimented portion of natural language. I confine myself to declarative sentences not involving any complicated adverbial constructions, minor sentences, intensional operators, deictic or indexical elements. Also, I do not take into account paradoxical sentences like, e.g., the Liar sentence. I only examine ordinary and harmless subject-predicate constructions like "Plato is a philosopher" or "Gaia is a mother". One could almost say that I discuss a hybrid of natural and formal language. In fact, I will not hesitate to use sentences like "$\forall x$ (x is a planet $\to$ x is eternal)," which combine elements from both natural language and the formal language of first-order predicate logic.

---

[6] See especially Montague 1970[a]: 188, and 1970[b]: 222.

This is a quite common methodology. Even Tarski, who prominently confined his research to formal languages, remarks that the formal languages he is interested in can be understood as 'fragments of natural language':

> I should like to emphasize that, when using the term 'formalized languages', I do not refer exclusively to linguistic systems that are formulated entirely in symbols, and I do not have in mind anything essentially opposed to natural languages. On the contrary, the only formalized languages that seem to be of real interest are those which are fragments of natural languages (fragments provided with complete vocabularies and precise syntactical rules) or those which can at least be adequately translated into natural languages. (Tarski 1960: 68)

I do not in any way want to suggest that the logical form of a sentence can be read off its surface appearance. Quite to the contrary: I hold the restriction to a very small portion of natural language to be necessary, because I am, like so many others are, convinced that "grammatical form misleads as to logical form" (Strawson 1952: 51).[7] The logical form of a sentence or an argument cannot be easily read off its surface structure and I do not intend to conceal that it often requires deep linguistic and philosophical efforts to uncover the logical form of natural language expressions. Indeed, I consider the relation between logic and natural language as one of the most intriguing and fundamental topics in philosophy. Here I simply bracket any associated problems and confine myself to a more unproblematic part of natural language in order to engage with the central questions concerning logical truth and consequence without being compelled to make unnecessary or distracting detours.

Let me outline the structure of the book. Chapter 1 explains the notions of interpretational and representational semantics in detail. It will be argued that, while Tarski's original definition of logical consequence has to be read interpretationally, our contemporary model-theoretic definition is ambiguous between both readings. The stand-

---

[7] There are innumerable examples to support the *misleading form* thesis. Let me here only depict one of the earliest ones from Plato's *Euthydemus*. The following arguments have the same surface structure, but not the same logical form: (i) This is a pen. This is blue. Therefore, this is a blue pen. (ii) That dog is a father. That dog is his. Therefore, that dog is his father.

ard semantics of first-order predicate logic does not allow the distinction between the interpretational and the representational understanding. In order to give a precise formulation of the difference between the two readings, I introduce an alternative semantics in Chapter 2. This semantics comes with a more fine-grained notion of a model, thereby providing the means to keep interpretational and representational factors apart. Importantly, however, the alternative semantics only serves the purposes of clarity and rigor and does not carry any argumentative weight: the arguments in the subsequent chapters do not depend on it.

I then discuss the interpretational and the representational definition successively, concentrating on the interpretational definition (chapters 3-6). Chapters 3 and 4 argue that we cannot demand that a logically valid argument must be truth-preserving in literally *all* interpretations. The central task is to demarcate the admissible from the inadmissible interpretations which constitutes *the problem of admissible interpretations*. Depending on the restrictions imposed, different arguments will be declared logically valid by the interpretational definition. I thereby challenge the classical view that draws a boundary between arguments that are deemed to be merely structurally valid (Chapter 3) or analytically valid (Chapter 4) and those classified as logically valid. Chapter 5 shows that the interpretationalist must make non-trivial metaphysical assumptions in order to prevent his definition of logical consequence from massive overgeneration.[8] If these assumptions are made explicit in terms of corresponding restrictions on interpretations, logical necessity – understood interpretationally – reduces to metaphysical necessity.

In Chapter 6, I argue that the desideratum of formality is, without further specification, unsubstantial. The distinction between formal and non-formal sentences depends itself on a demarcation of admissible from inadmissible classifications of the terms of the language. This throws us back to the very problem we started with: to demarcate the admissible from the inadmissible interpretations. The chapter ends with the observation that the standard reasons for preferring the interpretational over the representational definition are inconclusive

---

[8] We say that a definition *overgenerates* iff it is too wide. It *undergenerates* iff it is too narrow.

Introduction

at best: firstly, the interpretational definition is not free of metaphysics, and secondly, the criterion of formality does not speak in favor of the interpretational definition.

Chapter 7 discusses the representational definition of logical consequence. I first develop a more general understanding of the representational view according to which representational models are not to be identified with (partial) possible worlds, but with what I call "states." Truth-preservation in all states is demonstrated not to collapse into metaphysically necessary truth-preservation. It will be shown, however, that the representational definition must cope with a problem analogous to the central difficulty for the interpretational definition of logical consequence, namely *the problem of admissible states*. I will argue that the interpretational and the representational definitions are extensionally equivalent if analogous restrictions on admissibility are imposed. The real challenge of the philosophy of logic is to provide a demarcation of the admissible from the inadmissible models, regardless of whether they are read interpretationally or representationally.

In the final chapters 8 and 9, I address the problem of logical constants, a particularly interesting instance of the problem of admissible models. I discuss the most prominent criterion for demarcating the logical from the non-logical constants, namely the criterion of permutation invariance. Chapter 8 gives a unifying analysis of familiar counter examples to this demarcation criterion. To cope with these examples, I provide a modification of the criterion of permutation invariance which makes use of the findings of the preceding chapters in the final Chapter 9. However, this chapter also reveals the partly skeptical conclusion that the logical properties of the object language depend on the logical properties of the metalanguage. I will therefore end with an outlook on the nature of model theory, which relies on the possibility of a clear distinction between the object language and the metalanguage.

1 Models of Models: Interpretation and Representation

Valid arguments are truth-preserving. The truth value of a sentence depends on its truth conditions and on whether these are fulfilled. The truth conditions of a sentence are determined by semantics,[9] and whether they are fulfilled depends on what the relevant portion of the world is like. If the world is exhausted by facts there are two, and only two, factors that determine the truth value of a sentence, namely its meaning and the facts. If either meaning or facts are changed, the truth value may be changed as well. As Quine says right at the beginning of his classic *The Philosophy of Logic*:

> When someone speaks truly, what makes his statement true? We tend to feel that there are two factors: meaning and fact. A German utters a declarative sentence: "Der Schnee ist weiss." In so doing he speaks truly, thanks to the happy occurrence of two circumstances: his sentence means that snow is white, and in point of fact snow is white. If meanings had been different, if "weiss" had meant green, then in uttering what he did he would not have spoken truly. If the facts had been different, if snow had been red, then again he would not have spoken truly. (Quine 1970: 1)[10]

As truth of a sentence is dependent on two independent factors, two definitions of logical truth emerge based on the variation of either of them. The *interpretational definition* understands logical truth as truth independent of the meaning of the terms occurring in it, while the *representational definition* understands logical truth as truth independent of what the world is like. According to the interpretational view, a sentence is logically true iff it is true in the *actual world* under any *possible interpretation*. With respect to the representational account, a sen-

---

[9] Here I concentrate on truth conditional semantics and disregard alternative positions, such as semantic inferentialism as proposed, e.g., by Brandom 1994.
[10] In the above quote, Quine does not talk about the truth of a sentence, but the truth of an *utterance*. Unless indicated otherwise, we disregard the role of pragmatics in our discussion and pretend to be concerned with sentences alone.

tence is logically true iff it is true in all *possible worlds* under the *actual interpretation*.[11]

Etchemendy has illustrated these two definitions by reference to the different readings of the traditional truth-table definition of logical truth. The truth-table definition says that a sentence is logically true iff it is true in all rows of its truth table. For example, consider the truth table of the logically true sentence "snow is green or snow is not green":

Snow is green.	Snow is green or snow is not green.
T	T
F	T

The truth-table definition is illuminating only if we have an account of what is modelled by "truth in a row". Clearly, the first row stands for a situation where the sentence "snow is green" is true. As we have just pointed out, there are two factors determining the truth value of a sentence. Accordingly, we can turn on either screw to render the sentence true. We can understand the first row as modelling a case where the sentence "snow is green" means, e.g., that snow is white. We keep the facts, but alter the meaning. This corresponds to the interpretational conception. Alternatively, we can understand this row as modelling a case where "snow is green" means that snow is green, but in which snow is not white, but green. In such a possibility, we keep the standard meaning of the sentence, but alter the facts. This is the representational conception. (Of course, one can also combine these two readings by understanding the first row to model both at once, a different interpretation of the sentence and a different world. For example, one could understand the row as representing an interpretation of

---

[11] I agree with Stephen Read that "[t]he terminology of 'interpretation' versus 'representation' is not altogether a felicitous one. Talk of representations suggests unwanted mental models; representing things to ourselves; and in both cases, interpretations are what is at stake, on the one hand, keeping interpretations fixed but considering varying situations, on the other hand, keeping the situation fixed, by allowing the interpretation to vary" (Read 1994: 249). In order to avoid any terminological confusion, I nevertheless retain Etchemendy's terminology which is most common in the relevant literature.

Tarski's Definition

"snow is green" as meaning that snow is red and simultaneously to model a world where snow is indeed red.)

Ludwig Wittgenstein, who introduced the truth tables in his *Tractatus*, had the second, representational reading in mind. He understood the rows of the truth table to model different possibilities. Yet, this understanding yields odd consequences as the following example shows:

Snow is white.	Snow is green.	If snow is white, snow is not green.
T	T	F
T	F	T
F	T	T
F	F	T

I guess that most of us would take this to be a legitimate truth table. However, the first row of the above truth table cannot be understood in a representational way. In the represented world, snow would have to be both white and green, which is surely impossible. It appears, therefore, that this truth table requires an interpretational reading. Problems with a representational reading of a truth table arise as soon as one considers the tables for 'dependent' atomic sentences.

Wittgenstein mentions the specific instance of this problem deriving from dependent color propositions already in the *Tractatus*, but only addressed the problem explicitly in his "Some Remarks on Logical Form" (1929). He there proposes that, in cases of dependency, the problematic row should actually be deleted. Thus, the truth table for the sentence "if snow is white, snow is not green" would have to appear as follows:

Snow is white.	Snow is green.	If snow is white, snow is not green.
T	F	T
F	T	T
F	F	T

This truth table allows for a representational reading as any remaining row represents a possible way the world could be. There arises another problem, however. In this modified truth table, the sentence "if snow is white, snow is not green" is true in all rows. It is therefore logically true according to the original truth-table definition.

It shall not be decided here which reading of the truth table is the correct one. The truth-table definition only served to illustrate the two different readings of 'truth in a model/row'. I will now turn to Tarski's notion of 'truth in a model'.

1.1 Tarski's Definition

Alfred Tarski's definition of logical truth says that a sentence is logically true iff it is true in all models. According to Etchemendy 1990, this definition is often misunderstood as a representational definition, but must be read in an interpretational way:

> [M]any philosophers have assumed that Tarski, in defining the logical properties, had in mind something akin to representational semantics, a characterization of "x is true in W," for all possible worlds "W." For example, we find David Kaplan extolling the insight of "Tarski's reduction of possible worlds to models," a reduction Kaplan claims to be "implicit in" the analysis of the logical properties developed in Tarski's article. But this, as we will see, is just a confusion, one of several that lend undeserved credence to Tarski's analysis. (Etchemendy 1990: 23)[12]

I think that Etchemendy is right in characterizing Tarski's definition as an interpretational definition and in diagnosing that it is often misunderstood as a representational definition. However, I will only argue for the former claim.[13]

To prepare the ground for my analysis, I will closely look at Tarski's seminal paper "The Concept of Logical Consequence" (1935), in which he presents his famous definition of logical consequence for

---

[12] For the reference to Kaplan, see Davidson and Harman (eds.) 1975: 216.

[13] The following reconstruction of Tarski's views is mainly based on Tarski 1935 and Tarski 1936. In his paper, "Arithmetical Extensions of Relational Systems" from 1956, which is jointly authored by Tarski and Vaught, Tarski and Vaught seems to employ the standard contemporary model-theoretic notion of a model and of truth in a model.

Tarski's Definition 19

the first time. Tarski's aim is to devise a definition of logical consequence that captures our common concept of consequence:[14]

> The concept of logical consequence is one of those whose introduction into the field of strict formal investigation was not a matter of arbitrary decision on the part of this or that investigator; in defining this concept, efforts were made to adhere to the common usage of the language of everyday life. (Tarski 1936: 409).

He motivates the new search for such a definition by showing that the definition of logical consequence used by the logicians of his time does not capture the intuitive notion of consequence. The concept Tarski refers to here is a syntactic, proof-theoretic concept, which he dubs the *formalized concept of consequence*:

> [...] the proof of every theorem reduces to single or repeated application of some simple rules of inference – such as the rules of substitution and detachment. These rules tell us what transformations of a purely structural kind [...] are to be performed upon the axioms or theorems already proved in the theory, in order that the sentences obtained as a result of such transformations may themselves be regarded as proved. Logicians thought that these few rules of inference exhausted the content of the concept of consequence. Whenever a sentence follows from others, it can be obtained from them – so it was thought – in more or less complicated ways by means of the transformations prescribed by the rules. (Tarski 1936: 409 f.)

Tarski objects to the formalized concept of consequence that Gödel's incompleteness results have shown that it does not capture our pretheoretic notion of consequence.[15] Roughly, the first incompleteness theorem states that for any effectively generated consistent theory of a certain strength, there is a sentence that follows from the

---

[14] Most authors share the view that Tarski is indeed referring to the everyday concept of consequence (see, e.g., Bays 2001, Etchemendy 1990, Gómez-Torrente 1996, Sher 1991, 1996, Ray 1996). A notable exception is Jané 2006, who argues that Tarski refers to a restricted form of the concept of logical consequence as it is employed by the logicians of his time in suitable mathematical contexts.

[15] See Gödel's 1931 article "On Formally Undecidable Propositions of Principia Mathematica and Related Systems I" for the proof and a precise formulation of his two incompleteness theorems.

theory, but is not syntactically provable in the theory. This incompleteness theorem shows that "the formalized concept of consequence, as it is used by mathematical logicians, by no means coincides with the common concept" (Tarski 1936: 411)[16] Logical consequence does not coincide with derivability.

In the consecutive paragraphs, Tarski sets out to provide a precise and reductive definition of the pretheoretic concept of consequence. To do so, he first formulates the adequacy conditions on a formal definition of consequence by identifying the essential features of the pretheoretic notion of consequence. Tarski names two such conditions of which this one is the first:

> Consider any class K of sentences and a sentence X which follows from the sentences of this class. From an intuitive standpoint it can never happen that both the class K consists only of true sentences and the sentence X is false. (Tarski 1936: 414)

As already Etchemendy pointed out, the passage involves a modal scope ambiguity.[17] According to the one reading, Tarski subscribes to the Aristotelian idea that the conclusion of a valid argument follows from the premises by necessity, i.e., that logically valid arguments are necessarily truth-preserving. We can formalize this reading, with the obvious abbreviations, as follows: "$LC(K, X) \rightarrow \Box (K \rightarrow X)$." According to another reading, we have a wider scope for the necessity operator. We can interpret Tarski as saying that if X is a logical consequence of K then it holds necessarily that one element of K is false or X is true: "$\Box (LC(K, X) \rightarrow (K \rightarrow X))$." Under this reading, logical consequence guarantees truth-preservation. Incidentally, there is also a possible third: we can understand the condition as merely saying that *all* logically valid arguments are truth-preserving. According to this understanding, the "it can never happen" has no modal force at all, but only serves as an indicator of generalization. For all logically valid arguments it holds that one of the premises is false or the conclusion is true: "for all Y, for all Z: $LC(Y, Z) \rightarrow (Y \rightarrow Z)$".

---

[16] For a similar remark, see also Tarski 1933: 295: "The formalized concept of consequence will, in extension, never coincide with the ordinary one."

[17] To be precise, Etchemendy identifies the two readings with respect to a later passage in Tarski. See Etchemendy 1990: 87 f.

Here I am not interested in an exegesis of Tarski's passage. As already pointed out in the introduction, I think that our common concept of consequence obviously involves the notion of necessary truth-preservation. It demands that "LC(K, X) → □ (K → X)" holds (for arbitrary K and X). As Tarski is also interested in the common concept, he *should* take necessary truth-preservation to be a desideratum on a definition of logical consequence, i.e., he should have intended the passage according to the first reading. In the following, I will pretend that Tarski has meant to say what he should have said. Whether he also actually did do so, need not be our present concern.

Let's proceed to the second central feature Tarski takes the pretheoretic notion of logical consequence to have:

> Since we are concerned here with the concept of logical, i.e., formal, consequence, and thus with a relation which is to be uniquely determined by the form of the sentences between which it holds, this relation cannot be influenced in any way by empirical knowledge, and in particular by knowledge of the objects to which the sentence X or the sentences of the class K refer. The consequence relation cannot be affected by replacing the designations of the objects referred to in these sentences by the designations of any other objects. (Tarski 1936: 414)

According to Tarski, logical consequence is always *formal*. Unfortunately, Tarski never precisely captures the notion of formality involved. In particular, he quickly and perhaps illegitimately moves from an epistemic characterization (empirical knowledge has no influence) to a non-epistemic, linguistic one (independence of substitution of terms). At this point, we simply note that Tarski takes formality to be a feature of the common concept of consequence and defer a closer analysis of the relevant notion of formality to Chapter 6. Summing it up, the two essential features of our common concept of consequence are *necessary truth-preservation* and *formality*.

Tarski's first attempt at providing a definition of logical consequence then reads as follows:

> If, in the sentences of the class K and in the sentence X, the constants – apart from the purely logical constants – are replaced by any other constants (like signs being everywhere replaced by like signs), and if we denote the class of sentences thus obtained from K by "K'", and the sentence obtained from

X by "X'", then the sentence X' must be true provided only that all sentences of the class K' are true. (*Ibid.*: 415)

Tarski here preliminarily defines logical consequence as truth-preservation under all substitutions of the non-logical terms. We call this the *substitutional definition* of logical consequence.[18]

---

[18] We already find a very similar definition of logical consequence in Bolzano's *Theory of Science*: "[...] I say that propositions M, N, O... would be *derivable* from propositions A, B, C, D..., with respect to the variables *i, j*..., if every set of ideas which makes A, B, C, D... all true when substituted for *i, j*... also makes M, N, O... all true. For the sake of variety, I shall also sometimes say that propositions M, N, O... *follow from* or can be *inferred* or *concluded* from the set of propositions A, B, C, D... I shall call propositions A, B, C, D... the *antecedents* or *premises*, and M, N, O... which are obtained from them *consequences* or *conclusions*." (Bolzano 1837, §155) If we understand Bolzano's *propositions* as sentences and Bolzano's *ideas* as terms, the similarity with the substitutional definition becomes obvious. Bolzano's *variables* are those terms that may be substituted by different terms. Here we already encounter a distinction between terms that are open for substitution and terms that must remain fixed. Interestingly, Bolzano defines the notion of consequence as a relative one: a sentence follows from another sentence *with respect to a given set of fixed terms*. So, for example, the sentence "Gaia is female" follows from the sentence "Gaia is a mother" with respect to the variable "Gaia", i.e., if we only allow substitutions of the term "Gaia" and treat the terms "is female" and "is a mother" as fixed terms. On the other hand, "Gaia is female" does not follow from "Gaia is a mother" with respect to the variable terms "is female" and "is a mother" because we could, for example, substitute "is male" for "is female" and thereby generate a true premise and a false conclusion.

Bolzano's definition of logical consequence and his analogous definition of logical truth understand logical consequence and logical truth as relative notions. However, in §148 of his *Theory of Science*, Bolzano considers a very specific set of fixed terms (rather than using the term "logical truth", Bolzano prefers to speak of "general truth" or "analytic truth"): "We have some very general examples of analytic propositions which are also true in the following propositions: A is A, A which is B is A, A which is B is B, Every object is either B or not B, etc. [...] Nothing is necessary for judging the analytic nature of [these propositions] besides logical knowledge, because the concepts that make up the invariant part of these propositions all belong to logic." (Bolzano 1837, §148) Bolzano here recognizes the special role of those sentences in which only the logical constants are taken to be fixed. However, Bolzano neither states a criterion of demarcation for the logical from the non-logical terms, nor provides a list of them. Indeed, he points out that the demarcation of the logical from the non-logical terms is probably not so easy to be drawn: "To be sure, this distinction has its

Tarski's Definition

Tarski immediately observes that the substitutional definition is too broad. The definition can easily be satisfied due only to a lack of richness of the given language. For example, in a language with only the two individual constants "Venus" and "Mercury" and the one predicate constant "is a planet", the sentence "Mercury is a planet" is a logical consequence of "Venus is a planet" under the substitutional definition. The only available substitutions are the substitution of "Mercury" for "Venus" and the substitution of "Venus" for "Mercury". These substitutions obviously never change the truth values of the sentences. Tarski concludes that the substitutional definition "could be regarded as sufficient for the sentence X to follow from the class K only if the designation of all possible objects occurred in the language in question," but in the same breath he says that "[t]his assumption, however, is fictitious and can never be realized" (Tarski 1936: 416).

It is not obvious that Tarski's skepticism with respect to the possibility of languages with a term for every possible object is warranted. Of course, there are many formal languages that fail to satisfy this assumption. Consider natural language, however. Surely, we do not *actually* have a term for every possible object in natural language. Still, it seems that, in principle, we can introduce new names for the as-yet-unnamed entities. Our language is expansible. For example, we could use a linguistic trick and let each object name itself in a Lagadonian fashion.[19] It is, of course, difficult to imagine such a language being actually used. Also, a Lagadonian language can surely not be spoken, as the words (at least many of them) cannot be said. Nevertheless, in principle it seems possible that every object constitutes its own name. Such a language would fulfil the requirement that any object, and

---

ambiguity, because the domain of concepts belonging to logic is not so sharply demarcated that no dispute could ever arise over it." (Bolzano 1837, §148)
Interestingly, Tarski seems to have not been familiar with Bolzano's definition when delivering his talk in 1935. He only added a reference to Bolzano in a later reprint. At this point, it should also be remarked that the idea of defining logical consequence via truth-preservation under all substitutions can already be found in Abelard's works. See in particular Abelard's *Dialectica*, §255.

[19] See Lewis 1986[a]: 145 for a characterization of a Lagadonian language. The idea of such a language has been wonderfully exploited in Jonathan Swift's *Gulliver's Travels* 1735: 162 f.

maybe even any possible object (depending on your modal ontology), has a name.

There is, however, a better reason to abandon the substitutional definition. Tarski's aim is to provide a definition of logical consequence applicable to all languages, and it is beyond dispute that there are languages that do not have a name for every object (English, e.g., being such a language). Thus, a substitutional definition would overgenerate.[20]

Tarski thinks that the above impediment can be circumvented by a modification of the substitutional definition that makes use of the semantic apparatus he developed in "The Concept of Truth for Formalized Languages". Tarski there introduces the central notion of *satisfaction* of a formula, which allows for a recursive definition of truth for complex, and in particular, for quantified sentences. Satisfaction is a relation between a formula and a model. A *formula* is a well-formed sequence of terms, possibly containing variables of different order. For illustration, assume an alphabet containing the variables $x^1_1, x^1_2, \ldots, x^2_1, x^2_2, \ldots$, where the superscript indicates the order of the variable. A Tarskian *model* is an n-tuple of sequences of objects, such that the j-th sequence is a sequence of objects of order j: the first sequence is a sequence of individual objects, the second a sequence of sets of individual objects, etc.[21] To determine whether a formula is satisfied by a model, we interpret the variable x^j_i as referring to the i-th object of the j-th sequence of the model. A model satisfies a formula iff the state of affairs described under this interpretation actually obtains. Thus, a model satisfies a formula iff taking each free variable occurring in the formula as a name of the object assigned to it by the model turns the formula into a true sentence. The formula "x^1_1 and

---

[20] Interestingly, this objection does not apply to Bolzano's conception. Bolzano does not define logical consequence for some arbitrary formal language, but only for natural language, and he assumes that there is a natural language term for any object. (To be more precise, Bolzano assumes there to be an idea for every object and his logic is meant to deal directly with ideas. What this is supposed to mean and whether Bolzano's account is viable cannot be discussed here.)

[21] For technical reasons Tarski assumed the sequences to be infinite. We can here neglect this subtlety. See Popper 1955 for an extension of Tarski's notion of satisfaction to models with finite sequences.
Also, I omit complications having to do with relations of higher arities and concentrate on unary relations, i.e., on predicates.

x^1_4 are brothers" is satisfied by a model with <John, Johanna, Petra, Peter> as its first sequence iff John and Peter are brothers.[22]

Satisfaction of molecular formulas can now be defined in the well-known recursive way:
- The model $\mathfrak{M}$ satisfies "$\neg\varphi$" iff $\mathfrak{M}$ does not satisfy "φ".
- The model $\mathfrak{M}$ satisfies "$\varphi \wedge \psi$" iff $\mathfrak{M}$ satisfies "φ" and $\mathfrak{M}$ satisfies "ψ".
- The model $\mathfrak{M}$ satisfies "$\exists x^1_i\, \varphi$" iff there is a model $\mathfrak{M}'$ that satisfies "φ", where $\mathfrak{M}'$ is identical to $\mathfrak{M}$ except possibly at the i-th place of the first sequence.

The above definition of the notion of *satisfaction of a formula in a model* is only one step on our way to Tarski's definition of logical consequence. The second step consists in introducing the notion of a *sentential function of a formula*. A complete sentential function is generated from a formula φ as follows: one first chooses an injective function f from the set of non-logical constants occurring in φ to a set of variables that do not already occur in φ such that a constant of order n is mapped on a variable of order n.[23] The sentential function of an atomic formula can then be procured by substituting every non-logical constant with the variable on which it is mapped. The complete sentential function of the sentence "John and Peter are brothers" can be formulated as "$x^2_1\ x^1_1\ x^1_2$".[24] Complete sentential functions contain no non-logical constants, while incomplete sentential functions may contain non-logical constants.

Aided by the notion of a sentential function, we can define *truth in a model* as follows: a sentence φ is true in a model $\mathfrak{M}$ iff the complete sentential function of φ is satisfied in the model $\mathfrak{M}$. Let me illustrate. Assume that John and Peter are brothers and consider again Tarski's example "John and Peter are brothers" and two models having as their first sequence <John, Peter> and <Plato, Tarski>, respectively.

---

[22] See Tarski 1936: 416 for a similar example. This is, of course, only an illustration of the notion of satisfaction, no proper definition. A general definition of the notion of satisfaction is impossible, as it would invite semantic paradoxes.
[23] I again omit complications having to do with the arity of the terms.
[24] Of course, different choices of f yield different sentential functions of a given sentence. As logical truth demands truth in all models, it is, however, irrelevant which sentential functions one chooses. I will, therefore, allow myself to speak of *the* sentential function of a given formula.

To test whether this sentence is true in such models, we must first construct the sentential function of the sentence. For ease of presentation, I will consider the partial sentential function of the sentence only. To do so, we define a function f from the individual constants to individual variables such that $f(John) = x^1_1$ and $f(Peter) = x^1_2$. The resulting partial sentential function is "x^1_1 and x^1_2 are brothers". According to the first model, $g(x^1_1)$ = John and $g(x^1_2)$ = Peter. As John and Peter are brothers, the models with the sequence <John, Peter> as their first sequence satisfy the sentential function; thus, the sentence "John and Peter are brothers" is true in such models. With respect to models with <Plato, Tarski> as their first sequence, $g(x^1_1)$ = Plato and $g(x^1_2)$ = Tarski. The sentential function is obviously not satisfied by such models; thus, the original sentence is not true in those models.

To understand the Tarskian framework, it is utterly important to keep apart the notion of *satisfaction of a sentence by a model* and the notion of *truth of a sentence in a model*. A true sentence φ is trivially satisfied by every model, but it is not the case that every true sentence φ is true in all models. A model satisfies a sentence φ just in case the following holds: if the variables occurring in φ are interpreted as referring to the respective objects of the corresponding sequence of the model, φ is true. As a sentence has no free variables, a true sentence is trivially satisfied by every model. However, a sentence φ is true in a model only if the *sentential function* of φ is satisfied by the model. We then also say that the model is *a model of the sentence φ*.

The ground is now prepared for Tarski's revised definition of logical consequence:

> The sentence X follows logically from the sentences of the class K if and only if every model of the class K is also a model of the sentence X. (Tarski 1936: 417)

Tarski says that a sentence follows logically from a set of sentences iff there is no model that is a model of the set of premises but not of the conclusion. We can translate this definition as follows: a sentence X follows logically from the sentences of the class K if and only if X is true in all models in which all members of K are true. Tarski defines logical consequence as truth-preservation in all models. The analogous definition of logical truth says that a sentence is logically true iff it is true in all models.[25]

Tarski is confident that this definition adequately captures the common concept of consequence. In particular, he thinks that both intuitive desiderata on the definition of logical consequence, i.e., (necessary) truth-preservation and formality, are fulfilled by the given definition:

> It seems to me that everyone who understands the content of the above definition must admit that it agrees quite well with common usage. This becomes still clearer from its various consequences. In particular, it can be proved, on the basis of the definition, that every consequence of true sentences must be true, and also that the consequence relation which holds between given sentences is completely independent of the sense of the extra-logical constants which occur in these sentences. (*Ibid.*: 417)

Tarski takes the criterion of formality to be fulfilled because the consequence relation holds "completely independent of the sense of the extra-logical constants which occur in the sentences". Whether an argument is valid is solely determined by the sentential functions of the occurring sentences, and those do not contain any non-logical constants. Thus, non-logical constants have no influence on the logical properties of the argument. At least at a first view, this appears to capture the crux of the desideratum of formality.

The situation is less perspicuous with respect to the condition of (necessary) truth-preservation. Tarski says that "it can be proved [...] that every consequence of true sentences must be true", yet he does not spell out the proof to which he is alluding. Etchemendy suggests

---

[25] Tarski confines his definition to sentences, i.e., to formulas with no free variables. As I am concerned with natural language arguments and as there are no open formulas in natural language, this does not limit the scope of my discussion any further. Irrespective of this, one can extend the Tarskian definition to formulas in a straightforward way: a formula X follows logically from the formulas of the class K if and only if X is true in all models in which all members of K are true. The corresponding definition of logical truth goes as follows: a formula is logically true iff it is true in all models. Arguably, Tarski would object to this extension of his definition to formulas because he avoids talking of the *truth of formulas*. For Tarski, a formula is neither true nor false (in a model). A formula is only satisfied or not satisfied by a model.

that Tarski has the following, utterly trivial proof in mind (see Etchemendy 1990: 86 f.). Let K be the set of premises and X the conclusion and let K' be the set of sentential functions of the sentences of K and X' be the sentential function of X. Furthermore, let $\mathfrak{M}^*$ be the model which interprets the variables occurring in X' and in the elements of K' such that they are mapped on the same objects as the respective constants occurring in X and in the elements of K. Now assume for reduction purposes that all elements of K are actually true and X is actually false. Then, the model $\mathfrak{M}^*$ satisfies K', but does not satisfy X'. It follows that there is a model, namely $\mathfrak{M}^*$, in which all elements of K are true, but in which X is false. This contradicts the definition of logical consequence, which says that all models of K are models of X. It is thus shown that if an argument is not truth-preserving, it does not satisfy the Tarskian definition of logical consequence: the proof shows that "$\Box\,(LC(K, X) \to (K \to X))$" is true. However, the above proof does not show that if an argument is a logical consequence according to Tarski's definition, it is necessarily truth-preserving: the proof does not show that "$LC(K, X) \to \Box\,(K \to X))$" is true.[26, 27] It is thus still an open question whether Tarski's definition

---

[26] One might propose that we can indeed prove the condition of necessary truth-preservation by adding a plausible premise. The above proof shows that "$\Box\,(LC(K, X) \to (K \to X))$".
If we additionally assume "$LC(K, X) \to \Box\,(LC(K, X))$",
we can derive the desired "$LC(K, X) \to \Box\,(K \to X))$" (in every normal Kripke-model, i.e., in all frames that validate the K-axiom "$\Box(\varphi \to \psi) \to (\Box\varphi \to \Box\psi)$"). The additional premise "$(LC(K, X) \to \Box\,LC(K \to X))$" says that if something is a logical consequence, it is so necessarily. I do not want to judge here whether this route is a viable option.

[27] Etchemendy concludes from this that Tarski commits a modal fallacy by claiming that it can be proved that "every consequence of true sentences must be true". (see Etchemendy 1990: 85 ff.) I prefer a more sympathetic reading of Tarski's remark. As pointed out above, it is not clear whether Tarski really takes *necessary* truth-preservation to be a criterion of logical validity. Therefore, the above argument might be taken to indicate that Tarski understands only truth-preservation *simpliciter* to be a feature of our common concept of consequence. We need not, however, dwell on this exegetical question any further. (For a thorough discussion of this exegetical question as well as Tarski's fallacy in general, see in particular Sher 1996, Gómez-Torrente 1998, and Ray 1996, but also Etchemendy 1990: 90 f.)

of logical consequence fulfils the intuitive desideratum of necessary truth-preservation.

Tarski himself points the reader to another worry: his definition presupposes a demarcation of the logical from the non-logical constants. To construct the sentential function of a sentence, we replace all non-logical constants by variables, while leaving the logical constants untouched. This procedure draws on a distinction between logical and non-logical constants. The task of formulating and justifying criteria for the demarcation of the logical from the non-logical constants is known as *the problem of the logical constants*. Ever since Tarski's remarks, this problem has been in the focus of those searching for a definition of logical consequence. Tarski himself does not provide a solution for the problem, at least not in the mentioned article. Rather, the paper ends with the skeptical remark that we might not succeed in justifying the required demarcation.

After having familiarized ourselves with Tarski's original definitions, we are now prepared to address the initial question: should Tarski's definitions of logical consequence and of logical truth be read in an interpretational or a representational way? Tarski says that a sentence is logically true iff it is true in all models. Whether a sentence is true in a model is determined as described above: we first construct the sentential function of the sentence by mapping the non-logical constants on variables (call this function f) and then, in a second step, map the variables on objects of the model (call this function g). Let us define the function i as the composition of f and g: $i \stackrel{\text{def}}{=} g \circ f$. The function i directly maps the constants on objects provided by the model. A sentence is true in a model iff it is true when interpreted with i directly, i.e., iff it is true when the constants have as their semantic values the objects assigned to them by the function i.[28] (To account for the interpretation of open formulas and formulas containing bound variables, we should, more precisely, say that a sentence is true in a model iff it is true when interpreted with $<i, g>$, i.e., iff it is true when the constants have as their semantic values the objects assigned to them by the function i and the variables have as their semantic values the objects assigned to them by the function g.)[29]

---

[28] For a similar reconstruction, see Etchemendy 1990: 53 ff.
[29] Here, and in what follows, I intend to use the term 'semantic value' as neutral as possible. (For a similar use, see Dummett 1991: 24-25.)

Consider again Tarski's sample sentence "John and Peter are brothers" and two models having as their first sequence <John, Peter> and <Plato, Tarski>, respectively. We have seen before that in Tarski's original definition the sentence comes out as true in models of the first kind, and false in models of the second kind (with respect to the chosen f, which maps "John" on x^1_1 and "Peter" on x^1_2).[30] If we apply the function i directly to the sentence, we get $i(John) = g \circ f(John) = o^1_1$ and $i(Peter) = g \circ f(Peter) = o^1_2$ (where o^i_j is again the object at the j-th place in the i-th sequence of the given model). According to models of the first type, we thus interpret "John" as referring to John and "Peter" as referring to Peter. According to the models of the second type, we interpret "John" as referring to Plato and "Peter" as referring to Tarski. Obviously, the sentence is, as it should be, true in the models of the first type, though not in models of the second type.

In this reconstruction it becomes obvious that the evaluation of a sentence according to different Tarskian models amounts to the evaluation of the sentence as true or false under different interpretations i. Truth in all Tarskian models amounts to truth under all interpretations. Whether or not a given sentence is true in a model thus depends on the function i and on what the *actual* world is like. In our example, it depends on who is actually who's brother. Non-actual, merely possible worlds do not matter. A Tarskian model only determines the meaning of a sentence. The model does not determine whether or not a certain state of affairs obtains, i.e., it does not determine the worldly facts. The Tarskian definition of logical consequence has to be classified as an interpretational definition. This should, however, not come as a surprise. Tarski developed his definition out of the substitutional definition of logical consequence, which is, obviously, very close to the interpretational one.

1.2 The Model-Theoretic Definition

The contemporary model-theoretic definition of logical consequence is often traced to Tarski and in fact assumed to be identical with his

---

[30] Recap that g maps the variable x^i_j to the i-th object of the j-th sequence of the model.

The Model-Theoretic Definition 31

definition: after all, we do define logical consequence as truth-preservation in all models just as Tarski did. However, we employ a crucially different notion of a model and of truth in a model. It is worthwhile to precisely delineate the present conceptions of a model and of truth in a model from Tarski's.[31]

Let me begin with the standard contemporary model-theoretic definitions of logical truth and of logical consequence for first-order predicate logic (PL). Here are the syntax and the semantics of PL. The alphabet of PL consists of the following signs:

- Individual constants: $a_0, a_1, \ldots$,
- n-ary-relation constants: $R^n_0, R^n_1, \ldots$, (with $n \in \mathbb{N}\setminus\{0\}$)
- individual variables: $x_0, x_1, \ldots$,
- logical constants: $\neg, \vee, \exists$.[32]

The syntax rules of PL are given by the following rules:

- $R^n_k \tau_1 \ldots \tau_n$ is a formula (where τ_j (with $j \in \{1, \ldots, n\}$) is an individual constant or an individual variable, $n \in \mathbb{N}\setminus\{0\}$ and $k \in \mathbb{N}$),
- if φ is a formula, then $\neg\varphi$ is a formula,
- if φ and ψ are formulas, then $\varphi \vee \psi$ is a formula,
- if φ is a formula, then $\exists x_i\, \varphi$ is a formula (with $i \in \mathbb{N}$), and
- no other sequence of signs is a formula.

While the syntax tells us which sequences of signs constitute the well-formed formulas, the semantics delivers the truth conditions of the formulas. The semantics of PL is spelled out as follows. A structure $\mathfrak{S}$ is defined as a pair $\langle \mathfrak{D}, i \rangle$ consisting of a non-empty set $\mathfrak{D}$ (the *domain*) and an interpretation i with $i(a_j) \in \mathfrak{D}$ (with $j \in \mathbb{N}$) and $i(R^n_j) \subseteq \mathfrak{D}^n$ (where $n \in \mathbb{N}\setminus\{0\}, j \in \mathbb{N}$)). A variable assignment β is a function from the set of variables into the domain: $\beta(x_j) \in \mathfrak{D}$ (with $j \in \mathbb{N}$). A model $\mathfrak{M}$ is a pair consisting of a structure $\mathfrak{S}$ and a variable assignment β. We define (for $j \in \mathbb{N}, n \in \mathbb{N}\setminus\{0\}$): $\mathfrak{M}(a_j) = i(a_j)$;

---

[31] Etchemendy also argues that the model-theoretic definition cannot be identified with Tarski's definition (see especially Etchemendy 1988[b]). However, Etchemendy focusses on a different aspect of divergence than I do. While Etchemendy stresses that Tarski's definition does not yet involve the notion of a varying domain (see also fn. 118), my comparison will focus on the different definitions of truth in a model for atomic sentences.

[32] As is well known, the other logical constants can be defined in terms of these.

$\mathfrak{M}(R_i) = i(R_i)$; $\mathfrak{M}(x_j) = \beta(x_j)$. An atomic formula $\varphi = R^n_i \tau_1 \ldots \tau_n$ is true in a model $\mathfrak{M}$ (i.e., $\mathfrak{M} \vDash \varphi$) iff $<\mathfrak{M}(\tau_1), \ldots, \mathfrak{M}(\tau_n)> \in \mathfrak{M}(R^n_i)$. For complex formulas φ, truth in a model is defined recursively as follows:

- $\mathfrak{M} \vDash \neg\varphi$ iff $\mathfrak{M} \nvDash \varphi$,
- $\mathfrak{M} \vDash \varphi \vee \psi$ iff $\mathfrak{M} \vDash \varphi$ or $\mathfrak{M} \vDash \psi$,
- $\mathfrak{M} \vDash \exists x_j \, \varphi$ iff there is an o $\in \mathfrak{D}$ such that $\mathfrak{M} o/x_j \vDash \varphi$ (where $\mathfrak{M} o/x_j$ is the pair $<\mathfrak{S}, \beta o/x_j>$ with $\beta o/x_j$ defined as follows: $\beta o/x_j (x_k) = $ o for $j = k$ and $\beta o/x_j (x_k) = \beta(x_k)$ otherwise).

These are the standard model-theoretic definitions of logical truth and logical consequence:

DEFINITION: A formula φ is *logically true* iff for all models $\mathfrak{M}$ it holds that $\mathfrak{M} \vDash \varphi$.

DEFINITION: A formula φ *follows logically* from a set of formulas Γ iff for all models $\mathfrak{M}$: if $\mathfrak{M} \vDash \Gamma$, then $\mathfrak{M} \vDash \varphi$ (where $\mathfrak{M} \vDash \Gamma$ iff $\mathfrak{M} \vDash \psi_i$ for all $\psi_i \in \Gamma$).

Like in Tarski's original definition, logical truth is defined as truth in all models and logical consequence is defined as truth-preservation in all models. However, the contemporary notion of a model is not identical with the Tarskian notion. One glaring difference lies in the fact that a model-theoretic model comes with a domain of objects. Truth in all models thus also demands truth in all domains. A Tarskian model, on the other hand, is just a tuple of sequences of objects providing an interpretation of a sentence. This difference is particularly important when it comes to evaluating sentences regarding the size of the domain. Yet, for our present purposes we will ignore this difference and concentrate on further aspects. (But see Section 5.2.)

I want to show in particular that – in contrast to Tarski's original definitions – the standard model-theoretic definitions can be read both in an interpretational and a representational way. The model-theoretic definitions cannot be classified as either interpretational or representational; rather, they are ambiguous between the two accounts. The reason is that the formal semantics of PL is *extensional*: the interpretation function of a model maps each non-logical constant on its extension. Two models equipped with different interpretation functions therefore assign different extensions to the non-logical constants. However, the assignment of varying extensions may be due to two factors: varying intensions and varying matters of fact. Since an extensional semantics does not distinguish between these two factors, the classical first-order models of PL allow for an interpretational and a representational reading.

Let me first illustrate this with respect to the interpretation of predicate terms. Consider an interpretation function *i* with i(*married*) = {Plato, Kant, Descartes, Leibniz, Schopenhauer, Nietzsche}. Under the representational reading, this interpretation function stands for a world where Plato, Kant, Descartes, Leibniz, Schopenhauer, and Nietzsche are, contrary to fact, married.[33] The interpretation function assigns the term "married" the semantic value it would have in some possible world (namely a world in which the respective philosophers are married) given its actual meaning. Under the interpretational reading, however, this interpretation function says that the term "married" is interpreted as having the actual meaning of "unmarried" (or of some other term that has the respective set as its actual semantic value).[34] The term "married" is here understood as expressing the property of being unmarried. The interpretation function assigns the term "unmarried" the semantic value it would have in the actual world given some possible meaning.

The same ambiguity can be found in the interpretation of individual constants if only we presuppose a description theory of names. The name "Alfred Tarski" then could be identified with a description such as the following: "the person who was born in 1901, is the youngest person who ever completed a PhD at the University of Warsaw, and is the author of *The Concept of Truth for Formalized Languages*, etc."[35] Consider, however, the interpretation function *i* with i(*Alfred Tarski*) = Plato. According to the representational reading, this interpretation function represents a world where Plato was born in 1901, received his PhD from the University of Warsaw at a very young age, and wrote *The Concept of Truth in Formalized Languages*. According to the interpretational reading, on the other hand, the function stands for an interpretation of the language in which the term "Alfred Tarski" has the meaning usually assigned to the term "Plato",

---

[33] For the sake of simplicity, we say that someone is married iff s/he is married or has been married.
[34] Here we ignore that there are of course further unmarried persons.
[35] There are various refinements of the naïve description theory presented above. Fortunately, these need not bother us here.

i.e., the function *i* interprets the term "Alfred Tarski" as being synonymous with the description "the person who was born around 428 BC, is the founder of the Academy in Athens, is the author of the *Politeia*, etc".

An interpretational and a representational reading of the interpretation function of PL are both possible with respect to the interpretation of terms. Equally such readings are possible regarding the interinterpretation of sentences. For illustration, consider an interpretation function *i* which makes the sentence "Alfred Tarski is married" false: the semantic value of "Alfred Tarski" is thus not an element of the semantic value of "married". But what is modelled by i being such that i(*Alfred Tarski*) ∉ i(*married*)? What is modelled by the sentence "Alfred Tarski is married" being false under the respective interpretation? According to the representational reading, the sentence is false under the interpretation function i because i represents a world in which Alfred Tarski has not been married. Under the interpretational reading, the sentence is false because it describes an actually nonobtaining state of affairs. Classical PL semantics allows for both readings.[36] This is a radical break with Tarski's definition of truth in a model. In Tarski's conception, the model only determines the state of affairs described by a given sentence. Whether or not the state of affairs expressed holds is not determined by the model, but by the actual world.

As there are two different readings of what it means that a sentence is true in a model, there are also two readings of what it means

---

[36] Similarly, Menzel 1990 argues that we cannot keep meaning and fact apart in the semantics of PL: "Consider two models M and M' [...] and suppose a predicate P is assigned extension E relative to M and extension E' ($\neq E$) relative to M'. Intuitively, these changes in P's extension relative to the two models are supposed to reflect different ways the world could have been, different ways in which Pishness could have been exhibited. But how is this nailed down in the semantics? How is this to be distinguished from mere ambiguity, mere change in the linguistic meaning of P? Granted, that is not our *intention*. But there is nothing answering to this intention in the semantics itself. There is, in short, nothing in the semantics that captures the fixity of meaning, nothing stable across models, that pins down the meaning of the predicate. [...] [T]he reason [the interpretation, A. Z.] can't distinguish a change in the world from a mere change in meaning is that difference in extension (in general) accompanies both sorts of change." (Menzel 1990: 361 f.)

that a sentence is true in all models, i.e., logically true. In PL semantics we cannot vary meaning and facts independently. As a result, the classical model-theoretic definition of logical truth based on the standard PL semantics is ambiguously situated between a representational and an interpretational reading.

2 Interpretation and Representation: A Systematic Approach

To properly spell out the two competing definitions, the standard, extensional PL semantics is unsuitable; we need an intensional semantics. In this chapter, I will introduce an intensional semantics. "Form-logical semantics", as I will call it, enables us to provide two formal definitions of logical truth and logical consequence, respectively, one accounting for the representational intuitions and the other accounting for the interpretational intuitions.[37] Other intensional semantics, e.g., a standard Montague semantics, would also allow for this (see, e.g., Montague 1970[a] and 1970[b]). However, form-logical semantics is not only intensional, but has further features that will prove invaluable in later chapters. For example, it does not assume a bisection of the non-logical constants into individual and relation terms, but treats all terms equal. As the categorization of the non-logical constants into different types will become the central in later sections, it will be helpful to have a semantics that is as neutral as possible in this respect. Form-logical semantics is the ideal background theory in which to state the informal ideas more precisely. Importantly, however, form-logical semantics does not carry any argumentative weight. None of my arguments depends on the specific choice of the semantics.

2.1 An Alternative Semantic Theory: Form-Logical Semantics

The basic idea of form-logical semantics is straightforward: all non-logical constants, predicate and relation terms included, are mapped on elements of the domain. Semantically, all non-logical constants are thus treated alike. As in PL, a variable assignment maps the variables on elements of the domain. An atomic formula, i.e., a sequence of terms, is interpreted term-wise. The interpretation of a formula is a

---

[37] The formal semantics presented in this chapter is a simplified version of the semantics developed in Freitag & Zinke 2012. We there do not only formulate an alternative semantics, but spell out a logical system, called *form logic*, which is also based on an alternative syntax. The syntax of form logic does not presuppose that there are exactly two kinds of non-logical constants, namely individual constants and relation constants (of different arities), but allows for an arbitrary number of types of non-logical constants. We spell out a general syntax, provide a calculus and proof the strong completeness of all form-logical systems. We also show that classical first-order predicate-logic is a special case of form logic.

tuple of elements of the domain. Such a tuple of objects is here understood as constituting a Russellian proposition. The tuple <Pluto, the property of being a planet> constitutes the Russellian proposition that Pluto is a planet. Thus, the interpretation function tells us which proposition a sentence expresses. To account for the notion of truth in a model, we define a *state* as a set of tuples of elements of the domain. An atomic formula is true in a model iff the interpretation function of the model maps the sentence on an element of the state of the model. Truth for molecular formulas is defined in the usual recursive way.

Before spelling out the formal details of the semantics of form logic (*FL*), some preparatory remarks might be helpful. First, a note on terminology: I take Russellian propositions, which are here understood as tuples of objects, to represent states of affairs. My notion of a state of affairs is maximally liberal. I allow myself to speak of possible and impossible states of affairs, obtaining and non-obtaining states of affairs, and of simple and complex, e.g., negative or conjunctive states of affairs. For instance, the Russellian proposition <Pluto, the property of being a planet> represents the possible, though non-obtaining state of affairs of Pluto's being a planet. Instead of saying that a Russellian proposition represents an obtaining/non-obtaining state of affairs, I will also simply say that the Russellian proposition itself is obtaining/non obtaining.

Second, a note on ontology: As just said, in FL all non-logical constants are mapped on elements of the domain. In particular, a predicate is mapped on a property and a relation term is mapped on a relation. For example, the intended interpretation maps the predicate "is a mother" on the property of being a mother. The domain thus not only contains individuals, but also properties and relations. Properties and relations are not understood as higher-order objects, but are, at least in this respect, ordinary first-order objects.[38] Importantly, however, form-logical semantics remains silent about the ontological

---

[38] The models of algebraic semantics also have a domain containing properties and relations as entities *sui generis* (see in particular Bealer & Mönnich 1989: 222). For a philosophical defense of a first-order treatment of predicates, i.e., a defense of treating predicates as naming properties, see also Bealer 1982, Ch. 4. Note that the first-order treatment of properties and relations blocks familiar ways to paradox.

An Alternative Semantic Theory: Form-Logical Semantics

status of the elements of the domain and thereby about the ontological status of the properties and the relations it contains. The semantics in no way presupposes that the elements of the domain constitute the fundamental building blocks of reality or, to use a common phrase, that they 'carve nature at its joints'. For example, the fact that the predicate "is a mother" is mapped on the property of being a mother in no way indicates that the property of being a mother must be 'ontologically real'. Quite to the contrary, it seems plausible that this property is one of those which allows for further ontological analysis. The properties and relations in the domain figure as the semantic values of the predicates, and that's it.[39]

Having dispelled possible ontological worries, I now spell out the formalities of form-logical semantics.[40] We first define a *domain* $\mathfrak{D}$ as a non-empty set of arbitrary objects (individuals, properties, relations). We then define a function i, called the *interpretation function*, from the set of non-logical constants into the domain:

i(*a*) $\in \mathfrak{D}$ for all non-logical constants *a*.

The interpretation function thus interprets all non-logical constants as referring to an element of the domain. We define the *variable assignment* β as a function from the set of variables into the domain $\mathfrak{D}$:

i(x) $\in \mathfrak{D}$ for all variables *x*.

$\mathfrak{I}$ is defined as the pair (i, β) of an interpretation function and a variable assignment. A formula is interpreted term wise:

---

[39] In David Lewis' terminology, the properties in the domain are *abundant* properties: "Sometimes we conceive of properties as abundant, sometimes as sparse. The abundant properties may be as extrinsic, as gruesomely gerrymandered, as miscellaneously disjunctive, as you please. [...] The abundant properties far outrun the predicates of any language we could possibly possess. There is one of them for any condition we could write down, even if we could write at infinite length and even if we could name all those things that must remain nameless because they fall outside our acquaintance." (Lewis 1986[a]: 59 ff.) While the sparse properties carve out the joints of reality, the abundant properties have no ontological impact, but merely serve as the semantic values of the predicates. (See also Schaffer 2004: 92, for a defense of this view.)

[40] As only the semantics of form logic, not its syntax, is needed in the following, here I assume the syntax of PL. The interested reader is asked to consult Freitag & Zinke 2012.

- $\mathfrak{J}(\tau) = i(\tau)$ iff τ is a non-logical constant,
- $\mathfrak{J}(\tau) = \beta(\tau)$ iff τ is a variable,
- $\mathfrak{J}(\tau_1 \ldots \tau_n) = \langle \mathfrak{J}(\tau_1), \ldots, \mathfrak{J}(\tau_n) \rangle$ for all atomic formulas $\tau_1 \ldots \tau_n$.[41]

To define *truth in a model*, we choose a set $\mathfrak{S}$ of tuples of elements of the domain. $\mathfrak{S}$ is called a *state*. The triple $\langle \mathfrak{D}, \mathfrak{J}, \mathfrak{S} \rangle$ is called a model $\mathfrak{M}$. Truth in a model for an atomic formula is defined as follows:

$$\mathfrak{M} \vDash \tau_1 \ldots \tau_n \text{ iff } \mathfrak{J}(\tau_1 \ldots \tau_n) \in \mathfrak{S}.$$

Molecular formulas then receive recursively defined truth conditions as in PL:

- $\mathfrak{M} \vDash \neg \varphi$ iff $\mathfrak{M} \nvDash \varphi$,
- $\mathfrak{M} \vDash \varphi \vee \psi$ iff $\mathfrak{M} \vDash \varphi$ or $\mathfrak{M} \vDash \psi$,
- $\mathfrak{M} \vDash \exists x \, \varphi$ iff there is an $a \in \mathfrak{D}$ with $\mathfrak{M}a/x \vDash \varphi$ (where $\mathfrak{M}a/x$ is defined as $\langle \mathfrak{D}, \mathfrak{J}a/x, \mathfrak{S} \rangle$).[42]

The only condition that matters in the present context is the first one of our list, i.e., the definition of truth in a model for an atomic formula. An atomic formula is true in a model iff the tuple of objects resulting from a term-wise interpretation of the formula is an element of the state of the model.

Before illuminating the semantics with an example, let me make some remarks about the notion of a state. As mentioned above, a state is a set of tuples of elements of the domain. This definition presupposes neither that a state is 'complete' nor that it is 'metaphysically

---

[41] See Soames 1987 for a similar account: "[T]he proposition expressed by an atomic formula "$Pt_1, \ldots, t_n$" relative to a context C and assignment f is $\langle\langle o_1, \ldots, o_n\rangle, P^*\rangle$, where P^* is the property expressed by P and o_i is the content of t_i relative to C and f." (Soames 1987: 62) Soames also provides an independent defense of the view that Russellian propositions should figure as the semantic values of sentences.

[42] $\mathfrak{J}a/x$ is defined in the obvious way:
(i) $\mathfrak{J}(\tau) = i(\tau)$ iff τ is a constant,
(ii) $\mathfrak{J}(\tau) = \beta a/x\,(\tau)$ iff τ is as variable,
(iii) $\mathfrak{J}(\tau_1 \ldots \tau_n) = \langle \mathfrak{J}(\tau_1), \ldots, \mathfrak{J}(\tau_n) \rangle$ for all atomic formulas $\tau_1 \ldots \tau_n$.
As usual, $\beta a/x$ (with β being a variable assignment and $a \in \mathfrak{D}$) is defined as follows: $\beta a/x\,(y) = \beta(y)$ if $y \neq x$ and $\beta a/x\,(y) = a$ if $y = x$.

consistent'. A state 𝔖 is *complete* iff for every *n*-ary relation R and individual objects $o_1, ..., o_n$ it holds that $<R, o_1, ..., o_n> \in 𝔖$ or that $<-R, o_1, ..., o_n> \in 𝔖$, where -R is the complement of R (for example, the properties of being married and of being unmarried are complements of each other). States need not be complete; there is, e.g., a state 𝔖 with <the property of being married, Alfred Tarski> $\notin 𝔖$ and <the property of being unmarried, Alfred Tarski> $\notin 𝔖$ (although the domain of the respective model contains Alfred Tarski and both properties). States might also not be *metaphysically consistent*, i.e., they may represent metaphysical impossibilities; there is, e.g., a state 𝔖 with <the property of being married, Alfred Tarski> $\in 𝔖$ and <the property of being unmarried, Alfred Tarski> $\in 𝔖$. Also, there is a state 𝔖 with, e.g., <the property of being a mother, Alfred Tarski> $\in 𝔖$ and <the property of being male, Alfred Tarski> $\in 𝔖$. So far, there are no restrictions on states. In particular, a state must not be understood as a possible world or even as a part of a possible world. Furthermore, there are also no restrictions on the elements of a state considered individually. As of yet, any tuple of elements of the domain may figure as an element of a state. It is not required that a tuple contains an *n*-place relation and n individuals. For example, a state may contain a pair containing just two properties, or a one-place tuple containing only one individual. It might seem a bit as a stretch of the term, but I will nevertheless call all elements of a state 'Russellian propositions'.

To see how it works, let's apply form-logical semantics to a toy example. Assume an alphabet containing the individual constant "Alfred Tarski" and the predicate constant "is married". Let the model 𝔐 be given by the domain 𝔇 = {Alfred Tarski, Plato, the property of being married}, the state 𝔖 = {<Alfred Tarski, the property of being married>} and by the interpretation function i defined as follows: i(*Alfred Tarski*) = Alfred Tarski, i(*is married*) = the property of being married. We then have i(*Alfred Tarski is married*) = <Alfred Tarski, the property of being married>. It holds that <Alfred Tarski, the property of being married> $\in 𝔖$, and thus 𝔐 ⊨ *Alfred Tarski is married*.

Now consider the model 𝔐' = <𝔇', 𝔍', 𝔖'> with 𝔇' = 𝔇, 𝔖' = 𝔖, and 𝔍' = 𝔍 except that i'(*Alfred Tarski*) = Plato. Then, i'(*Alfred Tarski is married*) = <Plato, the property of being married>. It holds that <Plato, the property of being married> $\notin 𝔖'$, and thus 𝔐' ⊭ *Alfred Tarski is married*.

Finally, look at the model $\mathfrak{M}'' = \langle \mathfrak{D}'', \mathfrak{I}'', \mathfrak{S}'' \rangle$ with $\mathfrak{D}'' = \mathfrak{D}$, $\mathfrak{I}'' = \mathfrak{I}$, and $\mathfrak{S}'' = \langle$Plato, the property of being married$\rangle$. Then, i''(*Alfred Tarski is married*) = $\langle$Alfred Tarski, the property of being married$\rangle$. It holds that $\langle$Alfred Tarski, the property of being married$\rangle \notin \mathfrak{S}''$, and thus $\mathfrak{M}'' \nvDash$ *Alfred Tarski is married*.

Despite its simplicity, I think that form-logical semantics has no less a claim to the label 'Tarskian' as has PL semantics. Form-logical semantics differs from the semantics of PL only with respect to two aspects: firstly, it interprets predicates as elements of the domain, and secondly, it defines truth of an atomic sentence via membership of the expressed proposition in the respective state. Let me address these aspects successively and start with Tarski's view on the semantics of predicates.

Tarski develops his general ideas on semantics in most detail in his monograph "The Concept of Truth in Formalized Languages", but there focuses on truth conditions for sentences of certain formal languages and hence ignores the semantics of natural language sentences. The first formal language Tarski looks at is the *calculus of classes*. In this language there are no predicates in the immediate sense of the term, but only, to use Tarski's expressions, 'names of objects' and 'names of classes of objects'. See, e.g., the following passage in which Tarski explains his notion of a sentential function:

> [T]hey are certain complexes of constants, or relations, and of variables which represent names. The first sign of such a complex is always the name of a class [...] or a corresponding variable, and is called a (sentence forming) functor of the given primitive sentential function; the remaining signs are called arguments. (Tarski 1935: 212 f., Tarski's emphasis)

According to Tarski, the first sign in a sentential function is a name of a class, while the subsequent signs are names of objects. That a 'name of a class' gets assigned as its semantic value a class of objects, however, is trivial and does not justify the interpretation of predicates as having sets of objects as their semantic values. Incidentally, Tarski adds a footnote to the above passage indicating that he hesitates to identify names of classes with natural language predicates:

> The sentence forming functors which have names as arguments are here identified with the names of classes or relations [...]. This interpretation seems artificial with the interpretation

An Alternative Semantic Theory: Form-Logical Semantics 43

of the term "functors" which was given by some examples on p. 161, note 1; in any case it certainly does not agree with the spirit and formal structure of the language of everyday life. (Tarski 1935: 213)

The examples for functors that Tarski gives in the respective footnote 161 are "reads", "sees", and "the father of", which are typical examples of natural language predicates and relation terms. Since the identification of predicates with names for sets of classes is "artificial" and does not fit the "spirit of the language of everyday life", this identification surely is no essential part of Tarski's theory, nor is that plausibly his views on natural language predicates.

The second feature in which PL semantics and FL semantics differ is the truth-definition for atomic sentences: in PL semantics, an atomic sentence is true just in case the semantic value of the individual constant is an element of the semantic value of the predicate. A precondition of this definition is that predicates are mapped on sets. I just argued that Tarski seems to reject this view. Furthermore, there are also independent reasons to think that Tarski does not subscribe to the definition of truth for atomic sentences as given in PL semantics. Actually, Tarski does not really elaborate on the notion of truth in a model for atomic formulas, but concentrates on spelling out the recursive truth conditions for molecular and quantified formulas on the basis of those for atomic sentences. He only says that an atomic formula is true in a model iff its sentential function is satisfied by it. When I explained Tarski's definition of logical truth in the preceding chapter, I already pointed to the fact that Tarski's models only provide an interpretation of the language, but do not in themselves determine the truth value of a sentence. The truth value also depends on what the world is like. To illustrate: Tarski says that a model with <John, Peter> as its first sequence satisfies the sentential function "x and y are brothers" iff John and Peter are brothers. Whether or not John and Peter are brothers is, however, not decided by the model, but dependent on the actual facts. Compare also Tarski's remarks in Tarski 1935: "We shall say that the objects R, a, and b satisfy the function Xyz if and only if R is a relation and a and b are individuals [...] and a stands in the relation R to b" (Tarski 1935: 225). If we ignore the detour via the notion of satisfaction here, Tarski's idea can be reformulated as follows: "*Rab* is true if and only if R is a relation and a and b are individuals and a stands in the relation R to b."

Whether a stands in relation R to b is solely determined by the worldly facts. In PL semantics, however, the model alone determines the truth value. Thus, Tarskian PL semantics plausibly is not Tarski's own.[43] Tarski's view is at best neutral between PL and FL semantics, as it only says that an atomic sentence is true iff the state of affairs it describes obtains. Perhaps Tarski can even be said to lean towards form-logical semantics.

But let me not dwell further on the question of historical legitimacy of our two semantical schemes. Form-logical semantics appears to be theoretically as legitimate as PL semantics is. I use FL semantics simply because it has a great practical advantage: it allows us to clearly and precisely distinguish between interpretational and representational conceptions of logical consequence.

2.2 Definitions of Logical Consequence and Logical Truth

To spell out the interpretational and representational definitions, we first have to introduce the notions of an *intended state* and an *intended interpretation*. The intended state is that set $\mathfrak{S}^*$ of Russellian propositions that has all and only the actually obtaining propositions as elements. The intended state $\mathfrak{S}^*$ represents, so to speak, the actual world. The intended interpretation i* assigns to each constant the semantic value it actually has. The intended interpretation interprets "Bertrand Russell" as referring to Bertrand Russell, and it maps "being married" on the property of being married. $\mathfrak{J}^*$ is given by the intended interpretation i* and some arbitrary variable assignment β: $\mathfrak{J}^* = (i^*, \beta)$, for some arbitrary variable assignment β.

We are now in the position to provide the interpretational and the representational definitions of logical truth and logical consequence:

(IT) Interpretational definition of logical truth
      A sentence φ is logically true iff:
      $(\mathfrak{D}, \mathfrak{J}, \mathfrak{S}^*) \vDash \varphi$ for all $\mathfrak{J}$ and all $\mathfrak{D}$.[44]

---

[43] This is at least true for Tarski's early writings. Things might change with his "Arithmetical Extensions of Relational Systems" from 1956 (jointly authored by Tarski and Vaught).

[44] As the intended state $\mathfrak{S}^*$ is fixed in the interpretational definitions (IC) and (IT), we cannot consider literally all domains, but only those that at least contain the

Definitions of Logical Consequence and Logical Truth 45

(IC) Interpretational definition of logical consequence
A sentence φ follows logically from a set of sentences $\Gamma = \{\gamma_1, \ldots, \gamma_n\}$ iff:
for all $\mathfrak{I}$ and all $\mathfrak{D}$ it holds that if $(\mathfrak{D}, \mathfrak{I}, \mathfrak{S}^*) \vDash \gamma_i$ for all $i \in \{1, .., n\}$, then $(\mathfrak{D}, \mathfrak{I}, \mathfrak{S}^*) \vDash \varphi$.

(RT) Representational definition of logical truth
A sentence φ is logically true iff:
$(\mathfrak{D}, \mathfrak{I}^*, \mathfrak{S}) \vDash \varphi$ for all $\mathfrak{S}$ and all $\mathfrak{D}$.

(RC) Representational definition of logical consequence
A sentence φ follows logically from a set of sentences $\Gamma = \{\gamma_1, \ldots, \gamma_n\}$ iff:
for all $\mathfrak{S}$ and all $\mathfrak{D}$ it holds that if $(\mathfrak{D}, \mathfrak{I}^*, \mathfrak{S}) \vDash \gamma_i$ for all $i \in \{1, .., n\}$, then $(\mathfrak{D}, \mathfrak{I}^*, \mathfrak{S}) \vDash \varphi$.

The interpretational definition of logical truth says that a sentence is logically true iff it is true in the intended state *in all interpretations* (and all domains). The interpretational definition leaves the world fixed and varies the interpretation. The representational definition does exactly the converse. It defines a sentence as logically true iff it is true in the intended interpretation and *in all states* (and all domains). It leaves the interpretation fixed and varies the state. We thus arrive at precise definitions of logical truth and logical consequence which capture the pretheoretical ideas underlying the interpretational and the representational views.[45, 46]

---

objects figuring in the tuples of $\mathfrak{S}^*$. Analogously, the intended interpretation is fixed in the representational definitions (RC) and (RT). Here we only consider those domains that are supersets of the image of i*. As the role of the domain is irrelevant for the arguments in the next chapters, we need not dwell on these subtleties.

[45] I pointed out at the beginning of this chapter that also an intensional semantics a lá Montague allows for properly spelling out the interpretational and representational definitions. To illustrate the basic idea, assume a fixed set of worlds $\mathfrak{W}$ including the actual world ω^*, and a fixed non-empty domain of objects $\mathfrak{D}$. (For the sake of simplicity, I use a possibilist semantics where we have one domain of objects for all worlds. Furthermore, I only consider a language without variables.) We then define an *interpretation* $\mathfrak{I}$, which assigns an intension i to every non-logical constant: $\mathfrak{I}$ assigns a function from $\mathfrak{W}$ to $\mathfrak{D}$ to every individual constant, and to every n-place relation constant $\mathfrak{I}$ assigns a function mapping each world on a subset of $\mathfrak{D}^n$. (We also write $\mathfrak{I}(t, \omega)$ instead of $\mathfrak{I}(t)(\omega)$. $\mathfrak{I}^*$ is the in-

In the next chapters I will discuss the interpretational and the representational definitions one by one, concentrating on the interpretational definitions. I will argue that (IT) and (IC) are untenable as they stand. After all, however, this should not come as a surprise. We already noticed in the introduction that the interpretational definitions grossly undergenerate if we allow a reinterpretation of the logical constants: no sentence will then be logically true and no argument logically valid. To account for this, the interpretational definition of logical truth is usually formulated along the following lines: a sentence is logically true iff it is true under all interpretations *of the non-logical terms*. A logically true sentence need only be true independently of the meanings of the non-logical constants. Its truth may depend on the meaning of the logical terms.

As I will lay out in the next chapters, however, we cannot even reasonably demand truth under all interpretations of the non-logical terms. If we do not also restrict reinterpretation of non-logical constants, again, no sentence whatsoever will turn out to be logically true. To provide for the possibility of further restrictions on interpretations, I propose the following amendment of the interpretational definition of logical truth: a sentence is logically true iff it is true under all

---

tended interpretation function.) Truth in an interpretation at a world ω is then defined in the usual way, e.g., $(\mathfrak{I}, \omega) \vDash R^n(a_1, \ldots, a_n)$
iff $\langle \mathfrak{I}(a_1, \omega), \ldots, \mathfrak{I}(a_1, \omega) \rangle \in \mathfrak{I}(R^n, \omega)$, where R^n is an n-place relation constant and a_i (with $i \in \{1, \ldots, n\}$) are individual constants. In this framework, interpretational and representational logical truth can be defined as follows:

Interpretational definition of logical truth:
A formula φ is logically true iff for all interpretations $\mathfrak{I}$ it holds that $(\mathfrak{I}, \omega^*) \vDash \varphi$.

Representational definition of logical truth:
A formula φ is logically true iff for all worlds ω it holds that $(\mathfrak{I}^*, \omega) \vDash \varphi$.

[46] It has been suggested to combine the interpretational and the representational definition of logical truth (see, e.g., Shapiro 1998, Hanson 1997, McFarlane (unpublished), resulting in the following definition:

(CT) A sentence φ is logically true iff $(\mathfrak{D}, \mathfrak{I}, \mathfrak{S}) \vDash \varphi$ for all $\mathfrak{I}$ and all $\mathfrak{S}$ and all $\mathfrak{D}$.

(CT) says that a sentence is logically true iff it is true under all interpretations in all states (and with respect to all domains). As the discussion in the next chapters will show, nothing is gained by this synthesis of the interpretational and the representational definition.

admissible interpretations. The reformulated interpretational definition of logical truth thus reads as follows:

(IT*) A sentence φ is logically true iff:
　　　$(\mathfrak{D}, \mathfrak{I}, \mathfrak{S}^*) \vDash \varphi$ for all *admissible* $\mathfrak{I}$ and all $\mathfrak{D}$.

(IT*) is unbiased between different possible restrictions. The extension of the interpretational definition of logical truth will depend on the chosen restrictions. To mention just the two extreme cases: If all reinterpretations are deemed admissible, no sentence will be declared logically true by (IT*). If, on the other end of the spectrum, no reinterpretation is admissible, all true sentences will be defined logically true. We have to strike the balance between these two extremes. But we do not only strive for extensional adequacy. The restrictions on interpretations must not be unfounded, but thoroughly justified. The hard task is to draw the line between the admissible and the inadmissible interpretations and to justify it. We must solve *the problem of admissible interpretations*.

We already saw that interpretations reinterpreting the logical constants must be excluded from the admissible ones. This gives us the first restriction on admissible interpretations:

(I1)　Only those interpretations are admissible that do not reinterpret the logical terms.

Restriction (I1) presupposes a delineation of the logical from the non-logical constants.[47] So far, the literature mainly focused on possible demarcation criteria for logical constants.[48] The next chapters will show that this is an illegitimately narrow focus. We do not only have to decide between fixing a term totally, i.e., not allowing any reinterpretation of it, and not fixing it at all. We can, and must, also partly fix the interpretation of terms. Furthermore, certain cross-term re-

---

[47]　(I1) is already encoded in the interpretation function of most formal systems, such as, e.g., PL and FL: the interpretation function i is usually only defined on the non-logical constants. I discuss the dialectical differences already encoded versus not yet encoded restrictions in Sec. 6.2.

[48]　A notable exception is Sagi 2014. Sagi stresses the possibility of constraints on interpretations that go beyond (I1): "Even if a term is not to be completely fixed and considered as a logical term in a system in the standard sense, its range of interpretations can still be limited, and this option should have a place in a theory of logical reasoning." (Sagi 2014: 266)

strictions on the simultaneous reinterpretation of terms will be shown to be necessary. The problem of the logical constants, so prominently discussed in the literature, is merely a sub-problem of the deeper and much more general problem of admissible interpretations.

3 From Structural Truth to Logical Truth

Restriction (I1) confines the admissible interpretations to those treating the logical constants as fixed terms. Of course, this restriction is already implicit in the definition of the interpretation function i of standard formal languages. The interpretation function is usually only defined on the non-logical terms, while the logical terms are interpreted via the recursive definition of truth-in-a-model. In this chapter, I want to pinpoint a further restriction that we impose on admissible interpretations, albeit only implicitly: the reinterpretation of a sentence must not violate the grammatical categories of the occurring terms.

In the first section of this chapter, I will make this implicit restriction explicit. I present a generalization of the restriction in the second section and argue that its scope depends on the underlying notion of a grammatical category. In particular, under certain conceptions of grammatical categories so-called 'structural truths' will be declared logically true by the interpretational definition.

3.1 Grammatical Restrictions

The sentence "Pluto is a planet or Pluto is not a planet" is a paradigm case of a logically true sentence. If we impose restriction (I1), i.e., if we do not reinterpret "or" and "not", the sentence may appear true under all interpretations. For example, if we interpret "Pluto" as having Plato as its semantic value and "is a planet" as having the property of being a philosopher as its semantic value, the sentence expresses the proposition that Plato is a philosopher or that Plato is not a philosopher. Thus it is, again, true. Yet appearance is misleading. Consider an interpretation that treats the term "is a planet" as having Plato as its semantic value and interprets "Pluto" as usual. The sentence then no longer expresses a genuine proposition. It does not make any sense any more, but has become a meaningless sequence of words. This is a result of the fact that the considered interpretation does not respect the grammatical categories of the terms, as it interprets a predicate term as having an individual as its semantic value.

In claiming that a sentence is true under all interpretations, the type of reinterpretation just cited is implicitly ignored. Interpretations violating the grammatical categories are generally held inadmissible.[49]

To properly formulate the respective restriction on admissible interpretations, let $\tau^{[i]}$ stand for the term τ interpreted under i; $\tau^{[i]}$ is an interpreted term. For example, "*Pluto*$^{[i^*]}$" is the term "Pluto" considered under the intended interpretation. (Importantly, $\tau^{[i]}$ is to be distinguished from i(τ). i(τ) is the semantic value of τ interpreted under i, i.e., an object, whereas $\tau^{[i]}$ is an interpreted term.) Here is the grammatical restriction on interpretations:

(I2)   An interpretation i is only admissible if the following holds:
if $\tau^{[i^*]}$ is an individual constant, then $\tau^{[i]}$ is an individual constant, and
if $\tau^{[i^*]}$ is an *n*-ary relation constant, then $\tau^{[i]}$ is an *n*-ary relation constant.

(I2) restricts the admissible interpretations to those that are faithful to the distinction between individual and relation terms. An admissible interpretation must reinterpret an individual constant as an individual constant and an *n*-ary relation constant as an *n*-ary relation constant. The case in which "Pluto" is interpreted as referring to Plato is therefore excluded and our sample sentence "Pluto is a planet or Pluto is not a planet" defined logically true.[50]

---

[49] If we decide to assign a truth value to atomic sentences also under those interpretations that violate the categories of the terms, no problem for the definition of logical truth will arise from such interpretations. The sentence "Plato is a planet or Plato is not a planet" will then be true also under an interpretation that maps the predicate "is a planet" on the individual Plato. However, many philosophers, including me, prefer to say that sentences expressing no proposition do not even qualify as truth-value bearers; definitely, they should not be said to be true, let alone logically true.

[50] There is a hint at grammatical restrictions on interpretations already in Tarski 1936. Right after proposing his definition of logical consequence as truth-preservation in all interpretations, Tarski makes the following comment: "For the sake of simplifying the discussion certain incidental complications are disregarded, both here and in what follows. They are connected partly with the theory of logical types [...]." (Tarski 1936:4 15) The context of Tarski's work suggests that the "logical types" are the types from Russell's theory of types and Tarski explicitly relates Russellian logical types to grammatical categories in Tarski 1935: 215. One could thus read the above passage as already making explicit

To avoid any possible misunderstanding regarding the formulation of (I2), let me already point out that, once we consider natural language, we cannot first categorize non-interpreted signs into grammatical categories, and then, in a second step, interpret them in accordance with their grammatical categorization. In natural language, syntax and semantics are more deeply intertwined. Therefore, restriction (I2) is formulated for interpreted terms, and the grammatical category of a term is made dependent also on its interpretation. (I elaborate on this in the next section.)

The situation is wholly different with regard to formal languages. In standard formal languages, as, e.g., in PL, the grammatical category of a term is displayed already by the typographical form of the term. For example, individual constants are usually lower case letters, often from the beginning of the alphabet, such as a_j or c_k, while predicate and relation terms are chosen to be capital letters like F_j, or G_k. Already Tarski remarks that the grammatical category of a term can be read off its typographical form (Tarski uses the term "semantical category" instead of "grammatical category"):

> Thanks to a suitable choice of the signs used in the construction of the expressions of the language, the mere shape of the sign (and even of the composite expression) decides to which category it belongs. Consequently it is possible that in methodological and semantical investigations concerning a concrete language, the concept of semantical categories does not explicitly occur at all. (Tarski 1935: 217, fn. 1)

In most formal languages, the grammatical category of a term is exhibited by its form. Categorical differences are syntactically encoded.

---

that the admissible interpretations must be confined to those respecting the grammatical categories.

Similarly Bolzano seems to base his substitutional definition on a prior classification of the terms into grammatical categories. As Etchemendy points out, "Bolzano's test for logical truth requires a division of expressions into grammatical categories, basically into groupings whose members can be freely exchanged within sentences without risking ungrammaticality". (Etchemendy 1990: 39. For the original passage in Bolzano, see particularly Bolzano 1973, §189.) This quote by Etchemendy not only expresses the need for restricting the admissible interpretations/substitutions to those respecting the grammatical categories of the terms, but it also suggests a definition of the notion of a grammatical category. I will discuss this proposal in the next section.

Moreover, as restriction (I1), so is the grammatical restriction already implicit in the definition of the interpretation function of PL and related formal languages: every interpretation function i of PL maps individual constants on elements of the domain and relation constants on sets of (tuples of) elements of the domain. The interpretation function is defined in such a way that it automatically respects the grammatical categories of the terms. It is therefore all the more important to make explicit the grammatical restriction that is usually only implicitly imposed. (I2) does exactly this.

3.2 Structural Restrictions

(I2) restricts the admissible interpretations to those that reinterpret individual constants as individual constants and relation constants as relation constants. It thus presupposes the classical bisection of constants, on which the syntax of first-order predicate logic is based. However, we can think of different or more fine-grained classifications of terms. The traditional bisection of terms into individual and relation constants might not be justified, or – perhaps more likely – we might strive for finer distinctions resulting in further subcategories. We should thus make room for a more liberal understanding of the notion of a grammatical category and reformulate restriction (I2) such that it is neutral with respect to different possible classifications of terms.

Let the function f induce a partition on the set of terms. Intuitively, f groups the terms into their respective grammatical categories. The generalization of (I2) takes the following form.

(I2*) An interpretation i is only admissible if the following holds:
$$f(\tau^{[i]}) = f(\tau^{[i^*]})$$

(I2*) regards those interpretations as inadmissible that do not respect the grammatical categories of the terms. An interpretation must be faithful to the grammatical category of the term. Which interpretations are deemed inadmissible by (I2*) depends on the chosen classification of terms into grammatical categories. For example, grouping the terms into the category of individual terms and the category of relation terms yields restriction (I2).[51]

The proponent of the interpretational definition has to provide, and justify, a particular classification of terms into grammatical categories. To illustrate the potential difficulties, I will now look more closely at the notion of a grammatical category and possible classifications of terms, resulting in different instances of (I2*).

The term 'grammatical category' is used in various ways, also among different disciplines. Here, however, we are not interested in the notion of a grammatical category in general, but only in the concept of a grammatical category as it figures in restriction (I2*), i.e., the notion of a grammatical category captured by the function f employed in (I2*). We opt for a characterization of that notion of a grammatical category which is relevant for a definition of logical consequence. To make this limit in scope explicit, I will also speak of an *(I2*)-grammatical category*.

A common characterization of the relevant notion of a grammatical category employs the criterion of substitutability *salva congruitate*. Terms are substitutable *salva congruitate* just in case their mutual substitution never turns a well-formed formula into one that it not well-formed. See, e.g., Tarski 1935:[52]

> [T]wo expressions belong to the same [grammatical – A.Z.] category if (1) there is a sentential function which contains one of these expressions, and if (2) no sentential function which contains one of these expressions ceases to be a sentential function if this expression is replaced in it by the other. (Tarski 1935: 216)

---

[51] Both (I2) and (I2*) impose restrictions on interpretations of one term considered in isolation. We could also think of the grammatical and the structural restrictions as 'cross-term restrictions', i.e., restrictions that confine the simultaneous reinterpretation of two or more terms. This could result in a weaker constraint on interpretations, which only demands that the whole formula must be reinterpreted such that it is still grammatically well-formed.

[52] See also Quine 1970: 18: "[T]he category of an expression is the class of all the expressions that are interchangeable with it *salva congruitate*." A similar remark can be found in Carnap 1937, §46. (Carnap, however, calls terms that are substitutable *salva congruitate* 'isogenous' expressions and calls a class of isogenous expressions a 'genus'.)

Despite its intuitive appeal, it is far from trivial that the definition of a grammatical category via the notion of substitutability *salva congruitate* serves our purposes. To begin with, Etchemendy poses the following problem case (see Etchemendy 1990, Ch. 3, fn.13). The noun phrases "George Washington" and "every president" seem to be substitutable *salva congruitate* in all sentences. However, if we classify these two terms in the same (I2*)-grammatical category, paradigm cases of logically true sentences will not come out as logically true according to the interpretational definition. If we substitute "every president" for "George Washington" in the sentence "George Washington had a beard or George Washington did not have a beard", the resulting sentence would be false. (To avoid utterly cumbersome formulations, I speak of 'substitutions' rather than of 'reinterpretations' here.) Another interesting counter example is due to Mark Sainsbury.[53] Consider the following argument: "Human beings are sensitive to pain. Harry is a human being. Therefore, Harry is sensitive to pain." This argument will only be declared logically valid, if we exclude the following substitution instance from the admissible ones: "Human beings are evenly distributed over the earth's surface. Harry is a human being. Therefore, Harry is evenly distributed over the earth's surface." Thus, "being distributed over the earth's surface" and "being sensitive to pain" must not belong to the same (I2*)-grammatical category. It is far from obvious, however, that we cannot always substitute the one expression for the other *salva congruitate*.

Even if one could cope with examples like these, the criterion of substitutability *salva congruitate* is faced with a more fundamental worry. To determine whether two terms are substitutable *salva congruitate*, one must already know which sentences are ranked among the well-formed ones. The criterion thus ultimately rests on the notion of a well-formed sentence. In a formal language, there are explicit and exact formation rules for formulas. These formation rules, however, take recourse to the grammatical categories. In PL, for example, we define a formula as well-formed if the first term belongs to the category of n-ary relations and the next n terms all belong to the category

---

[53] See Sainsbury 1991, Ch. 6; however, Sainsbury introduces this example in a completely different context.

of individual terms. Obviously, the interpretationalist cannot presuppose a classification of terms in grammatical categories on pain of circularity here. The objective is to determine whether a formula is well-formed without employing the notion of a grammatical category. The criterion of substitutability *salva congruitate* demands a self-contained demarcation criterion for well-formed sentences.

In the present context, the notion of a well-formed formula cannot be spelled out syntactically, as this would presuppose the notion of a grammatical category. It seems that the interpretationalist must take recourse to a semantic notion of a well-formed formula. At least as far as natural language is concerned, the following criterion suggests itself: a string of terms is well-formed just in case it 'makes sense'. Here, a semantic demarcation criterion of sentences into well-formed ones and ill-formed ones is assumed, and then, in a second step, the grammatical categories are derived via the criterion of substitutability *salva congruitate*.

A famous objection to the semantic characterization of well-formed sentences immediately comes to mind: Noam Chomsky's example "Colorless green ideas sleep furiously" (Chomsky 1957). The crux of this example is exactly that it seems to be grammatically well-formed, though semantically nonsensical. However, we need not discard the semantic account of well-formedness so hastily. The Chomskyan example surely puts into doubt whether the notion of a grammatical category *in general*, or the notion of well-formedness in general, can be characterized in terms of making sense. Yet, as pointed out above, this is not the notion relevant here. We are only interested in the notion of an (I2*)-grammatical category. (I2*) was designed to exclude those interpretations from the admissible ones that interpret a sentence in a way such that it no longer qualifies as a truth value bearer. As long as we do not want to assign a truth value to the Chomskyan sentence, it is not well-formed in the relevant sense, i.e., it is not (I2*)-well-formed. Hence, the Chomskyan example does not force us to discard the proposal that a natural language sentence is (I2*)-well-formed iff it makes sense.

Let me recapitulate the findings of this chapter so far. In order to be logically true, a sentence need not be true under literally all interpretations. Not only interpretations reinterpreting the logical constants, but also interpretations not respecting the grammatical categories of the terms need to be excluded from the admissible ones.

To flesh out the respective restriction, the interpretationalist has to provide a classification of terms into grammatical categories. We tentatively proposed to define the notion of a grammatical category via the criterion of substitutability *salva congruitate*, which itself rests on a demarcation of the well-formed from the ill-formed sentences. On pain of circularity, we cannot define a well-formed sentence via the notion of a grammatical category in the present context. It seems that the only other plausible criterion of demarcation is a semantic one: a sequence of terms is well-formed iff it is meaningful.

I am fully aware that the above remarks do not even come close to providing a reductive analysis of the notion of a grammatical category, or even of an (I2*)-grammatical category. Firstly, I did not properly defend the criterion of substitutability *salva congruitate* against the mentioned alleged counter examples. Secondly, and probably more importantly, the proposed characterization of a grammatical category rests on an even more dubious notion, the notoriously cryptic notion of meaningfulness. Still, I did not mean to provide a precise analysis of (I2*)-grammaticality. My sole objective was to exemplify that the classification of terms into grammatical categories does not run by itself. There is plenty of room for discussion. We do not yet have a precise analysis of the notion of a grammatical category. As a consequence, it is still not settled which terms should be treated as belonging to the same category. However, once restriction (I2*) is imposed, whether or not certain sentences are declared logically true by the interpretational definition hinges on the grammatical classification of terms. This in particular affects certain paradigm cases of so-called *structural truths*. Let me explain.

The notion of structural truth is explained by Gareth Evans as follows: a sentence is structurally true iff its truth "depends merely upon the *kind* of semantic elements out of which a sentence is constructed, and its manner of construction" (Evans 1985: 60 f.). Paradigm examples of structural truths are, e.g., "If Lisa quietly left school, Lisa left school" and "If Snowball is a black cat, Snowball is a cat". It is usually argued that these sentences are not logically true as there are reinterpretations or substitutions which make them false. Substitution of "allegedly" for "quietly" in the first example, and of "fake" for "black" in the second, might make the respective sentences false. However, linguists still discuss whether manner adverbs like, e.g., "quietly", "quickly", and "slowly" belong to the same grammatical category as adverbs like "allegedly" and "partially". In particular, the criterion of substitution *salva congruitate* speaks against classifying manner adverbs and "allegedly"-type adverbs into the same grammatical category: for example, substitution of "allegedly" by "slowly" turns the well-formed sentences "Gonzo allegedly knows French" and "Kermit is allegedly allergic to peanuts" into ones that are not well-formed.[54] These data also indicate that manner adverbs do not uniformly function as verb-phrase operators. According to the operator approach of manner adverbs, the meanings of manner adverbs determine functions from verb-phrase meanings to verb-phrase meanings.[55] Yet it has also been proposed that modification by a manner adverb should rather be understood as an attributive use of an event-level adjective.[56] As this is implausible for 'allegedly'-type adverbs, manner adverbs would then have a different kind of semantic value than 'allegedly'-type adverbs. They are not verb-phrase operators but predicates of events. If syntax must answer to semantics, this could also count in favor of fine-graining the grammatical category of adverbs such that manner adverbs and 'allegedly'-type adverbs are not grouped together.

If we follow this line of reasoning and categorize manner adverbs in a different grammatical category than 'allegedly'-type adverbs, the sentence "If Lisa quietly left school, Lisa left school", a putative paradigm example of a merely structurally true sentence, will be true under all interpretations and hence a logical truth: if "quietly" may only be reinterpreted as having the semantic value of another manner adverb, such as, e.g., "slowly" or "loudly", there is no interpretation under which the sentence is false. Similarly, it has been proposed that attributive adjectives like "black" do belong to the same category as 'fake'-type adjectives. If we treat them as members of different grammatical categories, also the second cited paradigm case of a structural truth turns out to be a logical truth.

---

[54] See Balcerak-Jackson 2017: 30 for these examples. This paper also provides a good overview of further differences in the behavior of these adverbs that might indicate that they belong to different grammatical categories.
[55] See, e.g. Cresswell 1976, Montague 1970[a], Thomason and Stalnaker 1973.
[56] See, e.g. Eckardt 1998, Higginbotham 1985, Katz 2003, McConnell-Ginet 1982, Parsons 1990.

Yet observe that my target here is not to uncover the correct grammatical categories of the terms. This would be a huge and indeed quite comprehensive linguistic research program. My aim is to stress the possible consequences of the grammatical restriction (I2*). As the extension of the interpretational definition varies with the classification of terms in grammatical categories, restriction (I2*) might blur the boundaries between structural and logical truth.

4 From Analytic Truth to Logical Truth

Grammatical restrictions on interpretations are necessary, but they are not sufficient. We need also *identity restrictions*: interpretations must be 'uniform', i.e., all occurrences of a term must be interpreted alike. Again, I take myself not to formulate a new restriction, but one which has played an important role in everyday logical practice. It has only remained largely implicit – no doubt due to the fact that it is undisputed. I make this restriction explicit and argue that it is not as innocent as it might seem. In particular, the restriction will crucially involve the notion of word-identity. Depending on one's exact criteria for word-identity, certain further restrictions on interpretations can be motivated. As a result of these restrictions, some alleged paradigm cases of mere analytic truths will turn out to be logical truths according to the interpretational definition.[57]

4.1 Identity Restrictions

Consider again our paradigm case of a logical truth: "Pluto is a planet or Pluto is not a planet". This sentence is taken to be true under all interpretations (assuming that interpretations respect the grammatical categories and treat the logical constants as fixed terms). Yet, if we consider an interpretation that maps the first occurrence of "Pluto" on Pluto and the second occurrence on Venus, the sentence is false.[58] Of course, however, such reinterpretations are usually taken to be inadmissible on the grounds that they interpret two occurrences of

---

[57] In the proceeding chapter, I discussed 'structural truths', while I concentrate on 'analytic truths' in this chapter. One might argue that structural truths are also analytic, and I would not mind such a characterization. However, the truth of structural truths is due solely to their (grammatical) structure, while the truth of analytic truths is (also) due to the meanings of the terms. It is thus helpful to discuss structural truths and (genuine) analytic truths separately.

[58] As you know, Pluto is denied the status of a planet. The official definition of a *planet* set in 2006 by the *International Astronomical Union* states that, in the Solar System, a planet is a celestial body that "(i) is in orbit around the Sun, (ii) has sufficient mass for its self-gravity to overcome rigid body-forces so that it assumes a hydrostatic equilibrium (nearly round) shape, and (iii) has cleared the neighborhood around its orbit." (IAU 2006: *General Assembly: Resolutions 5 and 6*. 2006-08-24) Pluto has not cleared his neighborhood and was therefore expulsed from the unsoiled family of planets. Pluto is a dwarf planet. The IAU is explicit that dwarf planets are, despite their name, no planets.

one word differently. The admissible interpretations are restricted to those respecting the identities between the terms. We call this restriction the *identity restriction*.

As the restriction on the reinterpretation of the logical constants and the grammatical restriction were already implicit in our standard formal languages, so is the identity restriction. In both, PL and FL, the interpretation function is defined on the set of terms, not on the set of term occurrences. All occurrences of one term are thus automatically interpreted alike. One therefore tends to overlook the identity restriction. It is time to make it explicit.

Let the function f map each term occurrence on the term of which it is an occurrence, and let τ_j and τ_k be arbitrary term occurrences. Here is the identity restriction:

(I3) An interpretation i is only admissible if the following holds:
if $f(\tau_j^{[i*]}) = f(\tau_k^{[i*]})$, then $i(\tau_j) = i(\tau_k)$.

An admissible interpretation maps two term occurrences on the same semantic value, if the two term occurrences – considered under the intended interpretation – are occurrences of the same term. Under the intended interpretation, the two occurrences of "Pluto" in our initial example are occurrences of the same term. By restriction (I3), only those interpretations are admissible which interpret these occurrences uniformly.

Restriction (I3) imposes conditions on the *simultaneous* reinterpretation of term occurrences. In contrast to the restrictions presented so far, (I3) does not exclude interpretations that assign an illegitimate semantic value to term occurrences in isolation, but it excludes interpretations that do not respect a certain relation between different term occurrences. Such relational restrictions may be called *cross-term restrictions* (or *cross-occurrence restrictions*).[59]

The function f figuring in restriction (I3) maps each term occurrences on the term of which it is an occurrences. Which interpretations are excluded from the admissible ones by (I3), thus depends on the classification of term occurrences into terms: to apply (I3), one has to spell out the conditions that term occurrences must satisfy in

---

[59] This expression 'cross-term restriction' is borrowed from Etchemendy 1990, although he employs it in a different context. See my later remarks.

order to be occurrences of the same term. The proponent of the interpretational definition must determine the exact identity criteria for terms or words. He must specify which term occurrences count as being occurrences of the *same* term.

This is a notoriously difficult task. As meaningful items, words are very peculiar entities, somehow 'reaching out' to the world. The identity conditions of words are inscrutable. The word "word" itself appears to be polysemous. In some sense, "color" and "colour" are the same word, in another, they are different words. In some sense, Alfred Tarski and Alfred Nobel have the same first name, in another, they don't.[60] And in some sense, our word "planet" is the same as the one used years ago, in another, it is not. The question of word identity, at least if phrased in these general terms, lacks a unique answer. However, the proponent of the interpretational definition need not spell out the conditions of word identity in all its generality. The interpretationalist can concentrate on the particular notion of word identity, or term identity, figuring in restriction (I3). The notion of an *(I3)-term* must be defined. The interpretationalist is looking for that notion of term identity that is relevant for determining the logical properties of a sentence. This notion need not coincide with the (or a) common or pretheoretic notion of word identity.

To begin with, consider the question of term identity in formal languages. When we introduce a formal language, we begin with an alphabet. The alphabet contains a list of terms, which are not yet interpreted. All there is are signs with a certain typographical appearance. Thus, the only sensible way to define term identity in a formal language seems to be by reference to the typographical type of the term occurrences. This suggests the following criterion of term identity: two term occurrences are occurrences of the same term iff they are of the same typographical type.[61] We say that two term occurrences

---

[60] Kaplan 1990 would say that Tarski and Nobel share one *generic name*, but have different *common currency names*.

[61] The typographical type here stands exemplarily for further non-semantic types like, e.g., the phonetic type. However, I concentrate on written language here and thus focus on the typographical type. Interestingly, as Hawthorne and Lepore 2011 observe, while philosophers seem to focus on the typography of words, linguists tend to take the phonetics of words as authoritative for word identity (compare, e.g., Fiengo and May 2006: 54, Segas and Speas 1986).

are of the same *typographical type* iff they 'look the same', i.e., if they have the same graphical form. "a" and "a" are occurrences of the same constant because they are of the same typographical type.

Observe that in most formal languages term occurrences belonging to the same typographical type usually also have the same semantic value, i.e., the tokens are also of the same *semantic type*. In formal languages, the typographical type and the semantic type thus stand in an intimate relation. In fact, Tarski took it to be the essential feature of a formal language that sameness of typographical type guarantees sameness of semantic type:

> I restrict myself henceforth to formalized languages. These can be roughly characterized as artificially constructed languages in which the sense of every expression is uniquely determined by its form. (Tarski 1935: 165 f.)

Context shows that Tarski is referring to typographical form here. According to Tarski, it is a characteristic of formal languages that typographical identity implies sameness of semantic values.[62] However, this is a feature of formal languages alone. We cannot rely on it to be present in natural language.

Contrary to formulas of a formal language, natural language sentences are already interpreted. Whereas the terms of formal languages are non-interpreted signs, the words of natural language have an intended meaning. Furthermore, it is not the case that natural language terms of one typographical type are also of one semantic type: natural language contains homonymic expressions. With respect to natural language, the typographical type alone cannot determine the (I3)-term. Otherwise, all occurrences of homonyms would be of the same (I3)-term and far too many sentences would turn out to be logically true according to the interpretational definition. We can borrow one particularly neat example from Peter Strawson:

> [C]onsider two typographically identical occurrences of the sentence "He is sick." In one occurrence the sentence might be used to attribute a property of mind to one person, in the

---

[62] While Tarski takes it to be a defining feature of formal languages that sameness of typographical type implies sameness of semantic value, there certainly are possible alternatives. One could easily invent languages in which this is not the case and which plausible are regarded as formal languages themselves.

> other occurrence to attribute a condition of body to a different person. (Nor is this fact altered by replacing the pronoun "he" by a proper name, say, "John".) If now, keeping in mind two such uses for this expression, we frame the sentence "If he is sick, then he is sick", we obtain something which may be used to make statements some of which may be true and others false. (Strawson 1957: 117)

The sentence "he is sick" is ambiguous. It is so in two ways. The two occurrences of the pronoun "he" can refer to different persons, and the predicate "is sick" can mean different things: It can mean that the respective person is, say, depressed. Alternatively, it means that the person is physically ill. That the pronoun "he" can refer to different persons is a matter of the vagaries of indexical reference which I do not want to discuss here. However, as Strawson notes, the sentence remains doubly ambiguous even if we substitute "John" for "he". If we nevertheless take the two occurrences of "sick" and of "he" (or "John") to be of the same (I3)-term, then they may only be interpreted alike. Thus the sentence "if he is sick, then he is sick" (or "if John is sick, then John is sick") would be declared logically true, although it is only contingently true. (Just assume, e.g., that the sentence means that if John$_1$ is depressed, John$_2$ is physically ill and assume that the respective states of affairs obtain.)

Strawson's example shows that typographically identical natural language expressions might have different semantic values. Strawson's argumentative aim, however, is more ambitious and quite similar to mine. His paper is a critical reply to Quine's "Two Dogmas of Empiricism" in which Quine famously argues that the notion of an analytic sentence rests on the notion of synonymy: an analytic sentence is one that can be transformed into a logical truth by substituting synonyms for synonyms. In his reply, Strawson argues that Quine has to extend his critique to logical truths, as the definition of logical truth also rests on the notion of synonymy. As a consequence, Strawson says, "Quine's characterization of logical truth can be made coherent, and made to do its job, only by implicit use of notions belonging to the group which he wishes to discredit" (Strawson 1957: 126).

Strawson establishes this conclusion in two steps. He first argues by reference to the above example that sameness of typographical type is not sufficient for two occurrences of a term to be occurrences of the same term. He goes on to show that, second, it also does not suffice for sameness of term type that two term tokens are typographical identical and have the same extension. Even if, say, the set of depressed persons is identical to the set of ill persons, and thus that "sick" (in the sense of 'depressed') and "sick" (in the sense of 'physically ill') would be extensionally identical, the above sentence should not be declared logically true because it is still – we may assume – only contingently true.[63] Strawson suggests that two occurrence of one term need not only be of the same typographical term type and have the same "reference", but must also have the same "sense":[64]

> A statement is a truth of logic if it is true, and remains true under all reinterpretations of the components other than the logical particles, provided that, [...] in any reinterpretation of non-propositional components all those identities of sense and ref-

---

[63] Let me remark that Strawson and I are in subtly different dialectical situations. I argue that the interpretational definition of logical truth massively overgenerates if we take typographical identity to determine whether two term occurrences are occurrences of the same (I3)-term. This follows from the way in which I formulated the respective restriction (I3): only interpretations i are admissible such that $i(\tau_j) = i(\tau_k)$ if τ_j and τ_k belong to the same term type. If we take the two occurrences of "John" or of "is sick" in Strawson's example to be occurrences of the same (I3)-term, then the sentence "if John is sick, then John is sick" will come out as logically true, although it is only contingently true. Strawson, however, argues that if we say that occurrences of the same typographical type are occurrences of the same term, then the definition of logical truth undergenerates. It would not declare any sentence to be logically true. This dialectical difference has a straightforward explanation. Strawson thinks of the relevant restriction on admissible substitutions as formulated as follows (Strawson discusses the substitutional definition, not the interpretation one, but this is irrelevant for the present concern): only substitutions are admissible that substitute occurrences of one term with occurrences that are also occurrences of one term. Taking both occurrences of "is sick" to be occurrences of the same term, then allows one to substitute them for the two occurrences of "is a philosopher" in the sentence "Plato is a philosopher or Plato is not a philosopher", generating the sentence "Plato is sick or Plato is not sick". This sentence might well be false. Thus, the definition of logical truth fails to declare certain intuitively logically true sentences to be logically true. See Strawson 1957: 117.

[64] As he is replying to Quine, Strawson also says that occurrences of the same term must be "synonymous". See Strawson 1957: 120 f. Barrett 1965: 361 ff. also argues for the claim that the interpretational definition of logical truth must presuppose the notion of synonymy, i.e., it must base its identity conditions for terms on semantic considerations.

> erence which are represented in the original statement by typographically identical predicate expressions and referring expressions are preserved in the reinterpretation. (Strawson 1957: 128)

Typographical identity cannot suffice for sameness of (I3)-term. Along the lines of Strawson, I claim that sameness of semantic value is necessary for sameness of (I3)-term: two term occurrences that are occurrences of the same term, must have the same semantic value. Observe, however, that I use the term "semantic value" in a neutral sense. It allows for different specifications. Semantic values need not be identified with *Fregean* senses. (See the next section for more on this.) In any case, the identity conditions of terms cannot be given independently of semantic notions. Indeed, I want to tentatively suggest that the semantics does all the work in determining the identity conditions for (I3)-terms: two term occurrences are occurrences of the same (I3)-term just in case they are of the same semantic type. Thus, *pace* Strawson, I think that sameness of typographical-type is not even necessary for being occurrences of the same (I3)-term. Let me elaborate on this.

If one wants to stick to the criterion of sameness of typographical type, one has to spell the criterion out more properly. It is far from obvious how this should be done. It seems that we cannot literally demand *sameness* of graphical appearance – at least if we identify the graphical appearance of a term occurrences with the respective distribution of, say, black dots on white paper. Even the two occurrences of "Pluto" in "Pluto is a planet or Pluto is not a planet" probably do not have the same physical appearance in every detail. So, either *similarity* of physical appearance must suffice, or typographical identity must be spelled out along wholly different lines. At least since Goodman 1972, we know that any attempt to make the notion of similarity precise faces serious problems. We do not want to base our definition of logical truth on the difficult and probably also vague notion of similarity. Furthermore, at least according to my intuition, the color, size and font of a term occurrence seems to be wholly irrelevant for the logical properties of the respective sentences. The relevant notion of typographical identity must be approached differently. Maybe, we should say that term occurrences belong to the same typographical type iff they are spelled alike, i.e., iff the letter sequences constituting them have the same length and for every place of the sequences the respective letter tokens belong to the same letter type. As an immediate consequence of this approach, "color" and "colour" are occurrences of different terms and thus, e.g., the sentence "red is a color or red is not a colour" is not declared logically true by the interpretational definition. I find this result counterintuitive, but intuitions might diverge here. We need not dwell on this, as the proposal has to struggle with a more fundamental objection anyhow: it defers the problem of the identity of terms or words to the problem of the identity of letters. Under which conditions do two letter occurrences count as being occurrences of the same letter?

I do not want to start a discussion about the identity conditions of letters here. The typographical criterion gets us involved into questions that seems to have nothing to do with logic at all. Therefore, at least as far as natural language is concerned, it seems to be a nonstarter. Most importantly, however, I think that the reference to typographical identity is made for entirely the wrong reasons. It seems to be meant to prevent that certain a posteriori truths as "Hesperus is Phosphorus" are declared logically true by the interpretational definition. "Hesperus" and "Phosphorus" seem to have the same semantic values, but are, under any only remotely plausible notion of typographical identity, of different typographical term types. In the next section, I will face this possible consequence of a purely semantic notion of word identity.

4.2 Hesperus and Phosphorus

So far, I did not elaborate on the notion of a semantic value. Depending on what exactly one takes the semantic value of a term to be, the individuation of (I3)-terms via the semantic type of term occurrences will have different consequences. If one subscribes to a semantics of direct reference and takes the term's semantic value to be constituted by its object of reference, the claim that sameness of semantic value is sufficient for two occurrences to be occurrence of the same (I3)-term implies that Frege's infamous "Hesperus is Phosphorus" becomes a logical truth. The same holds for my preferred formal semantics, the semantics of form logic, where the semantic value of an individual constant is the object it stands for and the semantic value of a predicate is the property expressed by the predicate. In such a semantics, "Hesperus" and "Phosphorus" are occurrences of the same (I3)-term.

Thus, according to restriction (I3), they may only be reinterpreted by an interpretation that assigns the same semantic value to both term occurrences. The above identity statement would then be true under all admissible interpretations. Yet according to the standard view this sentence is synthetic and *a posteriori*. Surely, we do not want there to be synthetic or *a posteriori* logical truths.

I think that, contrary to the common opinion, we can indeed accept "Hesperus is Phosphorus" as a logical truth without running into any problems. However, before defending this, let me stress that the logical truth of the Fregean example does not follow from the proposed criterion for the classification of term occurrences into (I3)-terms. One need not identify the semantic value of a term with its object of reference. A Fregean may identify the semantic value of a term with its sense. Under the further assumption that "Hesperus" and "Phosphorus" do not have the same sense, the two term occurrences will not belong to the same (I3)-term. Nevertheless, I am sympathetic to a semantic theory of direct reference and want to at least allow for the possibility that the semantic value of a term is just its object of reference. Under this assumption, the Fregean sentence will indeed be logically true. I will argue that this consequence is less harmful than it might appear. To do so, we must carefully distinguish between a meta-linguistic and an objectual reading of "Hesperus is Phosphorus".[65]

According to the meta-linguistic reading, "Hesperus is Phosphorus" says that "Hesperus" and "Phosphorus" are co-referential. It thus makes a statement about the expressions "Hesperus" and "Phosphorus". The Fregean sentence then says the same as the sentence "'Hesperus' and 'Phosphorus' are co-referential". This reveals that not the terms "Hesperus" and "Phosphorus" actually occur in the Fregean sentence, but the terms "'Hesperus'" and "'Phosphorus'". These terms, however, do not have the same semantic value.

---

[65] There is a third possible reading, according to which "Hesperus" and "Phosphorus" are read as implicit definite descriptions. According to this reading, the sentence is obviously *a posteriori*. However, as a Russellian analysis of the descriptions shows, the terms must then not be understood as referring expressions in the sense relevant here. They thus cannot have the same semantic values and thereby are not occurrences of one and the same (I3)-term. No problem arises for the proposed semantic criterion of the individuation of (I3)-terms.

The semantic value of "'Hesperus'" is "Hesperus" and the semantic value of "'Phosphorus'" is "Phosphorus". The proposed criterion for the individuation of (I3)-terms does thus not exclude interpretations that interpret these term occurrences differently. Therefore, the sentence does not turn out to be logically true. The meta-linguistic reading does not pose any problem for the semantic individuation of (I3)-terms: the sentence is *a posteriori*, but not logically true.

Frege proposes the meta-linguistic reading himself in the *Begriffsschrift* (1879, §8), but rejects it a few years later in "On Sense and Reference" (1892). According to the objectual reading of the sentence, it says that the planets Hesperus and Phosphorus are identical. The Fregean sentence describes the state of affairs that Hesperus is identical to Phosphorus, which is, however, nothing other than the state of affairs that Venus is identical to itself. This latter state of affairs is not only necessary, but we know that it obtains *a priori*. I therefore propose that the Fregean sentence is *a priori*, if it is understood in an objectual way.

I expect strong reservations here. It just seems to be a brute fact that "Hesperus is Phosphorus" is *a posteriori*, even in an objectual reading. Competent English speakers must know *a priori* that "Hesperus is Hesperus" is true, but they need not know that "Hesperus is Phosphorus" is true. This is the common intuition, which I take, however, to be confused. Nathan Salmon instructively explains the source of this confusion with his distinction between "semantically encoded information" and "pragmatically imparted information":

> [The] nonlinguistic fact that if Hesperus exists then it is Phosphorus is just the fact that if Venus exists then it is it, and this fact (proposition, "thought" piece of information) is fully knowable, with complete certainty, by reason alone. Indeed, it is a truth of logic (in the derivative sense). In determining the (derivative) epistemological status of any sentence – in determining whether its content is a priori or a posteriori – it is crucial to bear in mind a sharp distinction between the key notion of semantically encoded information and the entirely irrelevant notion of pragmatically imparted information, such as the information that the sentence in question is true. The semantically encoded information may be knowable a priori even when the sentence's pragmatic impartations are knowable only a posteriori. Since sentences like "If Hesperus exists, it is Phosphorus" are analytic, in the traditional sense, it is to be expected

> that they are metaphysically necessary. By the same token, it should be small wonder that they are also a priori. (Salmon 1986: 137 f.)

Let me explain. An assertive utterance of "x is y" not only says that x is y, but it pragmatically imparts the meta-linguistic information that the sentence "x is y" is true. The sentence "x is y" is true just in case the respective occurrences of "x" and of "y" have the same referent. Thus, the assertion of "x is y" pragmatically imparts that the respective term occurrences are co-referential. This holds, *mutatis mutandis*, also for an utterance of "x is x", which is just a special instance of an utterance of "x is y". An assertive utterance of "x is x" not only semantically encodes the information that x is self-identical, but it pragmatically imparts the information that the two occurrences of "x" have the same referent.

If true, both an assertion of "x is y" and an assertion of "x is x" describe the very same state of affairs, namely that x is self-identical (or, which is the same, that y is self-identical). This state of affairs can be known to obtain *a priori*. However, the pragmatic impartations of the utterances differ. The fist utterance suggests that the respective occurrences of "x" and of "y" are co-referential, while the second utterance suggests that the two occurrences of "x" are co-referential. As far as natural language is concerned, the previous discussion has shown that neither the former nor the latter is knowable *a priori*. Natural language contains homonyms. The meta-linguistic information that is pragmatically imparted is only knowable *a posteriori*. However, as it is usually, or nearly almost, the case that two occurrences of "x" are co-referential, this information does not come as a surprise. We already expect the two occurrence of "x" to be co-referential and thus might mistake this information as already given, or *a priori*. This might be the reason why we take "x is x" to be *a priori*, and "x is y" to be *a posteriori*.

The sentences "Hesperus is Hesperus" and "Hesperus is Phosphorus" encode the same semantic content, namely the proposition that Venus is identical to itself. However, the utterances differ in their pragmatic impartations. An assertive utterance of "Hesperus is Hesperus" pragmatically imparts the meta-linguistic information that the sentence is true and thus that the two occurrences of "Hesperus" are co-referential. Analogously, an assertion of "Hesperus is Phosphorus" pragmatically imparts the meta-linguistic information that the respective occurrences of "Hesperus" and "Phosphorus" have the same semantic value. Usually, however, the former information is less interesting than the latter, because typographically identical term occurrences are often expected to be co-referential. Yet as the above discussion has shown, it is also not knowable *a priori* that the two occurrences of "Hesperus" have the same semantic value. This is non-trivial semantic information.

The sentences "Hesperus is Hesperus" and "Hesperus is Phosphorus", if read in an objectual way, have the same epistemic status. The state of affairs described by both sentences can be known *a priori*, but both sentences convey *a posteriori* semantic information. Thus, the sentences can be known to be true only *a posteriori*. Both sentences have the same epistemic status. This is also the punchline of a recent paper on Frege's puzzle by Glezakos.[66] I quote the relevant passage in full:

> Of course, if a speaker uses or encounters the name "Aristotle" on one occasion, uses or encounters "Aristotle" on a later occasion, and recognizes that the name is the same name on both occasions, then (given the characterization of name as a sign/referent combination) she can immediately know that "Aristotle = Aristotle" is true. But notice that the ability to recognize that the name is the same seems to involve the ability to recognize that the referent is the same. If this is the case, then an identity sentence of the form $a = a$ is not, in principle, recognizable as true in a way that differs from a true sentence of the form $a = b$. In both cases: once one knows that the referent is the same, one knows that the sentence is true. If one does not know this, or believes the referents to be different, then, whether the sentence is of the form $a = a$ or $a = b$, one does not know (let alone know a priori) that the sentence is true. (Glezakos 2009: 204 f.)

Glezakos concludes that "we ought not accept Frege's initial, supposedly 'puzzlement-inducing' claim: that sentences of the form $a = a$ and $a = b$ have distinct epistemic profiles. The truth of a sentence of either form can be denied by a perfectly competent language user; furthermore, for each sentence, recognition of its truth involves recognition that the names – either a twice, or a and b – have the

---

[66] Glezakos 2009. See also Freitag 2009: 299 f. for a detailed defense of this claim.

same referent" (Glezakos 2009: 205). We know neither of the two sentences *a priori*, because we might lack the necessary *semantic* information. However, both sentences describe the same state of affairs and we know *a priori* that this state of affairs obtains. If we want "Hesperus is Hesperus" to be declared logically true, then we should accept "Hesperus is Phosphorus" as a logical truth. Thus, even if one identifies the semantic value of an expression with its object of reference, restriction (I3) does not yield the consequence that sentences that are *a posteriori* in a relevant, i.e., non-semantic, sense are declared logically true.

4.3 Semantic Restrictions

According to (IT*), the modified version of the interpretational definition of logical truth, a sentence is logically true iff it is true under all admissible interpretations. We already formulated restrictions on interpretations motivated from the classification of terms into logical and non-logical constants, into grammatical categories, and from classifications of term occurrences into terms. We also suggested that the relevant notion of a term must involve semantic notions although this is not at the center of my structurally oriented claims. In this section, I bring into play a further plausible restriction drawing on this result.

Consider the sentence "mothers are female". This sentence is a paradigm case of an analytic sentence. Moreover, according to the standard view, it is not declared a logical truth by the interpretational definition. If we interpret "is female" as having the property of being male as its semantic value, and leave the interpretation of the other terms as it is, the sentence is false. Thus, the original sentence is not logically true according to the interpretational definition. This classification of the sentence as non-logical by the interpretational definition is widely welcomed. Most philosophers take the sentence to be a paradigm case of a sentence that is not logically, but merely analytically true. Only few disagree. For example, Stephen Read claims that in letting the interpretation of terms like "mother" and "female" vary independently we "overlook the fact that their interpretation is linked – their interpretation is not independent" (Read 1994: 250). He sees the need for a theory that takes these semantical connections into account:

> What is lost in interpretational semantics is the analytical linkage between expressions. For interpretational semantics properly to replace representational semantics we would need a theory which took account of these connections. (Read 1994: 253)

In this section, I try to provide the ground for such a theory. I propose a restriction on interpretations which confines the admissible interpretations to those that respect the analytical linkage between the terms.

An analytic sentence is famously characterized by Kant as a sentence in which "the predicate B belongs to the subject A as something that is (covertly) contained in the concept A".[67] The sentence "mothers are female" is analytically true because the predicate "female" is 'contained' in the subject-term "mother". Of course, the term "female" is not contained in "mother" as "other" is contained in it. The predicate expression "female" is not a syntactical part of the subject expression "mother". As Kant says, the predicate is 'covertly' contained in the subject term. The relevant notion of containment is *conceptual* or *semantical* containment.[68]

No doubt, the Kantian containment analysis of analyticity has its drawbacks. It at best provides an analysis of a sub-class of analytic sentences, as analyticity is obviously not always grounded in containment,[69] and we lack a precise analysis of the notion of containment itself. Nevertheless, a certain intuitive grasp of semantic containment can safely be presupposed: it is a platitude that the predicate "female" is semantically contained in "mother" – whatever this might mean

---

[67] Kant, *Critique* A: 6-7. As always, there are predecessors. In particular, one should mention Locke's *trifling propositions*, Leibniz' *truths of reason* and Hume's distinction between *relations of ideas* and *matters of fact*. However, to my knowledge, Kant was the first to use the terminology of 'analytic' and 'synthetic' sentences.

[68] Kant probably thinks of the notion of containment in epistemic terms. I do not follow him in this respect as I consider containment a purely semantic notion.

[69] Kant was aware of this and intended his analysis of an analytic judgment in terms of containment to be restricted to affirmative judgments. Non-affirmative analytic sentences demand a different analysis: "In the analytic judgment I remain with the given concept in order to discern something about it. If it is an affirmative judgment, I only ascribe to this concept that which is already thought in it; if it is a negative judgment, I only exclude the opposite of this concept from it." (Kant 1781, A 154/B 193)

exactly. Independently of its proper definition, it seems to be just another platitude that the containment-relation and the identity-relation are closely connected: Semantic identity is but mutual semantic containment. Concepts *A* and *B* are semantically identical if, and only if, *A* semantically contains *B* and *vice versa*. Semantic containment appears as a generalization of semantic identity.[70]

I will not, and need not, commit myself to a certain notion of containment here, but let me indicate the possible direction an analysis of semantic containment might take.[71] As laid out in the previous sections, I have semantic criteria for term identity. Therefore, I also propose semantic criteria for the partial identity between terms: two terms are partially identical iff their respective semantic values are partially identical. More precisely, two term occurrences that have partially identical semantic values belong to partially identical terms. Let us here focus on containment between predicates – which is the source of the analyticity of the paradigm examples for analytic sentences. If we assume semantic values of predicates to be properties, partial identity between terms can be defined by reference to partial identity between properties, which in turn can be understood along Armstrongian lines:

> [T]he notion of a part [...] was applicable to any complex entity, including complex universals. If (complex) universals have parts, then they are capable of *partial identity*. One universal may be a part of another or two universals may overlap. If *P&Q* is a conjunctive property, then *P* and *Q* are parts of it. And if *Q&R* is also a property, then it overlaps with *P&Q*. (Armstrong 1978: 59)

According to Armstrong, a conjunctive property, like the property of being a mother, is partially identical to its parts, i.e., the property of

---

[70] Interestingly, already Kant must have seen a close connection between the identity-relation and the relation of semantic containment, as he also gives the following characterization of analyticity: "Analytic judgments (affirmative ones) are [...] those in which the connection of the predicate is thought through identity, but those in which this connection is thought without identity are to be called synthetic judgments." (Kant 1781, A 7/B 10)

[71] For a different account of the relevant notion of containment, see in particular Katz 1986, Ch. 6. For yet another account, see de Jong 1995 and Anderson 2004, 2005, who spell out the notion of containment via the notion of the logical division of concepts with the aid of Porphyrian trees.

being female and the property of having children. The property of being a mother ontologically contains the property of being female. The partial identities between the complex properties, which are the semantic values of the respective predicates, induce the partial identity of the predicate terms themselves.[72]

Restriction (I3) imposes constrains on the simultaneous reinterpretation of term occurrences belonging to one and the same term, i.e., to the reinterpretation of occurrences of identical terms. The following restrictions (I3*) constrains the possible simultaneous reinterpretation of term occurrences that are occurrences of terms that stand in the containment relation – however semantic containment might be fleshed out in detail.[73] It secures that interpretations respect the analytical linkage between the terms. As before, let τ_j and τ_k be arbitrary term occurrences and let the function f map any term occurrence on the term it is an occurrence of:

(I3*) An interpretation i is only admissible if the following holds:
if $f(\tau_j^{[i^*]})$ contains $f(\tau_k^{[i^*]})$, then $f(\tau_j^{[i]})$ contains $f(\tau_k^{[i]})$.

If term A semantically contains term B under the actual interpretation, then only those interpretations are admissible under which A still contains B. Devised for occurrences, this reads as follows: If A is an occurrence of term A^*, and B is an occurrence of term B^*, and A^* semantically contains B^*, then only those interpretations are admissible under which A is an occurrence of a term that semantically contains the term of which B is an occurrence. If occurrences considered under the intended interpretation are occurrences of terms that stand in the relation of containment, then then the respective occurrences considered under i must be occurrences of terms standing in the rela-

---

[72] Complex properties must not be confused with so-called *structural properties* as discussed in, e.g., David Armstrong 1978. David Lewis also has a notion of structural properties which is different from both Armstrong's notion of structural properties and from the notion of complex properties relevant here. (See Lewis 1986[a]: 56 and Lewis 1986[b])

[73] Importantly, however, if one wants to reduce the notion of containment between predicates to containment between properties, and subscribes to a class-nominalism for properties, one must not understand containment as mere set inclusion.

Semantic Restrictions

tion of containment.[74] Condition (I3*) thus restricts the admissible interpretations to those respecting the containment relations between the terms. The restriction excludes, for example, an interpretation i that leaves the interpretation of "is a mother" as before, but interprets "is female" as having the property of being male as its semantic value.[75] Importantly, however, (I3*) does not fix the interpretation of "is

---

[74] If one subscribes to the semantic notion of containment sketched above in the main text, the following restriction (I3*') is equivalent to (I3*):

(I3*') Only interpretations i are admissible such that $i(\tau_j)$ contains $i(\tau_k)$ if $f(\tau_j^{[i^*]})$ contains $f(\tau_k^{[i^*]})$.

[75] Restriction (I3*) might remind us of Carnapian meaning postulates. Carnap defines logical truth (or "L-truth", or "L-analyticity," as he calls it) as truth in all state descriptions. A state description of a language L is a class of sentences such that for every atomic sentence φ of L, it either contains φ or $\neg\varphi$. A state description can be enriched by further, possibly non-atomic sentences, so called "meaning postulates." For example, if one wants the sentence "mothers are female" to be logically true, one adds to each state description the object language sentence "if x is a mother, x is female". The definition of logical truth is then relativized to a chosen set of meaning postulates: "Suppose that certain meaning postulates have been accepted for the system L. Let P be their conjunction. Then, the concept of analyticity [or "L-truth" or "logical truth", A.Z.] can now be explicated. We shall use for the explicatum the term "L-true with respect to P" and define it as follows: a statement S_i in L is L-true with respect to $P \stackrel{\text{def}}{=} S_i$ is L-implied by P (in L)." (Carnap 1952: 69. But see also Carnap 1947: 226.). Based on Carnap's notion of L-implication, we can reformulate the definition as follows: a sentence S is L-true with respect to P iff S is true in all state descriptions in which P holds. Whether one makes use of meaning postulates and, in case one does, which meaning postulates one imposes, is, for Carnap, a mere matter of choice. One need not make use of meaning postulates at all, but, on the other hand, one can arbitrarily choose any sentence as a meaning postulate. Although there are some similarities between meaning postulates and restrictions on interpretations, let me point to some crucial differences. First of all, meaning postulates operate in a wholly different framework. Carnap defines logical truth as truth in all state descriptions which, however, are very different from model-theoretic models. State descriptions are sets of object language sentences, models are metalinguistic entities. Accordingly, meaning postulates are sentences of the object language, whereas the restrictions on interpretations are formulated in the metalanguage. Furthermore, the restrictions on interpretations are much more general than meaning postulates. (I3*) demands that all semantic containment relations between the terms are respected. No reference to the particular terms "is a mother" or "is female" is involved. Meaning postulates lack this kind of generality. They therefore fail to account for the source of the logical truth of the respective sentences. As Katz observes, "an account of analytic

a mother" or of "is female" itself. It does not exclude all interpretations that reinterpret these terms from the admissible ones. It just demands that the reinterpretations are semantically tied. For example, it still allows the simultaneous reinterpretation of the term "is a mother" as having the usual meaning of "is a father" and of "is female" as having the usual meaning of "is male". As (I3), also (I3*) is a cross-term restriction.[76]

Obviously, (I3) and (I3*) are closely related. Indeed, if we understand identity of terms as mutual containment of terms, (I3) is just a

> entailments based on meaning postulates fails to exhibit the grammatical source of their validity". (Katz 1986: 43)
>
> [76] As pointed out before, we find the notion of cross-term restrictions already in Etchemendy 1990, especially Ch.5. Etchemendy argues that the standard model-theoretic semantics relies on cross-term restrictions because the interpretation of the quantifier confines the possible interpretation of the non-logical constants: "Demanding that our interpretation of 'Abe Lincoln' […] be constrained by the interpretation of 'something' (or 'thing') imposes a *cross-term restriction* on the class of models." (Etchemendy 1990: 68) Etchemendy also considers further cross-term restrictions: "Cross-term restrictions impose constraints on the simultaneous interpretation of two or more expression. There are, of course, innumerable such constraints we might imagine imposing. For example, we might require f('Abe Lincoln') be a member of f('was president'), or that f('was president') be a subset of f('had a beard')." (Etchemendy 1990: 71) However, Etchemendy thinks that cross-term restrictions contradict the very idea of interpretational semantics. If there are cross-term restrictions, so he argues, logical truth is not persistent under well-behaved expansions of the language, or logical truths do not remain true under all substitutions. (see Etchemendy 1990: 69) As the restrictions presented here (e.g., (I3*)) have substitutional counterparts, this objection does not apply in the present context: logical truths are still true under all *admissible* substitutions, even if we consider well-behaved expansions of the language.
>
> Etchemendy also claims that cross-term restrictions lack a motivation that is independent of the inferential roles of the terms. Thus, any definition of logical truth that rests on cross-term restrictions becomes circular as it reduces to something like this: "a sentence is logically true if it is true in all interpretations that do not falsify any sentences that seem logically true." (Etchemendy 1990: 73) I think that this is incorrect, and will present some independent possible motivation for particular cross-term restrictions in this and the next chapter. My main response to Etchemendy's circularity objection is, however, that he has to show why the objection only applies to restrictions involving cross-term restrictions, while not to all restrictions on interpretations, e.g., also to restrictions (I1), (I2), and (I3), which we all seem to accept.

special case of (I3*). While (I3) merely demands that the semantic identity relations between the terms must be respected, (I3*) demands that all semantic containment relations must.

As pointed out already in the beginning of this section, containment is just one source of analyticity. The truth of, say, the analytic sentence "mothers are not male" seems to be grounded in the semantic exclusion of the term "is male" from the term "is a mother". If we take care of the relation of containment, we should also impose a restriction to the effect that, e.g., the "exclusion" relations between the terms are respected. One could demand that admissible interpretations should not only adhere to the semantic relation of containment, but that they should respect all semantic relations. The following restriction accounts for this:

(I3**) Only interpretations i are admissible such that all semantic relations between the terms that hold under the intended interpretation i^* are respected.

(I3**) is a straightforward generalization of (I3*), which, in turn, was argued to be a natural generalization of (I3). As a consequence of (I3**) many, if not all, sentences that are usually considered to be merely analytically true, will come out logically true under the interpretational definition. I tentatively endorse (I3**) and hence the view that the notions of analytical and of logical truth coincide. Others might consider this consequence to be a reduction of (I3**). Yet abandoning (I3**) means either abandoning all restrictions based on semantic relations, and hence also such restrictions pertaining to two different occurrences of the same term, or it calls for an explanation why some semantic restrictions are to be accepted (e.g., (I3)) while other are to be rejected (e.g., (I3*) and (I3**)).

My main point is not, therefore, that one must endorse (I3**). My point is that none of the options comes for free. Moreover, it follows from our discussion that most widespread position with respect to the extension of logical truth – the position that holds "Hesperus = Hesperus" to be a logical truth, but excludes, say, "All mothers are female" – is theoretically the most difficult to defend: it requires an explanation of why some semantically based cross-term restrictions on reinterpretations are accepted, while others are rejected.

Let us recapitulate. On pain of trivialization, we cannot literally take all interpretations into account when evaluating the logical status of a sentence. We need to demarcate the *admissible* from the *in*admissible interpretations. In this chapter, I concentrated on a restriction on interpretations resulting from the requirement of uniform reinterpretation. It was shown that this restriction must be supplemented by criteria of term identity. I tentatively suggested a semantic identity criterion and, in the last section of this chapter, argued for a further semantic cross-term restriction: this latter restriction yields the consequence that many, if not all, analytic sentences would be declared logically true. As the classical boundary between structural truth and logical truth threatens to fade, so does the traditional demarcation of analytic truth and logical truth. The problem of admissible interpretations becomes ever more pressing.

5 From Necessary Truth to Logical Truth

Let us now turn to the relation between logical truth and metaphysically necessary truth. Logical truths must be metaphysically necessary – this is a commonplace. The reverse does not hold according to the vast majority of thinkers. It is usually assumed that only very few metaphysically necessary truths qualify as logical truths. At the end of the present chapter, I will challenge this view and tentatively claim that many metaphysically necessary truths also qualify as logical truths. But, as in the previous chapter, my aim is less to defend a claim about the extension of 'logically true', rather than uncovering the dependency of such an extension. The main focus of the chapter will therefore be the dependence of logic on metaphysics in general. More precisely, I will discuss the metaphysical presuppositions of the interpretational definition of logical truth.

I start with a critical discussion and argue that the interpretationalist must make certain non-trivial metaphysical assumptions. The second section compares my critique to the one found in Etchemendy 1990. The third section, finally, employs the findings of the first section to tentatively propose a further restriction on admissible interpretations which would attack the classical boundary between metaphysical and logical necessity: many, if not all, alleged paradigm cases of merely metaphysically necessary sentences would be declared logically true by the interpretational definition.

5.1 Metaphysical Presuppositions

The sentence "Alfred Tarski is married" is a paradigm case of a sentence that is, though true, not logically true. It is a perfectly ordinary contingent sentence. Any definition that declares it to be logically true must be discarded as obviously inadequate – at least if the definition still aims at capturing something only remotely resembling our pretheoretic notion of logical truth.

The interpretational definition of logical truth is usually taken to correctly classify this sentence as not logically true. There seem to be many admissible interpretations under which the sentence describes a non-obtaining state of affairs. For example, interpret "Alfred Tarski" as referring to Immanuel Kant. Under this interpretation the sentence says that Kant is married. For all we know, this is false. However, we might be mistaken. It might actually be the case that Kant was secretly wedded, unknown to anyone but the couple and without a noticeable trace for later generations. But if Kant was actually married, the proposed reinterpretation does not make the sentence false. Of course, the possible failure of a single reinterpretation does not constitute any problem yet, as there seem to be further, indeed many, reinterpretations that yield false sentences. Let "is married" express the property of being a musician. Then, the sentence says that Tarski is a musician, which is again false. Or is it? Maybe some secret society (definitely a super intelligent one) or an evil demon makes us all believe that Tarski spend his time on logic, mathematics and philosophy, while he was truly sitting in some bar, playing the guitar...

Let me generalize. According to the interpretational definition the sentence "Alfred Tarski is married" is not logically true if and only if there is some admissible interpretation under which the sentence is false. Yet, might it not be the case that, contrary to our expectations, every state of affairs the sentence describes under some admissible interpretation does in fact obtain? Suppose this is the case. Then, the interpretational definition of logical truth declares our sample sentence logically true. This would be an untenable consequence.

Before we can address possible answers to this problem, it is important to spell out the alleged challenge in all its generality. Only then we can see what it takes to answer it. The problem generalizes in two dimensions.

Firstly, it does not only apply to our sample sentence and further sentences of the subject/predicate-form, but generalizes to atomic sentences of all 'forms': For illustration, assume again that Kant indeed died as a bachelor. In this case, the sentence "Alfred Tarski is married" is not a logical truth, as it is false if we interpret "Alfred Tarski" as referring to Kant. However, this type of contingency does not guarantee that there is an admissible reinterpretation that makes, say, the atomic sentence "Mary is married to Harry" false. Under some reasonable categorization of terms into grammatical categories, we cannot interpret this sentence as expressing the atomic state of affairs that Kant is married: Let us divide the constants into individual and relation constants, and let atomic states of affairs take the form of atomic Russellian propositions each consisting of an n-place relation and n individuals. If we impose the grammatical restriction of PL, individual constants must always be assigned the semantic values of individuals, and n-ary relation constants must stand for n-ary relations.

As a consequence, sentences can only describe propositions of the corresponding form. It then holds that for every n such that there is a sentence of the form $R^n a_1 \ldots a_n$, the interpretationalist has to assume that there is a relation R and that there are n individuals $o_1, \ldots, o_n$, such that the proposition $<R, o_1, \ldots, o_n>$ does not obtain.

The interpretationalist has to presuppose something even stronger, if we assume further restrictions as those discussed in the last chapters. Let me just give one example. The form of the proposition that can be expressed by a sentence is not determined by the grammatical categories of the terms alone, but also by the identity relations between the terms. For example, a sentence consisting of a binary relation term and two occurrences of one individual constant only allows for interpretations that reinterpreting the occurrences of the individual constant uniformly. Thus, the sentence always says that an object stands in a certain relation to itself. In case there is no non-obtaining state of affairs of this very form, the sentence will be defined logically true by the interpretational definition. Thus, to prevent that an atomic sentence of a given grammatical form is declared logically true, there must be a non-obtaining state of affairs *of the corresponding form*. If also the interpretational definition of logical falsehood should be prevented from massive overgeneration, we must additionally assume that there is an obtaining state of affairs of every relevant form.

Secondly, even if there happen to be obtaining and non-obtaining states of affairs of every relevant form, the proponent of the interpretational definition is not yet on the safe side. Atomic sentences would then not be logically true or logically false, which is the desired result. But this outcome could still be a matter of mere luck. As long as it is *possible* that all relevant states of affairs of a given form are obtaining or that all are non-obtaining, the plausibility of the interpretational definitions rest on contingencies. Modal talk is tricky here, so let us be a bit more careful: A sentence is logically true if and only if there is no interpretation under which it is false, i.e., if and only if there is no interpretation under which it expresses a state of affairs that is not obtaining. Let w_α be the actual world. Then, there must be an interpretation under which the sentence expresses a state of affairs that is not obtaining in w_α. Assume that this is the case. If, however, there is a possible world w^* in which, say, all atomic states of affairs are obtaining, then the definition of logical truth yields the right extension by luck only: If we were inhabitants of w^* (i.e., if w^*, rather than w_α, were the actual world), we had to evaluate the sentence not in w_α, but in w*, and the sentence "Alfred Tarski is married" would turn out as logically true. Thus, the proponent of the interpretational definitions does not only have to assume that there are actually enough obtaining and non-obtaining states of affairs, but he has to show that this cannot be otherwise, i.e., that this is *necessary*. To sum up: The interpretationalist has to assume that, necessarily, there is an obtaining and a non-obtaining atomic state of affairs of every relevant form.

To illustrate that this is no innocent assumption, let me show that there are metaphysical positions that are incompatible with it. For example, assume a *Tractarian* ontology of atomic states of affairs. According to the view of Logical Atomism as it is proposed by the early Wittgenstein, each atomic state of affairs can be obtaining or non-obtaining, and there are no atomic states of affairs that are necessarily obtaining or necessarily non-obtaining. Furthermore, atomic states of affairs are said to be independent of one another:

> From the existence or non-existence of one state of affairs it is impossible to infer the existence or non-existence of another. (TLP 2.062)[77]

Although Wittgenstein phrases independence here in the epistemological term of inference, he clearly has ontological independence in mind. In his *A World of States of Affairs*, David Armstrong explains more explicitly what the principle of independence amounts to:

> States of affairs are independent of each other if and only if: (1) no conjunction of states of affairs, including unit conjunctions, entails the existence of any wholly distinct state of affairs; and (2) no conjunction of states of affairs, including unit conjunctions, entails the non-existence of any wholly distinct state of affairs. (Armstrong 1997: 139)

The principle says that states of affairs are independent of each other iff for any state of affairs p and any set P of states of affairs (with $p \notin P$), it holds that the obtaining of the elements of P neither entails

---

[77] See also TLP 5.135. Wittgenstein gives up on the principle of independence in Wittgenstein 1929.

the obtaining nor the non-obtaining of p.[78] Although Armstrong acknowledges that there are possible complications related to the principle of independence, he advocates it himself:

> It may be noted that even if Independence is false, as I trust that it is not, it can serve most useful as a measuring rod or yardstick. It seems clear that it holds for many, many cases. In general, for any two wholly distinct states of affairs neither will entail the other, and for possible wholly distinct states of affairs, neither will exclude the other. In general, Independence holds. If it fails, it fails in highly particular circumstances, which we will want to discuss and catalogue. We will want to say: Independence holds, with these exceptions. For myself, while recognizing the difficulties in the most sweeping claim of all, I have hopes that Independence holds unrestrictedly. (*Ibid.*: 174)

According to both Wittgenstein and Armstrong, whether or not a certain atomic state of affairs obtains is independent of the obtaining or non-obtaining of further atomic states of affairs. Thus, any subclass of the class of all atomic states of affairs may obtain. In the extreme cases, no atomic state of affairs obtains, or all atomic states of affairs obtain. Both cases generate unsurmountable problems for the interpretationalist.

Given reasonable grammatical restrictions on interpretations, an atomic sentence expresses an atomic state of affairs under any admissible interpretation. Under the assumption that *all* atomic states of affairs obtain, we will thus not find an admissible interpretation under which the sentence "Alfred Tarski is married" is false. In the opposite case in which no atomic state of affairs obtains, any atomic sentence will be false under all admissible interpretations, and thus will be declared logically false by the corresponding interpretational definition of logical falsity. It might actually be the case that the interpretational definitions do massively overgenerate. And even if they are extensionally correct, this is only a matter of contingency – at least if we assume the principle of independence.

---

[78] Armstrong speaks of "wholly distinct" states of affairs. It is not so clear what this means, but I assume that all atomic Russellian propositions are wholly distinct in the relevant way.

In order to prevent disastrous results, the interpretationalist must hence postulate the following metaphysical assumption (MA) holds:

(MA) Necessarily, there is an obtaining and a non-obtaining atomic state of affairs of every relevant form.

This postulate is obviously of a metaphysical sort. The intuitive plausibility of the interpretational definitions of logical truth and of logical falsity hinges on metaphysical assumptions. The interpretational definitions are not free of metaphysics!

Let me end this section with a possible objection. A proponent of standard PL semantics might oppose as follows: We can always find, he says, a reinterpretation of "Alfred Tarski" and "is married" such that the sentence "Alfred Tarski is married" turns out to be false. We simply map "is married" on a set that does not contain the respective semantic value of "Alfred Tarski". To make it simple, we can let the interpretation function map "is married" on the empty set. So, he concludes, there are no worries for the interpretational definition of logical truth.

Sure, from a purely formal perspective, this is correct. The existence of a model mapping "is married" on the empty set is guaranteed. However, this fact of set theory has nothing to do with my objection to the interpretational definition. If the definition of logical truth as truth in all models is meant to capture our intuitive notion of logical truth, we have to explain what a model stands for. According to the interpretational approach, models stand for interpretations of the language. The interpretationalist must say which interpretation is encoded by the model that maps "is married" on the empty set. He must provide a reinterpretation of "is married" such that its semantic value is a property that as a matter of actual fact is not instantiated. This, however, is impossible if all properties are actually instantiated.

For further illustration of this point, turn to the models of propositional logic, which simply assign a truth value to each atomic formula. Of course, there is a model which maps "Alfred Tarski is married" on the truth value FALSE. According to the interpretationalist, this model represents an interpretation of the language in which the sentence "Alfred Tarski is married" expresses an atomic state of affairs that is actually non-obtaining. If, however, actually all atomic states of affairs obtain, no such interpretation will be found. The model mapping the sentence on the truth value FALSE does not allow for an interpretational reading; it is no interpretational model.

To prevent his definition from massive overgeneration, the proponent of the interpretational definitions of logical truth and of logical falsity must presuppose that, by necessity, some atomic states of affairs are actually obtaining and that some are non-obtaining.

5.2 Etchemendy's Critique

I am not the first who holds that the interpretationalist has to make certain extra-logical assumptions. Most famously, Etchemendy claims that "Tarski's account remains dependent on completely non-logical facts" (Etchemendy 1990:110). Let us compare his critique to mine.[79]

Etchemendy prominently argues that the interpretational definitions of logical truth and of logical consequence do not provide an adequate analysis of the respective common concepts, neither at the intensional, nor even at the extensional level:

> [M]y claim is that Tarski's analysis in wrong, that his account of logical truth and logical consequence does not capture, or even come close to capturing, any pretheoretic conception of the logical properties. The thrust of my argument is primarily at the conceptual level, but again the main impact is at the extensional. Applying the model-theoretic account of consequence, I claim, is no more reliable a technique for ferreting out the genuinely valid arguments of a language than is applying a purely syntactic definition. (Etchemendy 1990: 6)

The main source of Etchemendy's critique of the model-theoretic definition of logical truth is the very division of interpretational and representational semantics. Etchemendy carefully carves out the details of this distinction and shows that Tarski's definition has to be read interpretationally. Once this is fully understood, it is obvious that

---

[79] The following does neither provide a comprehensive summary of Etchemendy's attack on Tarski's definition of logical consequence, nor of the huge amount of literature that critically discussed or further developed Etchemendy's arguments (see, e.g., Priest 1995, Ray 1996, Sher 1996, Gómez-Torrente 1996, 1998, 2009, Hanson 1997, Patterson 2008, but also Etchemendy 2008). The sole aim of this section is to provide the proper background and context for the arguments presented in the previous section.

there is no conceptual guarantee that sentences that are logically true according to Tarski's definition, i.e., sentences that are actually true under all interpretations, are also necessary.

To nail this down, Etchemendy confronts the interpretationalist with a number of examples whose target is to show that certain non-logical facts have to be presupposed by a proponent of the interpretational definition, or otherwise, the interpretational definitions are also extensionally inadequate. The examples thereby show that the interpretational definition of logical consequence does not capture our common concept of consequence, as there is no conceptual guarantee that it yields a plausible extension. As they deserve closer attention also independently of their relation to my own arguments, I will introduce Etchemendy's examples step-by-step, quite closely following his line of argumentation.

To begin with, Etchemendy concedes to the interpretationalist that no facts about particular individuals or properties play a role in the outcome of the interpretational definition of logical truth, if we presuppose the traditional demarcation of logical and non-logical constants. However, he thinks that there are further facts of a "nonlogical sort" on which the interpretationalist must rely:

> [I]t is clear, or at any rate relatively clear, that certain kinds of extralogical influence can be excluded by banning names and predicates from [the set of logical constants]. Certainly, it is hard to see how facts concerning specific individuals and particular properties could affect the outcome of the definition if there were no way to refer to those individuals or those properties. Still, not all facts of a nonlogical sort involve specific individuals or properties. (Etchemendy 1990: 111)

The "facts of a nonlogical sort" Etchemendy is primarily referring to in this quote are cardinality facts, i.e., facts about the size of the domain. Etchemendy asks us to consider the following sentence:

(E1) $\exists x \exists y (\neg x = y)$.

If the domain contains at least two elements, (E1) is true. Given that the existential quantifier, the negation operator, and the identity sign are logical constants, no non-logical constants appear in (E1). Therefore, (E1) is, if true, trivially true under all interpretations of the non-logical constants. There is simply nothing to reinterpret. Thus, if (E1) is true, it is also logically true according to the interpretational definition. However, Etchemendy claims, "[s]entence [(E1)] makes a perfectly ordinary claim about the world, one that has little, if anything, to do with logic" (Etchemendy 1990: 114). He concludes that the interpretationalist is in deep trouble. There is a sentence that is true in all interpretations, although it is, intuitively, not logically true.

As a first response one might turn the argument upside down and object that the example only shows that the identity sign should not be treated as a logical constant. If we treat the identity sign as a non-logical relation constant, it is open for reinterpretation and the above example does not pose any problem.[80] However, Etchemendy anticipates this reaction and supplies us with an example not involving the identity sign:

(E2) $\forall R \, [\neg \, (\forall x \forall y \forall z \, (xRy \land yRx \to xRz) \land \forall x \neg \, (xRx) \land \forall y \exists x \, (xRy))]$

(E2) says that all transitive, irreflexive relations have a minimal element. (E2) is formulated in a second order language, but let us not be concerned about this feature. The interpretational definition of logical truth should also yield the right results with respect to second-order sentences.[81]

If we consider standard PL semantics, then (E2) is true just in case the domain is finite. As (E2) does not contain any logical constants, it is, if true, trivially true under all admissible interpretations. Thus, if the domain is finite, (E2) is, contrary to intuition, a logical truth. According to Etchemendy (E2) thereby shows that we have to make extra-logical assumptions in order to guarantee the extensional adequacy of the interpretational definition of logical truth: we have to presuppose that the domain is infinite.

Etchemendy's examples (E1) and (E2) seem to take for granted that the interpretational definition of logical truth does not involve a variation of the domain, but that it evaluates the formulas with re-

---

[80] However, other problems crop up if the identity sign is not considered a logical constant. For example, it leads to the consequence that "$a = a$" is not a logical truth according to the interpretational definition.

[81] (E2) is second-order if we interpret it according to the standard semantics of PL where predicates are mapped on sets of elements of the domain. If we use FL semantics, where predicates are mapped on elements of the domain, (E2) is a perfectly standard first-order sentence: no quantification over sets is involved.

spect to a fixed domain.[82] One might thus be tempted to deal with these examples by introducing a varying domain. However, Etchemendy foresees also this objection and argues that it does not really provide any relief. To reconstruct his line of argumentation, we have to introduce Etchemendy's notion of a 'universe'. The universe contains everything in the most general sense: all elements of all domains are elements of the universe.[83] To say it differently: the universe contains all there is, and particular domains are understood as providing a restricted interpretation of the quantifiers. Assumptions about the cardinality of the domain now transfer to assumptions about the cardinality of the universe as a whole. The sentence (E2) is only false if it is evaluated with respect to an infinite domain. Obviously, there is only an infinite domain if the universe as a whole is infinite. If the

---

[82] There is an intense debate on the exegetical question whether Tarski originally assumed a fixed domain or not. Sher 1991: 41, argues that it is highly unlikely that Tarski intended all models to share one domain, because this assumption is incompatible with the most important model-theoretic results of that time, in particular the (upward and downward) Löwenheim-Skolem theorem(s). See also Gómez-Torrente 1996, 2009 and Ray 1996 for a defense of the claim that Tarski assumed a varying domain. I am inclined to accept this interpretation. As also Etchemendy remarks (Etchemendy 1988[b]: 70), Tarski explicitly addresses the notion of *truth in a domain* in Tarski 1935: "In all cases in which we are able to define satisfaction and the notion of true statement, we can – by means of a modification of these definitions – also define two more general concepts of a relative kind, namely the concepts of *satisfaction* and *correct sentence* – both *with respect to a given individual domain a*." (Tarski 1935: 239) He also adds that "[t]he concept of correct sentence in every individual domain deserves special consideration". (Tarski 1935: 239 f.) Hodges 1986: 138 suggests that Tarski might not have mentioned a varying universe in his 1936 talk on logical consequence, because this talk was directed at philosophers which might not have been interested in such technical subtleties. See, on the other hand, Corcoran and Sagüillo 2011 for a defense of Etchemendy's claim that Tarski did assume a fixed domain of discourse. Etchemendy not only gives exegetical reasons why he thinks that Tarski assumed a fixed domain, but he presents arguments which are intended to show that a varying domain contradicts the idea of the interpretational definition. See Etchemendy 1990, Ch. 5.

[83] If any set can figure as a domain, then the union of all domains, i.e., the universe, is no set. The notion of a universe containing 'everything' might sound paradoxical. I will not critically discuss Etchemendy's notion of the universe here, but see, e.g., the essays in Rayo & Uzquiano 2006 for remarks on the notion of 'absolutely everything' and the (im)possibility of quantifying over everything.

universe as a whole is finite, there is no infinite domain and the sentence (E2) is true not only in all interpretations, but indeed in all domains:

> If the universe is finite, the standard semantics mistakenly declares [(E2)] a logical truth. This becomes obvious, of course, if we once again adopt the finitist's perspective. If there are only finitely many objects, both physical and mathematical, than clearly no model will contain a transitive, irreflexive relation with no least element. For then the model would have to contain an infinite number of objects, and so too would the universe as a whole, contrary to our assumption. Thus, if the universe at large is finite, there will, as a matter of fact, be no models in which [(E2)] comes out false. (Etchemendy 1990: 119)

The infinity of the Etchemendyian universe, and thus the existence of infinite models, is guaranteed by the axiom of infinity. This axiom of Zermelo–Fraenkel set theory says that there is a set S that has the non-empty set as a member and, for any member of the set, the union of this member and its singleton is also in S: $\exists S\ (\emptyset \in S \wedge \forall x\ (x \in S \rightarrow ((x \cup \{x\}) \in S)))$.[84] If one takes the axiom of infinity to be part of logic, Etchemendy's example (E2) does not pose any problem to the interpretationalist.

However, although Etchemendy concedes that the axiom is necessary, he denies it the status of a truth of logic: "Even if our views about mathematical objects lead us to conclude that these [e.g., the axiom of infinity; A.Z.] are necessary truths, which I happen to believe, they are surely not logical truths"(Etchemendy 1990: 169). According to Etchemendy, it follows that, though (E2) might be necessarily true, its truth is not guaranteed by logic alone. Thus, (E2)

---

[84] The axiom of infinity only guarantees that there is an infinite domain if we allow sets as elements of the domain. Interestingly, Tarski 1941 does not do so: "It should be emphasized that V [i.e., the domain – A.Z.] is the class of all individuals but not the class containing as elements […] also classes of first order, second order, and so on. The question arises […] whether we may consider "inhomogeneous" classes not belonging to a particular order and containing as elements individuals as well as classes of various order." (Tarski 1941: 73) If we think of domains as only containing individuals, as we also tend to do when we are considering intuitive interpretations of natural language, the axiom of infinity does not guarantee that there is an infinite domain.

should not be declared logically true by an adequate definition of logical truth. (E2) thus shows that the interpretational definition is conceptually flawed.

The relation between logic and set theory poses a problem of its own, and I will not enter this discussion here. Anyway, Etchemendy's cardinality arguments are obviously of a very different kind then the argument I gave in the preceding section. They rely on the non-logical status of set theory. Although his focus lies on the type of arguments just presented, Etchemendy brings forward a further kind of argument aiming to show that the interpretationalist must make certain non-logical assumptions in order to prevent his definition from extensional inadequacy. He asks us to consider the following sentence (Etchemendy 1990: 121):

(E3) Lincoln was president → Washington was president.

Firstly, assume again a fixed domain approach and the standard PL semantics. Etchemendy argues that (E3) is logically true if the domain consists of just one object. If there is only one object, the terms "Lincoln" and "Washington" cannot but refer to the same object in all interpretations. Thus, "Washington is president" will have the same truth value as "Lincoln is president" in all interpretations. Therefore, (E3) will be defined logically true. So far, this example does not pose any problems beyond those posed by (E1) and (E2). We can answer it by demanding that a logically true sentence need not only be true under all interpretations, but also in all domains. Etchemendy concedes that once we consider domains with more than one object, the pair-set axiom guarantees the existence of a PL-interpretation which makes the sentence false. The pair-set axiom says that for any given objects x and y, there is a set containing just these two objects. As x and y may be identical, the axiom particularly guarantees that there is a singleton for every object. Assuming a domain of at least two objects a and b, there is a PL-interpretation i with i(*Washington*) = a, i (*Lincoln*) = b, and i(*is president*) = {a}. This interpretation makes (E3) false. However, as with respect to the axiom of infinity, Etchemendy suggests that the pair-set axiom does not rank amongst the logical truths. Thus, it is not guaranteed on logical grounds alone that (E3) is excluded from the logical truths by the interpretational definition.

It seems that (E3) has not introduced a genuinely new objection. It again shows that the extension of the interpretational definition hinges on certain set-theoretic assumptions. The situation changes, however, once we focus on a further remark by Etchemendy. Although Etchemendy mainly discusses (E3) in the context of standard PL semantics, he also makes the following comment: "If the satisfaction domain consists of properties, [(E3)] will be true just in case the universe contains only one type of object – that is, if all objects share the same properties" (Etchemendy 1990: 121). Etchemendy here considers a semantics in which the semantic values of predicates are properties, just as in form-logical semantics. Within this semantic picture, the truth of (E3) does not only demand that the domain contains more than one object, but, so Etchemendy's argument goes, that it is sufficiently diverse. If all objects in the domain share the same properties, it will be the case that the objects that are the semantic values of the terms "Lincoln" and "Washington", respectively, will either both have the property that is the semantic value of the term "is president" or neither will have it. In this case, (E3) will be true under all interpretations. To avoid the logical truth of (E3), the interpretationalist not only has to assume that the domain consists of more than one object, but also that the objects in the domain do not all have the same properties. The domain must be sufficiently diverse and this is not guaranteed by the mentioned set theoretic assumptions.

In a first approach, it seems that one can object to Etchemendy's example (E3) as before: not only truth in all interpretations, but also truth in all domains is required for logical truth. However, this maneuver misses the essence of Etchemendy's example. Even if one assumes a varying domain, Etchemendy's argument shows that the interpretationalist must take the universe to be rich enough – not only in number, but in kind. The interpretationalist must deny that all elements of the universe have the same properties. Otherwise, (E3) will turn out to be true not only in all interpretations, but in all domains.

By showing that the interpretationalist must presuppose that the objects in the universe are sufficiently diverse, Etchemendy gets to the heart of the matter, at least in my view. However, I think that Etchemendy underestimates the scope of his example. In particular, he grants the proponent of standard PL semantics, where predicates are mapped on sets, much too much. As described above, Etchemendy concedes that the pair-set axiom guarantees the existence of an interpretation which makes (E2) false. Our example was the interpretation i with i(*Washington*) = a, i(*Lincoln*) = b, and i(*is president*) = {a}. However, if one wants to keep the interpretational spirit of one's definition of logical truth, one has to explain what the predicate "is president" means with respect to an interpretation mapping "is president" to the singleton {a}. The interpretationalist has to verbalize the reinterpretation that is given by the interpretation function *i*. If all objects in the universe share the same properties, this will, however, turn out to be impossible. The pair-set axiom is of no help here at all. Contrary to Etchemendy's own suggestion, the impact of his example is independent of the chosen semantics. It therefore presents a serious objection to the interpretational definition of logical truth, irrespectively of the chosen semantical framework. The interpretationalist does not only have to make claims about the cardinality of the universe, but also about its very constitution: he must assume a universe containing objects with different properties.

To appreciate the full strength of Etchemendy's argument, we still have to get rid of one common misunderstanding regarding the notion of the universe. The universe contains all there is. Domains contain subsets of all there is. At least as far as interpretational semantics is concerned, however, domains do not contain any merely possible objects. If they did so, it would be less clear that the cardinality and the constitution of the universe are not a matter of logic. As Graham Priest observes:

> This argument obviously puts a lot of weight on the notion of a substantive fact; and a major problem is that it is not very clear what this is. That there are so many physical objects in the cosmos is clearly such a fact. That there are so many existent objects (where this might include mathematical objects) is less clearly so (at least to anyone who takes mathematics to be part of logic). But that there are so many objects in toto does not appear to be a substantive fact at all. At least arguably, this collection includes not only all actual objects, but also all possible, and maybe even impossible, objects. That there are exactly so many of these hardly seems to be a matter of any contingency or variability. Nor is it a truth about some special domain or other in any obviously objectionable sense. (Priest 1995: 291)

Priest's objection is based on a misunderstanding. Of course, the status of a claim about the number of possible objects, or maybe even impossible ones, is hard to access. I have no firm intuition whether this is a logical fact or not. Be that as it may, this is, contrary to Priest's suggestion, irrelevant for Etchemendy's argument. Etchemendy never tires of insisting that the reference to possible objects (not to think of impossible ones) is foreign to Tarski's definition. The whole point of the interpretational definition is to reduce the notion of logical truth to *actual* truth. Tarski intends his definition as a reductive definition not involving any modal notions. Domains do not contain merely possible objects; even less do they represent possible worlds. The domains merely provide the satisfaction domain for the quantifiers. Combining an interpretational semantics with a varying domain does not amount to evaluating sentences with regard to merely possible objects or to counterfactual situations. Sentences are still evaluated with respect to the actual facts, though under varying interpretations.

As Etchemendy shows, the interpretationalist must assume the actual world to be sufficiently diverse, or his definition of logical consequence will be extensionally inadequate. More precisely, as argued in the preceding section, the interpretationalist must assume the actual obtaining and non-obtaining of atomic states of affairs of every form. This is undeniably not a matter of logic. If anything deserves to be called a 'non-logical assumption', then it is an assumption about the actual obtaining or non-obtaining of atomic states of affairs.

5.3 Modal Restrictions

In the first section of this chapter, I argued that the interpretationalist must make the following assumption:

(MA) Necessarily, there is an obtaining and a non-obtaining atomic state of affairs of every relevant form.

Importantly, my aim thereby was only to show that there is a certain metaphysical assumption to be made, and thus that the proponent of the interpretational definition has to engage into metaphysics in order to justify his definition of logical truth. I did not then intend to suggest that (MA) is false. Quite to the contrary, I think that one can indeed show that (MA) is true. There are various metaphysical theories which imply (MA), and I will soon exemplarily introduce one. Before doing so, let me suggest that the interpretationalist makes explicit the background metaphysics used to establish (MA). There is a straightforward way to do so: we can restrict the admissible interpretations to those that do respect the metaphysical dependencies postulated by the theory put forward in order to justify (MA).

Let M stand for the metaphysical theory that the interpretationalist assumes in order to show (MA). I suggest that the interpretationalist imposes the following restriction on interpretations:

(I4) An interpretation i is only admissible if it respects those metaphysical dependencies that are implied by M.

Restriction (I4) yields the result that certain alleged paradigm examples of merely metaphysically necessary sentences turn out to be logically true. Exactly which sentences these are depends on the assumed metaphysics.

To illustrate (I4), I will now discuss a possible candidate for M. I will exemplarily introduce a metaphysical theory the interpretationalist might put forward in order to establish the metaphysical assumptions he has to make. More precisely, I will not justify (MA), but concentrate solely on establishing the weaker assumption (MA'):

(MA') Necessarily, there is a non-obtaining atomic state of affairs of every relevant form.

I will thus argue that there must be a non-obtaining state of affairs of every relevant form, but I will not show that there must also be an obtaining atomic state of affairs of every relevant form. However, once they have been presented, it should be obvious that my arguments can be straightforwardly translated into arguments for the obtaining of atomic states of affairs of every relevant form.

So, let me now adopt the dialectical position of the interpretationalist in order to see what it takes to establish (MA'). To show (MA'), I will argue that the Tractarian principle of independence is false: certain atomic states of affairs are dependent on one another. More precisely, I will argue that there are atomic states of affairs such that the obtaining of the one state of affairs implies the non-obtaining of the other state of affairs. If this holds for states of affairs of every relevant form, we have succeeded in establishing (MA'): there must then be a non-obtaining state of affairs of every relevant form.

A possible approach to such a metaphysics originates with William E. Johnson's famous distinction between determinables and determinates.⁸⁵ According to this view, the world unfolds in a determinable/determinate structure: some properties stand in the determinable/determinate relation. For example, the property of being colored stands in the determinable relation to the property of being red, which in turn stands in the determinable relation to the property of being scarlet. The determinable/determinate relation induces a strict order on the set of properties, i.e., it is irreflexive, transitive and antisymmetric. Here I leave it open whether there are minimal and maximal elements. (A minimal element of the relation would be a property F for which there is no property G such that F is a determinable with respect to G; a maximal element would be given by a property F for which there is no property G such that F is a determinate with respect to G.)⁸⁶

For illustration, we can contrast the determinable/determinate relation with the genus/species relation.⁸⁷ A *species* is defined by means of a *genus* and a *differentia*. The genus and the differentia are logically independent of each other. As an example, the species 'man' is sometimes defined by the genus 'animal' and the differentia 'rational'.⁸⁸ The

---

[85] See Johnson 1921, Ch. XI. Johnson does not discuss the determinable/determinate relation in the context of the principle of independence, but introduces the distinction in order to argue that sentences like "red is a color" must not be read as an adjectival predication: "What is most prominently notable about red, green and yellow is that they are different, and even, as we may say, opponent to one another. [...] [T]he ground for grouping determinates under one and the same determinable is not any partial agreement between them that could be revealed by analysis, but the unique and peculiar kind of difference that subsists between the several determinates under the same determinable, and which does not subsists between any one of them and an adjective under some other determinable. If this is granted, the relations asserted in the two propositions "red is a color" and "Plato is a man," though *formally* equivalent, must yet be contrasted on the ground that the latter but not the former is based upon an adjectival predication." (Johnson 1921: 175–176)

[86] See Johansson 2000 for a defense of the claim that there are minimal and maximal elements. Fine 2011 provides an extensive elaboration of the formal structure of the determinable/determinate distinction.

[87] For a defense of the claim that the determinable/determinate and the genus/species relations are something very different, see especially Searle 1967.

[88] With respect to any only plausible notion of rationality, this characterization of human beings seems to be both, too narrow and too wide. The characterization here only serves in its role as a standard example. Diogenes' proposal, according to which a man is a featherless biped, would do as well.

property of being white, however, cannot be defined via the property of being colored plus a certain differentia. Being white is a way to be colored; being white is not 'being colored plus something else'.

We also have to distinguish the determinable/determinate relation from the relation of mere property-entailment. A property F can entail another property G without F being a determinate of G. (A property F *entails* a property G iff necessarily all objects that are F are also G.) For example, the property of being green entails the disjunctive property of being green or round, but the former is not a determinate of the latter. A property might entail another without the former being a determinate of the entailed property. However, it holds that if a property F is a determinate of a property G, then F entails G.

There surely is a number of open questions concerning the notions of determinables and determinates. The concepts would have to be further justified and developed. With respect to our present concerns, it would be of particular importance to extend the framework from properties to relations in general. If the interpretationalist wants to base his assumption that there is an atomic non-obtaining state of affairs of every form on the distinction of determinables and determinates, then he has to extend the distinction to relations of arbitrary arity. With respect to binary relations, one could argue that, e.g., the relation of 'being exactly 2 meters taller than' is a determinate of the relation of 'being taller than'. Here I will not discuss these matters, but simply concede to the interpretationalist that the notion of determinables and determinates can indeed be clarified and justified and, furthermore, that there are relations of every relevant arity standing in the determinable/determinate relation.[89] Let us take the framework for granted and see how exactly it helps to justify (MA').

One of the core principles of the theory of determinables and determinates says that a determinable can only be determined by exactly one of its determinate properties. The determinable property of being colored can only be determined by the property of being white, or the property of being green, or the property of being red, etc., but not by two such properties. Of course, the determinable property of being

---

[89] This also involves the implicit assumption that there are at least two relations of every relevant arity, i.e., of every arity for which there is a relation term in the language.

colored can be determined by both the property of being red and the property of being scarlet. However, this is only possible because the properties of being red and of being scarlet are of the same *range*, i.e., one property is again a determinable of the other property. To provide a precise formulation, let X, Y, and Z stand for properties, let x range over individuals, let "Det(X, Z)" abbreviate "X is a determinate of Z" and let the box-operator "$\Box$" stand for metaphysical necessity. The following is a cornerstone of the theory of determinables and determinates:[90]

(D) $\Box \, [\forall X \forall Y \forall Z \forall x \, ((Xx \wedge \text{Det}(X, Z) \wedge \text{Det}(Y, Z) \wedge X \neq Y \wedge \neg \, \text{Det}(X, Y) \wedge \neg \, \text{Det}(Y, X)) \rightarrow \neg \, Yx)].$[91]

In words: necessarily, it holds that if an individual instantiates a certain property F that is a determinate of a property H, than the individual does not instantiate a further property G that is also a determinate of H but not of the same range as F. The property of being white and the property of being green are determinates of one determinable, namely the property of being colored, and they are not of the same range. Thus, according to (D), if something is white, it

---

[90] (D) is a generalization of Johnson's *Principle of Disjunction*, which is one of four dependence relations Johnson identifies with respect to the determinable/determinate relation. Let me quote all four relations (Johnson speaks of 'determinate adjectives', rather than of 'determinate properties'):
(1) *Principle of Implication*: If s is p, where p is a comparatively determinate adjective, then there must be some determinable, say P, to which p belongs, such that s is P.
(2) *Principle of Counterimplication*: If s is P, where P is a determinable, then s must be p, where p is an absolute determinate under P.
(3) *Principle of Disjunction*: s cannot be both p and p', where p and p' are any two different absolute determinates under P.
(4) *Principle of Alternation*: s must be either not-P; or p or p' or p'' ... continuing the alternants throughout the whole range of variation of which P is susceptible – p, p', p'' ... being comparatively determinate adjectives under P." (Johnson 1921: 237)
(D) is a generalization of Johnson's *Principle of Disjunction* because the *Principle of Disjunction* only excludes that an object instantiates two maximally determinate properties of one determinable, whereas (D) excludes that an object instantiates two determinates of one determinable that are not of the same range. Trivially, two maximally determinates of one determinable are never of the same range.
[91] Note that we said that the determinable/determinate relation is irreflexive, and therefore need not explicitly demand that $X \neq Z$ and that $Y \neq Z$.

cannot be green. Necessarily, the state of affairs of snow being white is non-obtaining or the state of affairs of snow being green is non-obtaining. (D) guarantees that there are atomic states of affairs of the individual/property form that exclude one another (assuming there are at least two determinates of one determinable and an individual). Supposing that (D) generalizes to relations of arbitrary arity, we have established (MA').

If the above reasoning is cogent, the interpretationalist can justify the necessary metaphysical assumptions. However, we should not forget that the claim that the world has a determinable/determinate structure is no innocent claim of logic, but pure metaphysics. As a consequence, any reasonable interpretationalist view rests on non-trivial metaphysical assumptions about the structure of the actual world.

Restriction (I4) suggests that we confine the interpretations such that they do not violate the metaphysical dependencies stated by the interpretationalist's metaphysical theory M. Let me exemplarily illustrate how such a restriction would look if one justifies (MA') in the way indicated above, i.e., with recourse to (D).

Let τ_j ($j \in \{1, ..., n\}$) be logical or non-logical terms. Thus $\tau_1...\tau_n$ stands for an arbitrary (possibly non-atomic) formula. (D) results in the following restriction on admissible interpretations, formulated in FL semantics:

(I4*) An interpretation i of a formula $\tau_1...\tau_n$ is only admissible if the following holds:
if there is a property A with $Det(i^*(\tau_j), A)$ and $Det(i^*(\tau_k), A)$ and neither $Det(i^*(\tau_j), i^*(\tau_k))$ nor $Det(i^*(\tau_k), i^*(\tau_j))$, then it must also hold that there is a property B with $Det(i(\tau_j), B)$ and $Det(i(\tau_k), B)$ and neither $Det(i(\tau_j), i(\tau_k))$ nor $Det(i(\tau_k), i(\tau_j))$
(for $j, k \in \{1, ..., n\}$).

(I4*) says that for every admissible interpretation i it must hold that if $i^*(\tau_j)$ and $i^*(\tau_k)$ are determinates of one determinable (that are not of the same range), then $i(\tau_j)$ and $i(\tau_k)$ must also be determinates of one determinable (that are not of the same range). Interpretations must respect the determinable/determinate relations between the properties. For example, restriction (I4*) excludes a reinterpretation of "if snow is white, snow is not green" as saying that if snow is white, it is not cold: the properties of being white and of being cold are not determinates of the same determinable though being white and being green are.

As the restrictions discussed in the previous chapter, restriction (I4*) is a cross-term restriction. It does not treat any term as fixed, but restricts the possible simultaneous reinterpretation of terms. Consider some examples. (I4*) allows a reinterpretation of the sentence such that it says, e.g., that if snow is black, it is not blue: being black and being blue are determinates of one determinable, namely, again, the determinable of being colored. Furthermore, restriction (I4*) does not even demand that the property of which $i(\tau_j)$ and $i(\tau_k)$ are determinates is the same property as the property of which $i^*(\tau_j)$ and $i^*(\tau_k)$ are determinates: it is admissible to reinterpret the sentence as saying that, e.g., if snow is cold, then it is not hot, or as saying that if Alfred Tarski is (exactly) 1.80m tall, he is not (exactly) 2m tall.

As a consequence of restriction (I4*), the sentence "if snow is white, snow is not green" turns out to be true under all admissible interpretations.[92] This paradigm case of a merely metaphysically necessary sentence would thus come out logically true according to the interpretational definition. Thus, given acceptance of (I4*) many 'merely metaphysical' truths are turned into logical truths.[93]

In the first section of this chapter, I argued that the interpretational definition of logical truth, often praised for its independence from metaphysics, relies on certain non-trivial metaphysical assumptions. In this section, I proposed that the interpretationalist must not stop half-way: he should make his metaphysical commitments explicit by formulating the respective restrictions on interpretations. As a result, certain allegedly merely necessary sentences turn out to be logically

---

[92] Here I presuppose that different terms may not be interpreted in the same way. The sentence "if snow is white, snow is not green" may not be reinterpreted as saying that if snow is white, snow is not white.

[93] The above sentence "if snow is white, snow is not green" is metaphysically necessary. Of course, there are also sentences which involve two determinates of one determinable that are not metaphysically necessary. Just consider, e.g., the sentence "snow is white or grass is green". Here (I4*) excludes an interpretation such that the sentence says, e.g., that snow is hot or grass is green. However, I do not see this as a problem, but merely as a harmless side-effect, as the sentence will not be defined logically true anyway: restriction (I4*) still allows, e.g., a reinterpretation of the sentence such that it expresses the proposition that snow is green or grass is white.

true. A strict boundary between logical and metaphysical modalities does not exist.

6 Logic and Formality

The interpretationalist is faced with the problem of admissible interpretations: he must distinguish between admissible and inadmissible interpretations, and he must formulate the respective restrictions on interpretation. In the preceding chapters, I discussed different such restrictions with the result that what are often considered to be merely structural, analytic or metaphysically necessary sentences turn out to be logical truths. Many will reject the suggested restrictions on the ground that logic is *formal*: logical truths are true in virtue of their form alone. If the truth of analytic or necessary truths is grounded not in form alone, they cannot be logical truths either. This then, for the argument under consideration, provides the demarcation criterion for interpretations. There is only one meta-rule with respect to the formulation of restrictions on interpretations: one should impose exactly those restrictions that do not violate the formality constraint.

My aim in this chapter is to show that this line of reasoning is correct only in an unavailing sense. While it may indeed be the case that the boundary between formally and non-formally true sentences coincided with that between logical and non-logical truths, the former is unable to ground the latter. There is no independent criterion of formality the interpretationalist may use. Formality does not provide a non-trivial criterion for logicality.

6.1 Schematic Formality

The slogan that logic is formal almost never receives proper attention.[94] Sometimes, at least, it is said that the formality of logical truths lies in the fact that logical truths are true solely in virtue of the meaning of the logical constants. It is then argued that sentences like "mothers are female" or "if snow is white, snow is not green" are not true in virtue of the meaning of the logical constants alone, but only in virtue of the meaning of the particular predicates appearing in them. This reasoning is, however, not quite correct. On the one hand,

---

[94] A notable exception is McFarlane [PhD dissertation] who provides an elaborated, historically informed discussion of the formality of logic. See also Dutilh Novaes 2011.

it ignores the fact that logical truths are not solely true in virtue of the meaning of the logical constants. Their truth depends, for example, also on the identity relations between the terms. On the other hand, it is also false to say that, for example, analytical sentences are true in virtue of the particular meanings of the non-logical constants occurring in them. In order to know that "mothers are female" is true, we do not have to know the specific meanings of the terms involved: it suffices to know that that the semantic values of "mother" and "female," whatever they are, are linked in a certain way, i.e., that the meaning of the one terms semantically contains that of the other. Analogously, we do not need to know the particular meaning of "is white" or "is green" to account for the truth of "if snow is white, snow is not green". All we have to know is that the respective properties are determinates of one determinable.

These very superficial observations are sufficient to indicate that formality has to be fleshed out much more carefully. So let us consider the most common account of formality in terms of *schematic formality*. According to this suggestion, a sentence is formally true iff it is an instance of a valid schema. As spelling out this suggestion properly is more intricate than it might seem at first glance, I will start from scratch.

Let me stress in advance that I confine myself to the discussion of fully regimented and reformulated sentences in which the logical form is already displayed at the surface. For example, instead of considering the sentence "if snow is white, snow is not green" I will only discuss the following reformulation: "(not: snow is white) or (not: snow is green)". This restriction does, however, not limit the scope of the results in a sense relevant to the present context.

Our object language is, as just said, a regimented form of natural language. In a first step, we have to identify the terms of natural language. A selection S tells us which parts of the language are its simple constituents, the terms. A selection S breaks down natural language into parts by determining a set T_S of terms. To begin with, a selection need not satisfy any general constraints. I demand neither that the terms are the smallest meaningful parts of the language, nor that a term may not also be a constituent of a further term, as is the case if both "married" and "married to Plato" are considered as terms. Furthermore, a selection may fragment expressions we intuitively take as one expression into different terms. For example, a selection may understand the natural language expression "everything" not as one term, but as two terms, namely a quantifier ("every") and a variable ("thing"). A selection of terms can be chosen wholly arbitrarily.

A *classification* C_S partitions the set T_S of terms into equivalence classes, so called *term classes* $t_{CS}j$ ($j \in \mathbb{N}$). (I usually omit the index to the selection S. Of course, not only the set of terms T, but the classification C, and the resulting term classes, are defined relative to a given selection S.) Intuitively, terms are in the same term class if they are of the same 'type'. Let me give you some examples of familiar selections and classifications. The selection associated with propositional logic defines the set of terms, T_P, as the class of all atomic sentences and the logical constants "or" and "not". The elements of T_P are classified in three term classes: t_P1, t_P2, t_P3. The term class t_P1 is the singleton of "or", {or}, t_P2 the singleton of "not", {not}, and t_P3 is the class of atomic sentences. The selection associated with PL looks different: T_{PL} consists of the logical constants "or", "not", "all", all individual constants, all predicate constants, and all the individual variables.[95] The associated classification looks as follows: $t_{PL}1$ is the singleton of "or", $t_{PL}2$ is the singleton of "not", $t_{PL}3$ is the singleton of "all", $t_{PL}4$ is the set of all individual variables, $t_{PL}5$ is the set of all individual constants, $t_{PL}6$ is the set of all one-place relation terms, $t_{PL}7$ is the set of all two-place relation terms, etc.

For any term class t_Ci we define a *corresponding parameter class* $t_C\mathbf{i}$, such that the parameters $\boldsymbol{\tau}_j$ in $t_C\mathbf{i}$ range over the terms τ_j in t_Ci. The function f_C maps each term on the term class it belongs to in accordance with its classification C, and the function g maps each parameter on its parameter class.

DEFINITION: A C_S-*schema* $\varphi = \boldsymbol{\tau}_1\ldots\boldsymbol{\tau}_m$ is a finite string of parameters (and auxiliary symbols) such that there is a sentence $\varphi = \tau_1\ldots\tau_n$ (with $\tau_i \in T_C$, $i \in \{1, \ldots, n\}$) ($m, n \in \mathbb{N}$) with

(i) $m = n$,

(ii) iff $\boldsymbol{\tau}_i = \boldsymbol{\tau}_j$ (for some $i, j \in \{1,\ldots, m\}$), then $\tau_i = \tau_j$,

(iii) $f_C(\tau_j)$ corresponds to $g(\boldsymbol{\tau}_j)$ for all $j \in \{1, \ldots, n\}$.

---

[95] Natural language sentences do not contain any variables in the strict sense. However, their regimented reformulations might well do so.

The first condition secures that the schema $\boldsymbol{\varphi}$ and the sentence φ are of the same length, i.e., they consist of the same number of parameters and terms, respectively. The second condition guarantees that identical parameters are instantiated by identical terms and different parameters by different terms. (Note that it is not allowed that different parameters are instantiated by identical terms.) The third condition says that the j-th term of φ must be of a term class that corre-corresponds to the parameter class of the j-th parameter of $\boldsymbol{\varphi}$.

Very roughly put, a string of parameters is a schema iff it has an instance. It is a C-schema iff its instance is given by a natural language sentence analyzed by the classification C (and the respective selection S). To illustrate the notion of a C-schema, assume first the selection and the classification of terms associated with propositional logic. Let $\boldsymbol{p}$ be an element of $\mathbf{t_P 3}$, the class of parameters ranging over $t_P 3$, the class of atomic sentences. Then, the schema "$\boldsymbol{p}$" has "Pluto is a planet" as an instance: "Pluto is a planet" is, according to the selection associated with propositional logic, only one term and thus condition (i) is fulfilled. Condition (ii) is trivially fulfilled and as "Pluto is a planet" is an element of $t_P 3$, condition (iii) is also fulfilled: $t_P 3$ corresponds to $\mathbf{t_P 3}$. Thus, "$\boldsymbol{p}$" is a P-schema.

Next, exemplarily consider the selection and the classification associated with PL. Let $\boldsymbol{a} \in \mathbf{t_{PL} 5}$ and $\boldsymbol{F} \in \mathbf{t_{PL} 6}$. Then "$\boldsymbol{aF}$" is a PL-schema that has "Pluto is a planet" as an instance: C_{PL} classifies "Pluto" into $t_{PL} 5$ and "is a planet" into $t_{PL} 6$. The schema consists of two parameters, and the sentence "Pluto is a planet" consists of two terms according to the selection associated with PL, too; thus, condition (i) is fulfilled. Condition (ii) is again trivially fulfilled and as the respective term classes and parameter classes correspond to one another, (iii) is fulfilled, too.

We are now prepared to spell out the remaining definitions of a *valid schema*, of *C-formal truth*, and of *formal truth*.

DEFINITION: A schema is *valid* iff all its instances are true.

DEFINITION: A sentence φ is *C-formally true* iff there is a valid C-schema of which φ is an instance.

The notion of formality, or formal truth, is, so far, defined as a relative notion. A sentence is formally true with respect to a C-schema, and thus, ultimately with respect to a classification C (and the corresponding selection S). The non-relative notion of formal truth is defined in terms of the notion of C-formal truth as follows:

DEFINITION: A sentence φ is *formally true* iff it is C-formally true for some C.

A sentence is formally true iff it is formally true according to some classification of the terms. For example, the sentence "if all planets are eternal and Pluto is a planet, then Pluto is eternal" is not P-formally true. There is no valid P-schema of which it is an instance. The sentence is nevertheless formally true, as it is PL-formally true. To qualify as formally true, there need only be some classification C with respect to which the sentence is C-formally true. The sentence need not be formally true with respect to all classifications. Otherwise, no sentence whatsoever would be formally true.

Equipped with this definition of formal truth, based on the familiar notion of schematic formality, we will now evaluate whether alleged paradigm examples of merely analytically true or merely necessary true sentences are formally true. Let's start with the familiar example "if snow is white, snow is not green", which reads, in its regimented form, as follows: "(not: snow is white) or (not: snow is green)". Consider the selection and the classification of propositional logic first. We have: "or" $\in t_p 1$, "not" $\in t_p 2$, "snow is white" $\in t_p 3$, and "snow is green" $\in t_p 3$. Let, again, $p \in t_p 3$, $q \in t_p 3$, $\mathbf{v} \in t_p 1$ and $\mathbf{\neg} \in t_p 2$.[96] We can easily determine that "(not: snow is white) or (not: snow is green)" is an instance of the P-schema "$\neg p \vee \neg q$". Obviously, however, this is not a valid schema, as it has false instances. The sample sentence is thus not P-formal. By considering P-formality alone, our sentence cannot be determined as logically true.

However, recall that a sentence is formally true iff it is an instance of a C-schema for *some* classification C. I will now show that there is such a classification C. To spell out the novel classification C_N, choose the selection of PL and let $t_N i = t_{PL} i$ for $i \in \{1, ..., 5\}$. The classification C_N thus sorts the logical constants and the individual terms exactly as C_{PL} does. However, C_N deviates from C_{PL} in the fol-

---

[96] A note on notation: I use "$\mathbf{v}$" and "$\mathbf{\neg}$" as symbols for (metalanguage) parameters. As before, their being bold means that the symbols are parameters. I chose "$\mathbf{v}$" and "$\mathbf{\neg}$" rather than, e.g. "$\mathbf{r}$" and "$\mathbf{s}$", to indicate the range of the parameters and thereby to facilitate readability.

lowing way: C_N does not put all predicate constants in the term class $t_N 6$, but only the color predicates; $t_N 6 = \{$is red, is green, is blue, is yellow, etc.$\}$.[97] All further predicates are classified into term class $t_N 7$. The relation terms are then classified according to their arity in the obvious way: $t_N n = t_{PL} n\text{-}1$ for all $n \geq 8$. Now, consider the N-schema "$\neg aG \vee \neg aF$", with $F \in t_N 6$ and $G \in t_N 6$ (the other occurring parameters are classified as in PL). It is straightforward to establish that "(not: snow is white) or (not: snow is green)" is an instance of this schema. Furthermore, the schema is valid as all instances of it are true. Thus, there is a valid schema of which the sample sentence is an instance. The sentence is N-formally true and therefore formally true according to the above definition of formal truth.[98]

A similar move will also establish the formal truth of our paradigm example of the analytic sentence "if Gaia is a mother, Gaia is female", which reads, in its regimented form, as follows: "(not: Gaia is a mother) or Gaia is female".[99] Obviously, this sentence is not an instance of any valid P- or PL-schema. To account for the formality of the sentence, we choose the classification C_A of the terms as follows: $t_A i = t_{PL} i$ for $i \in \{1, ..., 5\}$; $t_A 6$ is defined as the singleton of "is a mother", i.e., $t_A 6 = \{$"is a mother"$\}$, and $t_A 7 = \{$"is female"$\}$; $t_A 8$ is the set of all predicates except "is a mother" and "is female", and $t_A n = t_{PL} n\text{-}2$ for $n \geq 9$. As can easily be shown, the above sample sentence is an instance of the schema "$\neg aF \vee aG$", with $a \in t_N 5$, $F \in t_N 6$ and $G \in t_N 7$. As all instances of this schema are true, it is val-

---

[97] More precisely, $t_N 6$ only contains all color predicates such that no predicate is a determinable or a determinate of the other, i.e., no two color predicates in $t_N 6$ are of the same range.

[98] For a similar argument, see Sagi 2014. Sagi also rejects the traditional dichotomy between terms that are not fixed at all (the non-logical constants), and terms that are totally fixed (the logical constants), and argues that it should be replaced by a system of 'semantic constraints', allowing for partially fixed terms. The form of a sentence φ is then not determined by the logical constants occurring in φ (and the arrangements of all terms of φ) alone, but depends on the chosen semantic constraints.

[99] In order to keep the discussion as clear and simple as possible, I will discuss the sample sentence "if Gaia is a mother, Gaia is female" in lieu of the sentence "mothers are female". The regimentation of the latter sentence is a bit more complicated as it involves quantification and thus generates unnecessary distractions.

id. As our sample sentence is an instance of the schema, there is a classification, namely C_A, according to which there is a valid schema of which the sample sentence is an instance. Therefore, the sentence "if Gaia is a mother, Gaia is female" is formally true according to our definitions. Thus, paradigm examples of allegedly merely necessary or merely analytic sentences turn out to be formally true.

In some sense, my argument seems to be based on a cheap trick. The above classifications seem most unusual at the very least. For example, according to classification C_A, there is a term class with only one element: the term class $t_A 6$ contains only the predicate "is a mother". However, note that this is, as such, nothing particularly abnormal. The respective term classes of the logical constants "or", "not", and "all" are also singletons, e.g., in the standard classifications C_P and C_{PL}. Nevertheless, it is true that if we are allowed to build term classes with just one element, then every true sentence is formally true according to some classification: simply chose the trivial classification where every term has a term class of its own! Then, every schema has just one instance. As a result, every true sentence is formally true. The desideratum that logical truths must be formal trivializes.[100]

There is an obvious solution strategy: We distinguish between admissible and inadmissible classification and adapt our definition of logical truth such that a formally true sentence is an instance of a valid C-schema for some *admissible C*.

Yet now we have moved from the frying pan into the fire. We started with the aim of distinguishing admissible from inadmissible interpretations, resorted to the notion of formality, just to find that we would have to distinguish first between admissible and inadmissible classifications. We have not made any headway. The problem of admissible term classes is entirely analogous to the problem of admissible interpretations. Reasons for certain restrictions on interpretations translate into reasons for the corresponding restrictions on classifications of terms, and *vice versa*. For example, if we stick to restriction (I1) on interpretations and exclude interpretations that reinterpret the logical constants, we will also find a categorization

---

[100] This observation can also be found in McFarlane 2000: 39: "*Every* inference is schematic-formal relative to *some* pattern."

classifying the logical constants in their singletons legitimate. If we bisect the non-logical constants into individual and predicate terms, and therefore subscribe to restriction (I2), we will demand a classification that sorts the individuals and predicates in different term classes. And if we think that restriction (I3*) is legitimate, we will also buy into classification A. Whether or not a sentence is declared formally true depends on the demarcation of admissible from inadmissible classifications, just as it depends on the demarcation of the admissible from the inadmissible interpretations whether or not a sentence is declared logically true.

In general, the restriction on interpretations that is particularly relevant for the logical truth of a sentence, and the classification of the terms under which this sentence is formally true, seem to share the same motivation. The demand that logical truths must be formally true may approach the topic of logical truth from a slightly different angle, but it has to cope with essentially the same difficulties. The criterion of formality does therefore not provide an autonomous desideratum on a definition of logical truth or logical validity. Pointing out that logical truths are formal is either unavailing or false.

6.2 Restrictions in Formal Languages

Throughout the book, I have articulated the problem of admissible interpretations with recourse to natural language sentences. This might generate the impression that the demarcation problem is confined to natural language sentences only and that, once the sentences are formalized, the formal apparatus takes care of the rest. Indeed, this thought is natural. Consider exemplarily the interpretation function of PL. It is only defined on the non-logical constants, so no logical constant gets reinterpreted by choosing a different interpretation function: no need for restriction (I1). It also treats individual and relation terms differently by definition, so we can omit restriction (I2). Furthermore, as the interpretation function is defined on term types rather than on term token, restriction (I3) is superfluous. There is no need to impose any of these restrictions on interpretations. As I mainly motivated the new restrictions by their respective similarity to (I1) – (I3), there seems to be no reason to accept them. The problem of admissible interpretations seems not to arise at all.

Although it undoubtedly has some initial plausibility, I will now argue that this line of reasoning is seriously flawed. Contrary to what is supposed above, the recourse to formal languages does not provide any relief at all. The reason is simple. Different formal languages may encode different restrictions in their interpretation function. Lest the choice is arbitrary, any proponent of that view must say why he prefers a formal language in which, say, restrictions (I1) to (I3) are encoded, to a language in which they are not encoded. By recourse to formal languages, one only shifts the demarcation problem to a different level, but does not get away from it.

I will defend this claim by showing that there is no principled obstacle to defining interpretation functions that do not implement (I1), (I2) or (I3), and, on the other hand, that one can define interpretation functions where the new restrictions are implemented. Let me be clear, however, that my aim is not to change the common practice of encoding exactly (I1), (I2) and (I3). Rather I want to show that we cannot draw any theoretical consequences about the legitimacy of the restrictions from this practice. No doubt, there are good practical reasons for implementing exactly those restrictions that are usually implemented: It helps to keep things simple. But these practical reasons do not by themselves provide any theoretical justification for the particular choice of restrictions in place.

I will first show how the interpretation functions of PL and of FL can be reformulated, such that they do not automatically conform to (I1), (I2), and (I3), beginning with (I1). Restriction (I1) on the reinterpretation of the logical constants is implemented in the interpretation function of both PL and FL because these functions are only defined on the set of non-logical constants. The logical constants get assigned their semantic value not by the interpretation function, but via the recursive truth definition. Thus, the interpretation of the logical constants trivially remains constant under all interpretations. In order to free the interpretation functions of the respective restriction (I1), we must only include the logical constants in the domain of definition of the interpretation functions. These interpretation functions then map, say, the conjunction sign on the conjunction relation. They assign a semantic value to the logical constants by mapping them on elements of the domain or, in the case of PL, on set-theoretic constructions of elements of the domains. With regard to FL semantics, we would simply postulate that the logical constants be mapped on 'logical objects', as, e.g., conjunction, negation, etc. which themselves are elements of the domain. Of course, this might seem odd, but at least from a purely technical point of view, there is no principled objection to treating the logical constants as referring to logical objects.[101] (See also Section 7.1, where I extensively discuss the notion of logical objects and the prospects of extending the domain of definition of the interpretation function to the logical constants.)

Let's turn to the more interesting case, the grammatical restriction (I2). Note that the interpretation function of form logic maps any constants on an arbitrary element of the domain and does thus not semantically distinguish between the different grammatical categories of the terms. The grammatical restriction (I2) is actually *not* implemented in the interpretation function of FL. We don't have to change anything.[102] The case is different with respect to PL. The interpretation function of PL assigns an element of the domain to any individual constant and a set of n-tuples of elements of the domain to an n-ary relation constant. There is no interpretation function that assigns, say, an element of the domain to a relation constant or a set of elements of the domain to an individual constant. All interpretation functions of PL respect the bisection of the non-logical constants into individual and relation terms by definition. To get rid of the implementation of the grammatical restriction (I2) within the framework of PL, we simply allow for each term that the interpretation function maps it on an element of $\mathfrak{D}$, or a subset of $\mathfrak{D}$, or on a set of n-tuples of $\mathfrak{D}$ (for arbitrary $n \in \mathbb{N}$). Such an interpretation function may for example map an individual constant on a set of ordered pairs of elements of the domain, or it may map a predicate constant on an element of $\mathfrak{D}$. The redefined interpretation function no longer automatically respects the grammatical categories of the terms.

---

[101] Although we would, of course, have to adapt the definition of truth in a model for 'molecular' sentences.

[102] I only introduced a simplified version of form-logical semantics in Chapter 2. The original form-logical semantics is actually designed to allow for various categorizations of the terms into grammatical categories. In the general semantics of form logic we have an arbitrary number of different semantical categories. See Freitag & Zinke 2012 for an elaborated version of form-logical syntax and semantics.

The identity restriction (I3), finally, is implemented in both the interpretation functions of PL and of FL. Both interpretation functions automatically map all occurrences of one term type on the same semantic value. This is due to the fact that they are defined on the set of terms, not on the set of term occurrences. However, we can in principle also define the interpretation functions on term occurrences. In spelling this out, we encounter some practical problems, because occurrences are unrepeatable by nature. This makes it difficult to explicitly state an interpretation function defined on term tokens. Yet, we can circumvent this problem by indirectly describing the occurrences, rather than using them. Consider, for example, the following definition of an interpretation function i (for a variant of either PL or FL): i maps the j-th occurrence of the individual constant a on the object o_k if j is even and on the object o_l if j is odd. (The occurrences of all other constants are interpreted arbitrarily, conforming to the usual conditions of PL and FL semantics, respectively.) This interpretation function is occurrence-sensitive in the required way: it does not map all occurrences of one term on the same semantic value.

Restrictions (I1), (I2), (I3) are internal restrictions with respect to the standard interpretation functions of PL and FL (with the exception of (I2) for FL). However, as I have just shown, we can straightforwardly modify the interpretation functions such that they no longer automatically obey the restrictions. Let me now argue that, conversely, we can also modify the interpretation functions such that they encode the newly proposed structural, analytic, or metaphysical restrictions, discussed in the last chapters. There is nothing in the notion of a formal language as such that determines which restrictions are encoded.

The structural restriction (I2*) is a generalization of the grammatical restriction (I2). (I2) demands that interpretations respect the dichotomy of individual and relations constants, whereas (I2*) states that interpretations must respect the grammatical categories of the terms – whichever categories these are. In principle, there are two ways to elaborate on the traditional individual/relation-picture, giving rise to different ways to modify the interpretation function of PL: (i) one can allow for additional grammatical categories, while either keeping or abandoning the traditional ones, or (ii) one can allow for finer categorizations with further sub-categories (or, of course, one can do both (i) and (ii)). If one allows additional grammatical categories, (I2*) can be implemented by redefining the interpretation function of PL such that the terms of the new categories are assigned set-theoretic entities different from elements of the domain (the values of individual constants) and from sets of tuples of elements of the domain (the values of relation constants): for example, the interpretation function could map some constants on functions from sets of tuples of elements of the domain to sets of tuples of elements of the domain, and the interpretation function could map constants of a yet different grammatical category on sets of sets of elements of the domain. (In principle, the latter is done in second-order predicate logic, where one allows there to be predicates of predicates.) There is a myriad of possibilities. If one choses the second way and deviates from the traditional PL-categorization of terms by fine-graining the category of individuals or relation constants, one will implement (I2*) differently. For preparation, one first groups the members of the domain into different sub-categories. For example, one can sort all individual objects located in space-time in one ontic category, and all abstract objects in another. One then restricts the interpretation function such that individual constants can only be mapped on elements of the domain belonging to a suitable ontic category, while predicates are only mapped on sets of objects of a suitable ontic category. For example, a color predicate may only allow for reinterpretations such that it always has as its semantic value a set of objects belonging to the ontic category of extended objects. We could then not assign to it a set of objects containing, say, numbers. Independently of whether (I2*) is fleshed out along the lines of (i) or (ii), it can easily be implemented into the definition of the interpretation function of PL.

The case is exactly analogous with respect to the interpretation function of FL. As you remember, in FL all terms are mapped on elements of the domain. However, we can redefine the interpretation function of FL such that it maps some terms on set-theoretic constructions of the elements of the domain, or – more in line with the spirit of form-logical semantics – sort the elements of the domain in ontic categories and restrict the possible semantic values of a term to the members of suitable ontic categories. We can thus implement the structural restriction (I2*) into both FL and PL in a straightforward fashion. As a consequence of such a modification of the interpretation functions, certain structurally true sentences of PL and FL will turn out to be true under literally all interpretations i.

Turn to restriction (I3*), which confines the admissible interpretations to those that respect the semantic containment relations between the terms. To implement (I3*) into the interpretation function of PL, we mutually constrain the possible values of predicates.[103] The modified definition of the interpretation function looks as follows.

Let the interpretation function *i* be a function from the set of non-logical constants such that:

- for all individual constants τ: $i(\tau) \in \mathfrak{D}$,
- for all predicate constants τ: $i(\tau) \subseteq \mathfrak{D}$ such that if $\tau_k^{[i*]}$ semantically contains $\tau_m^{[i*]}$, then $\tau_k^{[i]}$ semantically contains $\tau_m^{[i]}$ (for arbitrary $m, k \in \mathbb{N}$),
- for all *n*-ary relation constants τ (with $n > 1$): $i(\tau) \subseteq \mathfrak{D}^n$.

The interpretation of individual constants and of relations of higher arity remains as before, but predicates may now only be interpreted such that the semantic containment relations that hold under the intended interpretation are preserved. The respective modification of the interpretation function of FL looks just the same, except that all constants are mapped on elements of the domain. The modified definitions of the interpretation functions of FL and PL guarantee that a predicate which semantically contains another predicate under the intended interpretation will do so under any arbitrary interpretation. Restriction (I3*) can thus be implemented in the definition of the interpretation functions in a plain and simple manner. Assuming the redefined definition of an interpretation function *i*, many allegedly merely analytically true sentences will turn out to be true under literally all interpretations.

Finally, turn to restriction (I4*), which is an instance of the more general metaphysical restriction (I4). Restriction (I4*) excludes those interpretations from the admissible ones that violate the determinable/determinate relations. More precisely, it says that predicates that are determinates of one determinable under the intended inter-

---

[103] The modification of the interpretation function for PL only considers semantic containment relations between *predicates*. This accounts for all the examples of 'merely analytic' sentences that are usually discussed. If there are also semantic containment relations between relation terms of higher arity, or between individual terms, one must further change the interpretation function accordingly.

pretation may only be reinterpreted such that they are again determinates of one determinable. The following redefinition of the interpretation function i of PL implements (I4*).[104]

Let the interpretation function i be a function from the set of non-logical constants such that:
- for all individual constants τ: $i(\tau) \in \mathfrak{D}$,
- for all predicate constants τ: $i(\tau) \subseteq \mathfrak{D}$ such that if $\tau_k^{[i*]}$ and $\tau_m^{[i*]}$ are determinates of one determinable, then $\tau_k^{[i]}$ and $\tau_m^{[i]}$ are determinates of one determinable (for arbitrary $m, k \in \mathbb{N}$),
- for all n-ary relation constants τ (with $n > 1$): $i(\tau) \subseteq \mathfrak{D}^n$.

Individual constants and relations of higher arity are thus interpreted as usual, but the interpretation of predicates is confined to those respecting the determinable/determinate relations.

Finally, restriction (I4*) can be implemented into the interpretation function of FL in an analogous manner. However, as the interpretation function of FL maps predicates on elements of the domain, there is also an even more direct way to account for (I4*). We can partition the domain into subdomains such that two objects are in the same subdomain iff they are determinates of the same determinable (and not of the same range).[105] More precisely, let there be a partition of the domain $\mathfrak{D}$ into subdomains ∂j ($j \in \mathbb{N}$) such that:

- all elements of $\mathfrak{D}$ that are not determinates of any determinable are in the subdomain $\partial 0$,
- iff $o_m \in \partial j$ and $o_n \in \partial j$ (with $o_m, o_n \in \mathfrak{D}$, $j \in \mathbb{N} \setminus \{0\}$), then o_m and o_n are determinates of one determinable (and not of the same range).

The cells of the domain thus contain all determinates of one determinable that are not of the same range.[106] For example, $\partial 1$ may contain

---

[104] I again only take into account determinable/determinate relations between predicates, not between relations.
[105] As before, I use the terms 'determinate' and 'determinable' as applying to linguistic entities (predicates or relation terms) and non-linguistic entities (properties or relations) equally.
[106] This generates a partition because we assume that no property is a determinate with respect to different determinable properties. However, nothing hinges on this assumption.

the property of being white, the property of being green, and the further color properties, whereas $\partial 2$ may contain the property of weighing exactly 1 kilo, the property of weighing exactly 2 kilos, etc. Indi- Individuals such as Venus, Pluto, and Plato are grouped together with maximal determinables (if there are any) into $\partial 0$. This partition of the domain induces a partition of the set of terms into equivalence classes t_j as follows: if $i^*(\tau) \in \partial_j$, then $\tau \in t_j$ (for all $j \in \mathbb{N}$). If the semantic value of a term under the intended interpretation is in the subdomain ∂_j, then the term is classified in the corresponding class t_j. Finally, we can redefine the interpretation function i of FL as follows.

> Let the interpretation function i be a function from the set of non-logical constants such that for $\tau \in t_j$: $i(\tau) \in \partial_j$ (for $j \in \mathbb{N}$).

Terms are no longer mapped on arbitrary elements of the domain, but are interpreted within the confines of their respective subdomains. The subdomains are defined such that the following holds: if a term is mapped on a determinate of a determinable property F according to the intended interpretation, the interpretation function must again map it on a determinate property of the determinable property F. So, for example, the predicate "is white" can only be assigned a color property as its semantic value. The metaphysical restriction (I4*) is successfully implemented into the interpretation function of FL.[107] As a result of such modification of the interpretation function, many allegedly merely metaphysically necessary sentences of PL or FL will turn out to be true under literally all interpretations.[108] The restrictions tentatively proposed in the preceding chapters can thus be implemented into the interpretation functions of FL and PL.

Let me summarize the results of this chapter on the relation between formality and logicality. In the first section, I argued that the notion of formality rests on a demarcation of admissible from inad-

---

[107] To be precise, a restriction slightly stronger than (I4*) is implemented. According to the above redefinition of the interpretation function, a predicate which is a determinate of a determinable F may only be reinterpreted as being a determinate of F again. (I4*), however, allows determinates of a determinable F to be reinterpreted as determinates of a different determinable G. As already pointed out, the slightly more liberal restriction (I4*) can be implemented into form logic in a way analogous to the one spelled out for PL.
[108] I again assume that different terms are interpreted differently.

missible classifications of terms. The class of formally true sentences depends on the demarcation of admissible from inadmissible classifications of terms. It turns out that the problem of admissible classifications of terms is perfectly analogous to the problem of admissible interpretations. Formality is therefore of no help when it comes down to justifying the demarcation between admissible and inadmissible interpretations. In the second section, I discussed the distinction between internal and external restrictions on interpretation functions in formal systems. Some important restrictions are usually always entailed by the chosen interpretation functions themselves. Yet as shown, which restrictions are internal to the interpretation function and which are external is a matter of choice. Nothing in the nature of the restrictions determines whether they are external or internal. No doubt, our choice will often be based on practical considerations.

The problem of admissible interpretations is not confined to natural language. While interpretation functions determine the admissible interpretations for formal languages, we can determine which interpretation function to choose and hence which restriction to (implicitly) apply. Hence recourse to formal language does not solve the difficulty that the extension of 'logical truth' depends on a distinction between admissible and inadmissible interpretations which not only must be drawn, but also justified.

7 Representational Definition

According to the common view, the representational definition of logical truth declares all necessary sentences to be logically true, while the interpretational definition selects the formal amongst the necessary sentences. I argued extensively that this characterization is misleading at best as far as the interpretational definition is concerned: the extension of the interpretational definition depends on the chosen restrictions on interpretations, just as the extension of formality depends on the chosen classification of terms. The present chapter is devoted to the representational definition. I will reject the claim that, unconditionally, all and only the necessary sentences are declared logically true by the representational definition. Furthermore, I will show that the representational definition is confronted with *the problem of admissible states*, which is analogous to the demarcation problem of the interpretational definition.

Firstly, however, we have to spell out the representational definition properly. According to the standard view, the representational definition identifies logical truth with truth in all metaphysically possible worlds. For instance, we find this identification of representational models with worlds in Etchemendy 1988[a]:

> Models are just abstract representations of the world, both as it *is* and as it *might have been*. To use a rather loaded term, models represent possible worlds. (Etchemendy 1988[a]: 95)[109]

If representational models are identified with possible worlds, or representations thereof, representational logical truth boils down to metaphysically necessary truth straightaway.

Given the identification of representational models with possible worlds, it is hardly surprising that the representational definition is usually not regarded as a promising candidate for a definition of logical truth. The representational definition is then not only based on the notoriously cryptic notion of a 'possible world', but one gets the impression that a representationalist who identifies models with metaphysically possible worlds without further argument does not really accept the challenge to provide a definition of genuine *logical* truth. As John McFarlane says: "Representational semantics is clearly inappro-

---

[109] We find a similar comment already in Popper 1965: 432.

priate for an analysis of *logical* truth: truth in all [representational models – A.Z.] is just truth in all possible worlds, or *necessary* truth" (McFarlane, [unpublished]: 7).

As the previous chapters have indicated, I do not in principle object to the idea that, in the end, the traditional boundary between logical truth and metaphysically necessary truth might not hold up. We might not be able to justify the restrictions on models necessary to keep the two modalities apart. I do object, however, to identifying logical truth with metaphysically necessary truth unconditionally. The representational definition deserves to be treated more carefully. If one can preserve the initial representational idea of logical truth as truth independently of what the actual world is like, without bluntly identifying representational logical truth with necessary truth and thereby inviting the critique given above, one should do so.

Indeed, we already did so when we spelled out the representational definition of logical truth in Chapter 2 as follows:

(RT) A sentence φ is logically true iff $(\mathfrak{D}, \mathfrak{J}^*, \mathfrak{S}) \models \varphi$ for all $\mathfrak{S}$ and all $\mathfrak{D}$.

According to (RT), logical truth amounts to truth under the intended interpretation in all states (and all domains). A state was defined as a set of tuples of object of the domain. The notion of a state is thus *prima facie* quite different from the notion of a possible world – regardless of whether we think of possible worlds in Lewisian or Wittgensteinian terms. States neither qualify as possible *worlds*, nor as *possible* worlds: they neither claim to be complete, nor possible. States are defined as sets of Russellian propositions, understood as sets of tuples of elements of the domain. As of yet, there are no restrictions on propositions considered individually, and there are no cross-propositional restrictions. In particular, it is not demanded that the propositions that are elements of one state are compossible.

By distinguishing representational models from possible worlds, we have made room for a more liberal understanding of the representational definition in terms of (RT). In particular, without further qualification, it is not true that all metaphysically necessary sentences turn out to be logically true under the representational definition. For example, the sentence "if snow is white, snow is not green" is not true in all states, as there are states having both the proposition that snow is white and the proposition that snow is green as elements.

In the next sections, I will discuss the representational definition in the form of (RT), and argue that the problem of the demarcation of admissible from inadmissible states arises. Before I discuss the problem of admissible states, however, I will show that not only the interpretationalist, but also the representationalist is confronted with the problem of the logical constants. The representational definition cannot be spelled out solely in representational terms.

7.1 The Problem of Logical Objects

According to the representational definition, a sentence is logically true iff it is true independently of the facts, given its intended interpretation. As no reinterpretations are considered, it is usually assumed that the representational definition need not distinguish between logical and non-logical terms. In the present framework, this view is not correct. The demarcation between logical and non-logical terms need not only be presupposed to identify the terms that may be reinterpreted, but it already underlies any semantics that only treats the non-logical constants as genuinely referring terms and gives the meaning of the logical constants via the recursive truth definitions. This already presupposes a distinction between logical and non-logical terms.

Let us explore what happens if no such demarcation is assumed, and the logical and non-logical constants are therefore semantically treated on a par. The logical constants must then be treated as referring terms. Although the view that the logical constants refer to objects is widely neglected at least since Wittgenstein's famous dictum that the "'logical constants' do not stand for anything" (Wittgenstein 1921, § 4.0312),[110] it has, in more recent times, been prominently de-

---

[110] Wittgenstein contrasts his view that the logical constants do not refer with Russell's and Frege's view: "There are no 'logical objects' or 'logical constants' (in Frege's and Russell's sense)" (Wittgenstein 1921, § 5.4). McBride also ascribes to Russell the view that logical constants refer to logical objects. These logical objects may even fare as constituents of Russellian propositions: "If the logical constants are conceived as Russell conceived of them, i.e., as names of objects (logical objects), then the logically complex propositions must be taken to be descriptions of logically complex facts whose constituents include these special objects, e.g. the aforementioned negative fact includes negation as a constituent." (McBride 2011: 91) However, we should note that later Russell gave up the view that the logical constants refer to worldly objects that can figure as constit-

fended, e.g., by Gila Sher who views "logical terms as genuinely denoting terms" (Sher 1996: 674).[111] It is instructive to illustrate this idea within the framework of FL semantics. (A comforting comment in advance: I am not going to entertain this semantic position, but only want to see how it would look.)

In order to treat all terms semantically on a par, the interpretation function then maps every constant, whether logical or non-logical, on an element of the domain. The definition of truth in a model for atomic sentences then extends to *all* sentences (including those that traditionally would be called 'molecular'): a sentence $\varphi = \tau_1...\tau_n$, where τ_j ($j \in \{1, ..., n\}$) may stand for an arbitrary constant, be it a logical or a non-logical constant, is true in $\mathfrak{M} = (\mathfrak{D}, \mathfrak{I}, \mathfrak{S})$ iff $\langle i(\tau_1), ..., i(\tau_n) \rangle \in \mathfrak{S}$. Let me use this section to present the consequences of this semantics for the representational definitions of logical truth and logical consequence.

---

uents of propositions. In his *Theory of Knowledge*, Russell explicitly says that "[i]t would seem that logical objects cannot be regarded as 'entities.' [...] 'Logical constants', which might seem to be entities occurring in logical propositions, are really concerned with pure form, and are not actually constituents of the propositions in the verbal expression of which their names occur." (1913: 97 f.) The Russell of *Our Knowledge of the External World* makes a similar comment: "Such words as or, not, if, there is, identity, greater, plus, nothing, everything, function, and so on, are not names of definite objects like 'John' or 'Jones,' but are words which require a context in order to have meaning. All of them are formal, that is to say, their occurrence indicates a certain form of proposition, not a certain constituent." (Russell 1914: 208) And here is the Russell of the *Philosophy of Logical Atomism*: "You must not look about the real world for an object which you can call 'or', and say, 'Now, look at this. This is 'or.'" (Russell 1918: 39) Russell explicitly withdraws from his earlier views on logical constants also in the introduction to the second edition of the *Principles of Mathematics* (1938): "Logical constants [...], if we are to be able to say anything definite about them, must be treated as part of the language, not as part of what the language speaks about. In this way, logic becomes much more linguistic than I believed it to be at the time when I wrote the "Principles". It will still be true that no constants except logical constants occur in the verbal or symbolic expression of logical propositions, but it will not be true that these logical constants are names of objects, as "Socrates" is intended to be."

[111] For a similar view, see also Hossack 2007.

The Problem of Logical Objects

We will call the objects on which the logical constants are mapped under the intended interpretation *logical objects*.¹¹² The logical objects can be understood as certain kinds of relations and properties. Let me explain this with respect to the relation of negation, conjunction and generality, beginning with negation. The relation of negation, i.e., the semantic value of the negation connective, is a relation holding between the constituents of a Russellian proposition that represents a non-obtaining state of affairs.¹¹³ For example, the relation of negation applies to Pluto and the property of being a planet. As there are non-obtaining Russellian propositions of different arity, negation has, of course, to be understood as a multigrade-relation, i.e., a relation with a variable arity.

The semantic value of the conjunction connective is the relation of conjunction. If the Russellian proposition φ and the Russellian proposition ψ both represent obtaining states of affairs, then the constituents of φ and ψ stand in the relation of conjunction.¹¹⁴ Of course, the relation of conjunction must not just hold between the objects constituting φ and the objects constituting ψ, but it must be sensitive to the structure of the respective propositions. Conjunction is a *structural relation* in the Russellian sense. The notion of a structural relation was originally introduced by Russell as a means to analyze propositional attitudes (see Russell 1912, Ch. 12). He understood judging or believ-

---

¹¹² In my terminology, the logical objects are the semantic values of the logical constants. Sometimes the term 'logical object' is used in a much wider or even in a totally different sense. See, e.g., Russell who uses the term 'logical object' to refer to a wide range of philosophical or theoretical terms (1913: 97): "Many such terms have occurred in the last two chapters, for instance, particulars, universals, relations, dual complexes, predicates. Such words are, no doubt, somewhat difficult, and are only understood by people who have reached a certain level of mental development. Still, they are understood and this shows that those who understand them possess something which seems fitly described as 'acquaintance with logical objects.'"

¹¹³ See also Hossack 2007: 64: "[…] consider the property a proposition has, if no fact combines its constituents. This property of a proposition induces a relation in which its constituents stand to each other, if no fact combines them. My suggestion is that negation is this relation on the constituents of propositions." (This is only Hossack's preliminary definition of negation.)

¹¹⁴ See again, e.g. Hossack 2007: 71: "I suggest that conjunction is the multigrade relation that obtains between some things θ and some other things φ if and only if a fact combines θ and a fact combines φ."

ing, for instance, as structural relations between the believer and the objects constituting the believed proposition. Structural relations relate objects with further objects *qua* objects forming one proposition. To illustrate, consider Russell's example of the proposition that Cassio believes that Othello loves Desdemona. Here the relation of believing not merely holds between the four objects Cassio, Othello, Desdemona and the property of loving. Rather, it respects the 'glue' between Othello, Desdemona and the property of loving: it relates Cassio, on the one hand, to Othello, Desdemona and the property of loving on the other *qua* objects forming one proposition. Furthermore, structural relations respect the 'direction' of a proposition: the proposition that Cassio believes that Othello loves Desdemona can be distinguished from the proposition that Cassio believes that Desdemona loves Othello, as the relation of believing respects the direction of the believed propositions. The relation of conjunction has the same feature. It relates the objects of φ with the objects of ψ such that the propositional character and the fine-structure of φ and ψ are preserved.

Finally, turn to the relation of generality, which is the semantic value of the universal quantifier. We can understand it in a *Fregean* way: a property has the property of generality iff everything instantiates it. In the semantic view under discussion, the universal quantifier will refer to the higher-order property of generality. Note, however, that in the framework of FL semantics, where properties are not understood as set of elements of the domain, but simply as elements of the domain, the property of generality is no genuine higher-order property. (The same holds, of course, for further classical 'higher-order' properties.) The semantic value of the universal quantifier is then treated as an ordinary property, i.e., it is an element of the domain. It is not clear how such a purely referential semantics that also treats the quantifiers as genuinely referring entities will handle more complicated constructions involving, e.g., iterated or embedded quantifiers. Fortunately, this need not be our concern as we will abandon this view anyway. First, however, let us recapitulate.

In the view under discussion, which results from neglecting the demarcation of logical from the non-logical constants, the constant "for all" refers to a property, and the logical constants "not" and "and" to structural multi-grade relations. The semantic values of the other logical constants can be understood along similar lines. Just like

The Problem of Logical Objects 123

ordinary properties and relations, the logical objects are elements of the domain. Since a Russellian proposition was earlier defined as a tuple of elements of the domain, the logical objects can now figure as constituents of Russellian propositions. The negative proposition that Pluto is not a planet is then represented by the tuple <the relation of negation, Pluto, the property of being a planet>. The conjunctive proposition that Venus is a planet and that Plato is a philosopher can be understood as the tuple <Venus, the property of being a planet, the relation of conjunction, Plato, the property of being a philosopher>.[115] We call propositions containing logical objects *molecular propositions*. They represent complex states of affairs.

Whether there are complex states of affairs is one of the core questions of ontology. At the one end of the spectrum, there are the logical atomists, who, following the early Wittgenstein, promote an ontology of atomic states of affairs only. At the other end there are views that take every (complex) sentence to describe a state of affairs, thereby acknowledging arbitrarily complex states of affairs.[116] Of course, the answer to this fundamental question can, and need not be given here. I only want to explore the possible consequences of the different alternatives for the representational definitions. In particular, I want to illustrate that the representational definitions of logical truth and of logical consequence get into serious trouble, once we acknowledge molecular Russellian propositions containing logical objects. A state was defined as a set of Russellian propositions. If there are also molecular propositions, then a state may contain molecular propositions. This generates very odd states indeed! For example, there would be states containing impossible propositions, such as the conjunctive proposition that Pluto is a planet and that Pluto is not a planet. There would also be 'non-closed' states that contain, say, the conjunctive proposition that Pluto is a planet and that Plato is a philosopher without containing the proposition that Pluto is a planet.

---

[115] Of course, we could also represent these propositions by choosing a different order of objects. For example, we could let the relation of conjunction take the first place in the tuple. We also have to spell out rules such that more complex propositions can be represented in a non-ambiguous way. The notation used is purely arbitrary.

[116] For the latter view, see, e.g. Pollock 1984; Pollock does, however, not understand states of affairs as tuples of objects.

Furthermore, there would be states that contain both the proposition that Pluto is a planet and the proposition that Pluto is not a planet. Once we allow molecular propositions to be elements of states, impossibilities abound.[117]

The results for the representational definitions would be disastrous. To begin with, apart from arguments in which the conclusion is one of the premises, no argument would be declared logically valid by the representational definition of logical consequence. The reason is simple: there will always be a state containing all propositions expressed by the premises, though not the proposition expressed by the conclusion. For example, as already pointed out, there will always be a state containing a certain conjunctive proposition, though not containing the propositional conjuncts. Similar problems arise, of course, for the representational definition of logical truth. No proposition will be a member of every state. For every proposition, there will be some state not containing it. Thus, not a single sentence would turn out to be logically true.

As a first reaction to the problem of impossible states, one might suggest to restrict the admissible states such that the above deviant states are excluded from the admissible ones. However, this strategy is obviously viciously circular. To guarantee the right result for the representational definition of logical consequence, one would have to demand that states are 'logically complete', i.e., that states contain all propositions that are implied by the members of the state by logical necessity. (We say that a proposition p (logically) implies a proposition q iff it is (logically) impossible that the state of affairs represented by p obtains while the state of affairs represented by q does not obtain.) To

---

[117] Observe that this reasoning can be read as turning a familiar problem associated with impossible worlds, or impossible states, upside down: It is often seen as a problem for a framework allowing impossible worlds that we can no longer maintain a compositional semantics. Take, for example, the standard semantics for negation: $\omega \models \neg \varphi$ iff $\omega \not\models \varphi$. Consider an impossible world where both φ and $\neg \varphi$ hold. φ is true in that world and, by the above clause and the assumption that $\neg \varphi$ holds in the world, φ is not true in the world. A genuine contradiction! So, it is argued, once we allow impossible worlds, we can no longer subscribe to a compositional semantics. I argued just the other way around: If we have no prior distinction between logical and non-logical constants, a compositional semantics is unmotivated and we have to treat logical and non-logical terms semantically on a par. Doing so, however, yields impossible worlds.

make sure that the representational definition of logical truth yields the desired results, one would have to demand that every admissible state contains all 'logically necessary propositions'. This already presupposes the notion of logical necessity. A definition of logical truth that is spelled out in terms of logical necessity is, however, of little theoretical value.

We can elegantly prevent these shortcomings by assuming a demarcation of the logical from the non-logical constants. With this distinction, the path is paved to interpret truth for molecular sentences via the recursive satisfaction conditions in the usual way. We no longer have to assume the existence of logical objects which can figure as constituents of Russellian propositions. States will then be sets of atomic propositions only. The problems discussed in this section do not arise once we treat the logical and the non-logical constant semantically different. I conclude that not only the interpretationalist, but also the representationalist has to presuppose a solution to the problem of logical constants.[118]

7.2 Restrictions on States

A state is defined as a set of Russellian propositions, where a Russellian proposition is just a tuple of objects of the domain. If we reject logical objects, a state will only contain propositions with 'ordinary' objects, i.e., proposition we would usually call *atomic*. But such a restricted class of states still allows very much, as we have neither put forward any constraints on atomic propositions considered in isolation, nor have we formulated any cross-propositional constraints. Any tuple of objects whatsoever can up to now be considered an atomic proposition, even, e.g., <Plato, Pluto> or <Pluto, the relation of having more mass than>. Furthermore, we still allow for 'impossible' states, e.g., containing the proposition that Gaia is a mother without containing the proposition that Gaia is female, or states containing

---

[118] Of course, this conclusion only applies to the representational definition as I understand it, i.e., in terms of (RT). If one understands the representational definition as saying that a sentence is logically true iff true in all possible worlds then, of course, the representationalist need not presuppose a demarcation of the logical from the non-logical terms. However, I already dismissed such a formulation of the representational definition on independent grounds.

both the proposition that snow is white and the proposition that snow is green.

Our definition of a state is still very liberal. One might want to restrict the admissible states to those containing only 'well-formed' propositions or to those that are conceptually or metaphysically possible. To make room for such restrictions, I propose the following reformulation of the representational definition:

(RT*) A sentence φ is logically true iff $(\mathfrak{D}, \mathfrak{I}^*, \mathfrak{S}) \vDash \varphi$ for all *admissible* $\mathfrak{S}$ and all $\mathfrak{D}$.

To be logically true, a sentence need not be true in literally all states, but only in the admissible ones. Obviously, a problem paralleling the problem of admissible interpretations will emerge for the representational definition: the problem of demarcating the admissible from the inadmissible states. Let me elaborate on this parallel, focusing on the problem of 'ill-formed' propositions first.

With respect to the interpretational definition of logical truth we distinguished those interpretations that respect the grammatical categories of the terms from those that violate them. A logically true sentence need only be true under well-behaved interpretations, i.e., interpretations that reinterpret the terms in the confines of their respective grammatical categories. Analogously, one may want to exclude states containing tuples like <Plato, Pluto> from the admissible ones. Such states need not be considered when evaluating whether a sentence is true in all states.

According to the traditional view, a Russellian proposition consists of a property and an individual (or of an n-place relation and n individuals). The tuple <Plato, Pluto> however consists of two individuals. It does not constitute a proposition in the intuitive sense because the objects are not of the required ontological categories. Recall that (I2) excluded interpretations that do not respect the traditional dichotomy between individual and relation terms. The parallel restriction (R2)[119] excludes those states from the admissible ones that do not conform to the traditional view that a Russellian proposition consists of an n-place relation and n individuals:

---

[119] For the sake of straightforward comparability, I chose the same numbering for the representational restrictions as for the corresponding interpretational restrictions.

(R2) A state $\mathfrak{S}$ is only admissible if the following holds: for all elements $<o_0, ..., o_n>$ of $\mathfrak{S}$ (with $o_i \in D$) it holds that o_0 is an n-place relation and o_i is an individual (with $i \in \{1, ..., n\}$).

Once restriction (R2) is imposed, all admissible states only contain atomic propositions consisting of an n-ary relation and n individuals.

With regard to the interpretational definition, I also discussed a generalization of (I2), namely the structural restriction (I2*), which allows for different or more fine-grained grammatical categories. Similar generalizations are possible for (R2). Such generalizations might be advisable on metaphysical grounds. As one can question the bisection of terms into relation and individual terms, one can question the ontological claim that there are exactly two kinds of things, relations (or properties) and individuals. The ontological set-up of the universe might not be exhausted by the categories of individuals and properties, or more complicated combinatorial rules for well-formed propositions might be necessary. Let me briefly discuss such a generalization.

The notion of an 'ontological category' is the metaphysical counterpart of the linguistic notion of a grammatical or semantical category. As we preliminarily characterized the concept of a grammatical category via the notion of substitution *salva congruitate*, we analogously say that two objects belong to the same *ontological category* iff the substitution of one object for the other in a well-formed Russellian proposition always results in a well-formed Russellian proposition.[120] This characterization of an ontological category is neutral in two important ways: it neither determines which ontological categories there are, nor does it specify any category-related combinatorial rules. To preserve this generality within the respective restriction, let $\mathfrak{O}$ be a set of finite sequences of ontological categories. Intuitively, $\mathfrak{O}$ represents all legitimate 'forms' of atomic propositions. To illustrate: Let O_0 be the ontological category of individual objects (i.e., the set of individuals), and let O_n be the ontological category of n-place relations (for

---

[120] We already find this characterization of an ontological category in Russell's writings (Russell uses the expression 'logical type' rather than the term 'ontological category'): "The definition of a logical type is as follows: A and B are of the same logical type if, and only if, given any fact of which A is a constituent, there is a corresponding fact which has B as a constituent, which either results by substituting B for A, or is the negation of what so results." (Russell 1918: 137)

$n \in \mathbb{N} \setminus \{0\}$). Under the assumption that we subscribe to the traditional view that a proposition is formed by an n-place relation and n individuals, we will define $\mathfrak{D}$ as follows:
$\mathfrak{D} = \{<O_1, O_0>, <O_2, O_0, O_0>, <O_3, O_0, O_0, O_0>, \ldots\}$.

To spell out (R2*) in a straightforward way, we let the function f map every object on its ontological category:

(R2*) A state $\mathfrak{S}$ is only admissible if the following holds:
for all elements $<o_1, \ldots, o_n>$ of $\mathfrak{S}$ it holds that
$<f(o_1), \ldots, f(o_n)> \in \mathfrak{D}$.

Restriction (R2*) guarantees that all states containing 'ill-formed' propositions are excluded from the admissible ones. We can illustrate this for the traditional picture: a state containing <Plato, Pluto> is excluded from the admissible ones by (R2*), because $<f^T(\text{Pluto}), f^T(\text{Plato})> = <O_0, O_0>$ and $<O_0, O_0> \notin \mathfrak{D}^T$ (where f^T is the traditional categorization of objects into ontological categories and $\mathfrak{D}^T$ represents the traditional view on well-formed propositions).

Compare the function of this restriction on possible representations with the role of its interpretationalist analogue. Restriction (I2*) guarantees that we do not have to evaluate sentences under interpretations that do not respect grammar. However, rejecting restriction (I2*) does not have the consequence that the definition of logical truth over- or undergenerates as long as we take ill-formed sentences to be false. Something analogous holds for restriction (R2*) on admissible states. If we impose (R2*), we do not have to evaluate sentences with respect to states containing 'ill-formed' propositions. Considering states containing 'ill-formed' propositions would, however, not have the effect that the definition of logical truth over- or under-generates. Nevertheless, as one might be reluctant to evaluate a sentence with respect to a state containing 'ill-formed' propositions, I tentatively suggest that we impose restriction (R2*).

Assuming restriction (R2*), the admissible states will only contain tuples that represent genuine propositions. Yet, (R2*) still does not impose any conditions on the simultaneous membership of different propositions in the same state. Even given (R2*), there are 'impossible' states. For instance, (R2*) does not regard states as inadmissible that contain the proposition that Gaia is a mother without containing the proposition that Gaia is female, or states containing both the proposition that snow is white and that it is green. As a consequence, the sample sentences "if Gaia is a mother, Gaia is female" and "if snow is white, snow is not green" do not turn out to be true in all states if only restriction (R2*) is in play. Without further restrictions, these necessary truths are not declared logically true by the representational definition in form of (RT*).

This contradicts with the standard view of the representational definition which is usually deemed to identify logical necessity with metaphysical necessity. As (RT*) and the underlying conception of states show, the unqualified claim that all metaphysically necessary truths are true under the representational definition is simply false.

However, as we further restricted the range of admissible interpretations, we can, of course, also motivate additional restrictions on states. In particular, one might want to exclude states containing the proposition that Gaia is a mother though not containing the proposition that Gaia is female. Importantly, the motivation for the respective restriction need not just be that those states are impossible. There are more elaborated, intrinsic reasons. For instance, one could argue that Russellian atomic propositions consist of 'simple' objects and that the property of being a mother is not simple. As a conjunctive property it stands in need of further analysis and is thus no legitimate constituent of atomic Russellian propositions. Furthermore, one might also want to exclude states containing both the proposition that snow is white and that snow is green. A motivation for doing so could be that states should not contain mutually 'dependent' propositions, where color propositions are taken to be mutually dependent. Of course, such a move asks for an elaboration of the notion of dependency between propositions. I will neither try to deliver one here, nor will I go into any details of the motivations for possible further restrictions on states. My primary aim in this chapter was solely to broaden our conception of the representational definition and to highlight the structural similarities between the interpretational and the representational definition.

Like the interpretational definition, the representational definition allows for various restrictions on models. Importantly, the mentioned restrictions on states are not inherent in the representational definition; they must be argued for on independent grounds. As the interpretationalist must demarcate the admissible from the inadmissible interpretations, so must the representationalist demarcate the admissible from the inadmissible states. The representationalist is confronted with the *problem of admissible states.*

Let us put this result into context. In the preceding chapters the two definitions of logical truth, the interpretational and the representational one, were discussed separately. I concentrated on the interpretational definition and extensively argued that it falls prey to the problem of demarcating the admissible from the inadmissible interpretations. In this chapter, I transferred the findings from the previous chapters to the representational definition. I showed that it is not unconditionally true that the representational definition declares all and only the necessary sentences to be logically true. Without any restriction on states, and without a demarcation of the logical from the non-logical constants, no sentence will be declared logically true. With a standard semantics for the logical constants and restriction (R2), the same sentences will be declared logically true with respect to the representational definition, as with respect to the interpretational definition accompanied by the standard restrictions on interpretations. As there may be good reasons for further restrictions on interpretations, so one might justify corresponding restrictions on states. As a consequence of these restrictions, more sentences will turn out to be logically true under the interpretational and the representational definition, respectively. Both definitions behave perfectly analogously. Under corresponding restrictions, the two definitions declare the same class of sentences to be logically true.

8 The Problem of Logical Constants

The first restriction on admissible interpretations (I1) confines the admissible interpretations to those not reinterpreting the logical constants. It generates the problem of logical constants, the most prominent problem for the interpretational definition of logical consequence. The problem is that of providing and justifying a criterion for delineating the logical from the non-logical constants.

As argued in the preceding chapter, I hold, contrary to the common view, that not only the interpretational definition, but also the representational definition presupposes a demarcation of the logical from the non-logical terms – even if only indirectly. However, as the interpretational definition is more straightforwardly related to the problem of logical constants, and, furthermore, more frequently acknowledged and discussed in the literature, I will assume an interpretational definition while discussing the problem of logical constants.

The problem of logical constants is only a sub-problem of the more general problem of demarcating the admissible from the inadmissible interpretations. But although it is only a sub-problem, it deserves special attention. Even in the new framework developed, logical constants play a distinguished role: they are the only terms that may not be reinterpreted at all. All other terms may be reinterpreted, though only within certain boundaries spelled out by the respective restrictions. Logical constants thus lie at the end of a spectrum: their interpretation is held totally fixed.

Let me once again stress the centrality of the problem of the logical constants for the interpretational definition. Depending on where the line of demarcation is drawn, different sentences will turn out to be logically true. This is best illustrated with respect to two extreme cases: If no term is considered to be a logical constant, then no sentence whatsoever will qualify as logically true and no argument as logically valid.[121] Already Tarski observed that the interpretational

---

[121] This is not quite correct. Whether a certain sentence is declared logically true does not only hinge on the demarcation of the logical from the non-logical terms, but on the demarcation of the admissible from the inadmissible interpretations in general. If we chose, say, a grammatical restriction so strict that each term belongs to a different grammatical category, then every true sentence will trivially be true under all admissible interpretations, even if no term is treated as

definition fails to capture our common concept of logical truth if we treat some paradigm cases of logical constants as non-logical terms: "If, for example, we were to include among the extra-logical signs the implication sign, or the universal quantifier, then our definition of the concept of consequence would lead to results which obviously contradict ordinary usage" (Tarski 1936: 418).[122] If, on the opposite end of the spectrum, we take all constants to be logical constants, all truth-preserving arguments would qualify as logically valid: "In the extreme case we could regard all terms of the language as logical. The concept of *formal* consequence would then coincide with that of *material* consequence. The sentence X would in this case follow from the class K of sentences if either X were true or at least one sentence of the class K were false" (Tarski 1936: 418 f.). These cases show the importance of drawing an adequate distinction between the logical and the non-logical constants.

As the targets of this book are the notions of logical truth and logical consequence as applied to natural language sentences, the demarcation of the logical from the non-logical terms has to be done in natural language. Let me stress, however, that we are still investigating only a severely regimented natural language. Otherwise, a strict demarcation of the logical from the non-logical constants would be simply impossible. Just consider the term "and". It plays very different roles already in the sentences "Ann goes to the theatre and Ben goes to the cinema", "Ann falls in love with Ben and they go on holiday" (in contrast to the sentence "Ann and Ben go on holiday and Ann falls in love with Ben"), and "Ann and Ben are carrying the piano". In an utterance of the first sentence "and" will often be used as a purely truth-functional connective. In the second sentence, it seems

---

a logical constant. Furthermore, there are also ways to design the other restrictions such that some, though not all sentences are logically true, again without assuming that there are any logical constants at all. In the above comment I assume a sensible formulation of the other restrictions.

[122] We find a similar observation already in Bolzano (although Bolzano speaks of "ideas" rather than of "constants" and presupposes, of course, a substitutional definition): "For if we could change all the ideas in a proposition as we pleased, than we could transform it into any other proposition whatsoever, and consequently we should surely sometimes make a true proposition out of it, sometimes a false one." (Bolzano 1837, §148)

to have some additional temporal or causal meaning.[123] In the third sentence, "and" is not even a sentence connective, but connects singular terms. To account for the various roles of "and", we could propose that there are different "and"-terms in natural language, each of which has its own syntax and semantics. This would, however, already be the first step to turning natural language into a formal language. Yet this neither is nor has to be my objective, since I am concerned exclusively with a strongly regimented form of natural language sentences anyway. When I say, for example, that "and" is a logical constant, I implicitly restrict the claim to those occurrences of "and" in which it is used in a purely truth-functional manner.

The problem of logical constants does not merely consist in demarcating the logical from the non-logical constants, but it also consists in justifying this demarcation. A mere listing of the logical constants would perhaps be a first step, but certainly not the last. We need a well-motivated criterion for demarcating the logical from the non-logical constants if we aspire to resolve possible disputes over contested cases as, e.g., certain modal operators, higher-order quantifiers, or, most famously, the membership relation.[124]

Let me make one final preliminary remark to avoid any possible misunderstanding. We need to be aware of the fact that it is an arbitrary – though pragmatically helpful – feature of natural language that it really contains a term for, say, conjunction. In principle, our language could express conjunction very differently. We could, for example, subscribe to the convention that there is a conjunction between two written sentences if there is no space between them. Then, "Pluto is a planetPlato is a philosopher" says the same as our "Pluto is a planet and Plato is a philosopher". In the imagined language, there is no term that represents a conjunction and can possibly be classified as a logical constant. Ramsey puts forward the same thought with respect to negation: "We might, for instance, express

---

[123] One could argue that the temporal or causal aspect does not belong to the semantics of "and", but is merely a pragmatic feature. For explanations along these lines, see Grice 1991.

[124] Especially in the heyday of logicism, it was very important to give a justification for one's classification of terms as logical terms. Whether or not, say, the reduction of arithmetic to set theory counts as a reduction to logic crucially depends on whether the membership relation qualifies as a logical constant.

negation not by inserting a word 'not', but by writing what we negate upside down. Such a symbolism is only inconvenient because we are not trained to perceive complicated symmetry about a horizontal axis [...]." (Ramsey 1927: 161 f.) As Ramsey also observes, this convention would have the interesting effect that the logically equivalent expressions '*p*' and 'not not *p*' could not be distinguished. Or, to refer to a famous case, it is well known that all truth-functional connectives can be defined by reference to the Sheffer stroke. Any formula of propositional logic can be translated into a formula containing the Sheffer stroke ("|") as the sole connective. However, if we have only one connective, it seems dispensable: we could write "*p*|*q*" as "*pq*" (which is to be distinguished from "*p q*" (with a space in between)). Scope distinctions could be indicated with brackets. In such a language, there are no logical constants in the narrow sense, i.e., there are no elements of the alphabet which are classified as logical. The only logical notion there is, is not represented by a sign of the alphabet, but by the particular way the terms are arranged. Nevertheless, this would make only for a notational variant. Such a language does not differ from a language with the Sheffer stroke in any relevant way. We are unable to classify a *term* as logical in a case like this, but this does not mean that there are no logical constants in a wider sense in such a language. In the language just described, a grammatical construction rule has to be characterized as logical. Strictly speaking, the problem of logical constants should therefore not be understood as restricted to drawing a line between the logical and the non-logical terms of the alphabet.[125] While it is important to keep this in mind, I will neverthe-

---

[125] Dutilh Novaes 2012 describes the standard view on logical constants and logical form as implicitly (and unconsciously) subscribing to a view she calls "logical hylomorphism". According to logical hylomorphism, the 'matter' and the 'form' of a sentence are both mereological parts of it: the matter is provided by the non-logical terms (and the order of their occurrence), while the form is given by the logical constants. This would mean that the form of a sentence is literally a part of it. Dutilh Novaes then criticizes this view by pointing out that the terminology of matter and form is borrowed from Aristotle, and Aristotle never thought that the form of a thing is a mereological part of it. In as much as a language without logical terms falls in the vicinity of the standard view on logical constants, the above reasoning indicates that Dutilh Novaes' description of the traditional view is inadequate. It is obvious that the classical view should not,

less continue to speak of the problem of logical constants and say that it focuses on drawing and justifying the line of demarcation between the logical and the non-logical terms. This not only helps keep the discussion simple, it is also legitimate as far as one is solely concerned with natural language where we indeed have terms representing the logical notions.

8.1 The Criterion of Permutation Invariance

The criteria usually proposed to demarcate the logical from the non-logical constants divide into proof-theoretic and semantic criteria. The gist of the proof-theoretic tradition consists in defining those terms as the logical constants that can completely be defined via their inferential roles given by their introduction and elimination rules. For example, the term "and" is understood as being completely characterized by its introduction rule "$\varphi, \psi \mid \varphi$ and ψ" and its elimination rules "φ and $\psi \mid \varphi$" and "φ and $\psi \mid \psi$". This view has been challenged in Arthur Prior's celebrated paper "The Runabout Inference Ticket" (1960), where he introduced the operator "tonk" defined by the following introduction and elimination rules: "$\varphi \mid \varphi$ tonk ψ," "φ tonk $\psi \mid \psi$." "Tonk" leads straight to triviality: by applying the inference rules for the connective "tonk", we can infer an arbitrary formula ψ from an arbitrary formula φ. This seems to be untenable as the inferences legitimized by the calculus shall satisfy certain intuitive criteria, e.g., they should be analytic and *a priori*. The main focus of the proof-theoretic tradition therefore lies in formulating certain harmony conditions that must be satisfied by the rules for introduction and elimination of the logical constants, but are in fact not satisfied by "tonk".[126]

I will not enter into the discussion of proof-theoretic attempts to define the logical constants here, but exclusively focus on the most prominent and promising *semantic* demarcation criterion, namely the criterion of permutation invariance. This criterion has received con-

---

and, I think, does not necessarily understand logical constants to be terms and hence mereological parts of sentences in the way described by Dutilh Novaes.

[126] The term "harmony" for the desired relationship between introduction and elimination rules was coined by Dummett 1973, 1991.

siderable attention in comparatively recent literature,[127] but it traces back already to Mautner 1946, Mostowski 1957, and to Tarski's posthumously published writings from 1986 and 1987. Mautner discusses the permutation invariance of the Boolean connectives of propositional logic, while Mostowski is particularly interested in formulating a formal system with generalized quantifiers. Tarski, who seems to have arrived at his results independently of Mautner and Mostowski, is the first to propose permutation invariance as a criterion for the demarcation of the logical from the non-logical terms. In "What are logical notions?" Tarski presents the following approach:[128]

> Consider the class of all one-one transformations of the space, the universe of discourse, or "world" onto itself. What will be the science which deals with the notions invariant under the widest class of transformations? I suggest that they are the logical notions, that we call a notion "logical" if it is invariant under all possible one-one transformations of the world onto itself. (Tarski 1986: 149)

The idea of defining the logical notions as the permutation invariant ones is inspired by Felix Klein's *Erlanger Program* (Klein 1893), where Klein systematically characterizes different geometries with respect to the groups of transformations under which the geometries are invariant. The more transformations there are under which a theory is invariant, the more general the theory is said to be.[129] Logic, so it is

---

[127] See for example Belnap 1962, van Benthem 1989; Sher 1991, 2008; Feferman 1999, 2010; McGee 1996; McFarlane 2009, 2000; Bonnay 2008 and Bonnay and van Benthem 2008.

[128] This paper is a transcript of a 1966 lecture. Already in 1936, Tarski and Lindenbaum proved the *Tarski-Lindenbaum theorem* saying that, given a basic universe U, all the objects in derivative universes of U which can be defined in the language of the simple theory of types are invariant under all permutations of U. (See Lindenbaum & Tarski 1936) In spite of this result, Tarski did not propose to use permutation invariance as a demarcation criterion for logical constants before 1966.

[129] The central notions of *Euclidean geometry* are invariant under the absolute location of the objects, rotations of the objects, and under dilations. Two lines remain parallel after uniformly changing their absolute location and two triangles remain congruent after shrinking by a factor of 3. Euclidean geometry is thus invariant under all 'similarity transformations', i.e., under all transformations that preserve the angles of the objects and only change distances in the same ratio.

thought, is the most general discipline. Its notions should be invariant under all permutations of the objects of the domain. This is also meant to capture the idea that the logical terms are those that are not distinguishing the identity of objects, but are topic-neutral.

To facilitate the reading of the following sections, the notion of permutation invariance has to be made precise. We first define the notion of a permutation:

DEFINITION: A *permutation p of the domain* $\mathfrak{D}$ is an isomorphism from $\mathfrak{D}$ onto itself.

A permutation is a bijective function that maps elements of the domain on elements of the domain. A permutation p on a domain $\mathfrak{D}$ determines a *p-transform function* p^*:

DEFINITION: The *p-transform function* $p^*(x)$ is defined as follows:
- if $x \in \mathfrak{D}$, then $p^*(x) = p(x)$,
- if x is a set, then $p^*(x) = \{y: \exists z\, (z \in x \wedge p^*(z) = y)\}$,
- if x is an n-tuple $\langle x_1, \ldots, x_n \rangle$, then $p^*(x) = \langle p^*(x_1), \ldots, p^*(x_n) \rangle$.[130]

These clauses can be applied recursively to define the p-transform function for sets of ordered tuples of elements of $\mathfrak{D}$, sets of sets of elements of $\mathfrak{D}$, etc.

We define the notion of invariance under a permutation p for an entity x in this hierarchy as follows:

DEFINITION: x is *invariant under the permutation p of the domain* $\mathfrak{D}$ iff $p^*(x) = x$, where $x \in \mathfrak{D}$, or x is an item in the set-theoretic hierarchy over $\mathfrak{D}$.

Affine geometry is defined by invariance under all affine transformations, i.e., under all transformations of the form '$x \mapsto Ax+b$'. As all similarity transformations are affine transformations, affine geometry is 'more general' than Euclidean geometry in the sense that affine geometry abstracts from more aspects than Euclidean geometry does.

[130] This and the following definitions are adopted (with slight changes) from McFarlane 2009. Note that clause (iii) of the definition of a p-transform-function is redundant if tuples are defined in the *Kuratowskian* way, e.g., $\langle x, y \rangle$ as $\{\{x\}, \{x, y\}\}$.

To familiarize ourselves with these definitions consider some straightforward examples. Let the domain 𝔇 be the set {1, 2, 3, 4} and let the permutation p be the following function: {<1, 1>, <2, 3>, <3, 4>, <4, 2>}. With regard to the elements of the domain, only 1 is invariant under p, because p*(1) = 1, but p*(2) ≠ 2, p*(3) ≠ 3, and p*(4) ≠ 4. The set {1, 2, 3, 4} is invariant under p, because p*({1, 2, 3, 4}) = {1, 3, 4, 2}. However, because of p*({1, 2}) = {1, 3}, the set {1, 2} is not invariant under p. Finally, the tuple <1, 2> is not invariant under p, but <1, 1> is.

We have defined the notion of invariance under a permutation in a domain 𝔇 for items in the set-theoretic hierarchy over 𝔇. However, we are ultimately interested in a definition of logical constants, i.e., we are looking for a criterion of demarcation for linguistic entities. We will follow the common strategy and define a constant as logical iff its semantic value is permutation invariant in all domains.[131] To do so, however, we must, first, define the semantic value for all kinds of terms, and second, provide a definition of the notion of permutation invariance for all items that figure as semantic values.

The semantic value of a non-logical constant is the entity on which the constant is mapped by the interpretation function. In standard PL semantics, the semantic value of an individual term is an element of the domain and the semantic value of an n-place relation constant is a set of n-tuples of objects of the domain. In FL, both individual and relation constants are mapped on elements of the domain. Thus, the semantic values of individuals and of relation constants are, according to both semantics, elements of the domain or sets of (tuples of) elements of the domain.

We have not yet specified the semantic values of sentential connectives and quantifiers. An n-ary connective or quantifier is an operator which produces formulas out of formulas. The semantic value of an operator will be that operation the respective operator stands for.[132] The operation expressed by an n-ary connective or quantifier is

---

[131] It is usually said that a term is permutation invariant iff its *extension* is permutation invariant in all domains. As I will explicitly define the semantic value of all terms in the following paragraphs, no confusion should arise by using the more neutral term *semantic value*.

[132] In the context of Chapter 7, I should remark that this does not assume anything about the ontological status of the semantic values of the logical constants. In

a function that maps an *n*-place sequence of sets of variable assignments to a set of variable assignments. (A variable assignment is a function from the set of variables to the domain. A set of variable assignments satisfies a formula iff every variable assignment in the set satisfies the formula. An *n*-place sequence of (sets of) variable assignments satisfies an *n*-place sequence of formulas iff the (set of) sequence(s) at the *i*-th place of the sequence of (sets of) variable assignments satisfies the formula at the *i*-th place of the sequence of formulas (i ∈ {1, ..., *n*}).) Let $<\varphi_1, ..., \varphi_n>$ be the sequence of component formulas out of which the *n*-ary connective or quantifier "¤" forms the complex formula "¤ $(<\varphi_1, ..., \varphi_n>)$" (or "¤*x* $(<\varphi_1, ..., \varphi_n>)$" if "¤" is a quantifier). The operation expressed by "¤" then maps the sequence of sets of variable assignments that satisfies $<\varphi_1, ..., \varphi_n>$ to the set of variable assignments that satisfy "¤ $(<\varphi_1, ..., \varphi_n>)$".

The semantic value of the unary negation connective is the unary operation that assigns each set of variable assignments the complementary set of variable assignments. The semantic value of the binary connective of conjunction is the binary operation that, given an ordered pair of sets of variable assignments such that the first set of variable assignments satisfies the first component formula and the second satisfies the second component formula, yields the intersection of the sets of variable assignments. The semantic value of the existential quantifier "∃*x*" is the unary operation that takes a set *B* of assignments that satisfy the formula to which "∃*x*" is applied, to the set of all variable assignments that agree with a variable assignment in *B* except possibly at "*x*".[133]

---

particular, it is not assumed that they constitute logical objects that can figure as elements of Russellian propositions.

[133] There are still terms for which we have not yet defined a semantic value, most prominently intensional operators as, e.g., the modal operators. Of course, there are proposals regarding the definition of the semantic values of these operators, and also suggestion how to extend the notion of permutation invariance to these terms. For example, we could say that, very roughly speaking, a modal operator is a logical notion iff it is invariant under all permutations of the worlds (for the exact definition, see McCarthy 1981 and van Benthem 1989). This definition determines those modal operators as logical constants that work on frames with a universal accessibility relation, an empty accessibility relation, and identity accessibility relation (i.e., the relation that relates every world only to it-

140   The Problem of Logical Constants

We are now prepared to define the notion of permutation invariance for n-ary operations:

> DEFINITION: An n-ary operation $*$ is *invariant under the permutation p of a domain $\mathfrak{D}$* iff for any n-tuple $<B_1, ..., B_n>$ of sets of variable assignments it holds that $p(*(<B_1, ..., B_n>)) = *(<p(B_1), ..., p(B_n)>)$, (where $p(B_i) = \{p(\beta_j) \mid \beta_j \in B_i\}$ with $i \in \{1, ..., n\}$).[134]

To illustrate the definition, let me walk you through an example. We consider the domain $\mathfrak{D} = \{$Ann, Ben, Cen$\}$ and the permutation p defined as follows: p: Ann↦Ben, Ben↦Cen, Cen↦Ann. We assume that the language consists of the three individual constants "Ann", "Ben", "Cen", the two predicates "is a philosopher" and "is married," the variables "x" and "y", and the usual connectives and quantifiers. Assume the intended interpretation of the non-logical constants. Let us check whether the semantic value of the conjunction connective is invariant under the given permutation p on the given domain $\mathfrak{D}$.

For ease of presentation, I list all of the possible variable assignments of this language: β_1: x↦Ann, y↦Ann; β_2: x↦Ann, y↦Ben; β_3: x↦Ann, y↦Cen; β_4: x↦Ben, y↦Ann; β_5: x↦Ben, y↦Ben; β_6: x↦Ben, y↦Cen; β_7: x↦Cen, y↦Ann; β_8: x↦Cen, y↦Ben; β_9: x↦Cen, y↦Cen. Now consider the following formulas:

(i) x is a philosopher.
(ii) y is married.

Let $B_{(i)}$ be the set of variable assignments satisfying (i) and let $B_{(ii)}$ be the set of variable assignments satisfying (ii). Let $*_\wedge$ be the semantic value of the two-place conjunction connective "∧". $*_\wedge$ maps a pair of variable assignments to its intersection. To test whether the conjunction connective is invariant under the permutation p, we actually have to check for *any* ordered pair of sets of variable assignments of which one can consistently assume that it satisfies <(i), (ii)> whether the

---

self). Thus, e.g., the S5 modal operators are declared logical constants, though not, say, the S4 modal operators. Here I do not have the space to discuss the plausibility of these results any further.

[134] β is a variable assignment, i.e., a function from the set of variables to the domain. $p(\beta(x))$ is the composition of β and p: $p(\beta(x)) = (\beta \circ p)(x)$. So, $p(\beta)$ is also a function mapping variables on elements of the domain, i.e., a variable assignment.

equation "$p(*_\wedge(<B_1, ..., B_n>)) = *_\wedge(<p(B_1), ..., p(B_n)>)$" holds. I will only do so exemplarily for one pair of sets variable assignments, namely $<B_{(i)}, B_{(ii)}> = <\{\beta_1, \beta_2, \beta_3, \beta_4, \beta_5, \beta_6\}, \{\beta_3, \beta_6, \beta_9\}>$. This pair represents the case that only Ann and Ben are philosophers and only Cen is married. It holds that $p(*_\wedge(<B_{(i)}, B_{(ii)}>) =$ $p(*_\wedge(<\{\beta_1, \beta_2, \beta_3, \beta_4, \beta_5, \beta_6\}, \{\beta_3, \beta_6, \beta_9\}>)) = p(\{\beta_3, \beta_6\})$ $= \{p(\beta_3), p(\beta_6)\} = \{\beta_4, \beta_7\}$, on the other hand we have $*_\wedge(<p(B_{(i)}), p(B_{(ii)})>) = *_\wedge(<p(\{\beta_1, \beta_2, \beta_3, \beta_4, \beta_5, \beta_6\}), p(\{\beta_3, \beta_6, \beta_9\})>) =$ $*_\wedge(<\{\beta_5, \beta_6, \beta_4, \beta_8, \beta_9, \beta_7\}, \{\beta_4, \beta_7, \beta_1\}>) = \{\beta_4, \beta_7\}$, and therefore $p(*_\wedge(<B_{(i)}, B_{(ii)}>) = *_\wedge(<p(B_{(i)}), p(B_{(ii)})>)$. If the conjunction connective is invariant under the permutation p, we get this result for arbitrary pairs of sets of assignments that can satisfy $<(i), (ii)>$ and also for arbitrary formulas (i) and (ii).

So far, we have defined the conditions under which a semantic value, or, as we will say with Tarski (1986), a *notion* (i.e., an individual object, a set of (tuples of) individual objects, or an operation) is invariant under a permutation p on a domain $\mathfrak{D}$. We can now define a notion as logical as follows:

> DEFINITION (O): A notion is a *logical notion with respect to a domain* $\mathfrak{D}$ iff it is invariant under all permutations of $\mathfrak{D}$.

The concept of a logical notion is thus relativized to a domain. A notion may be invariant under all permutations of one domain, though not under all permutations of a different domain: the object o_1 is trivially invariant under all permutations of the domain $\mathfrak{D} = \{o_1\}$, though o_1 is not invariant under all permutations of the domain $\mathfrak{D} = \{o_1, o_2\}$.

We are finally prepared to spell out the definition of a logical constant:

> DEFINITION (C): A constant c is a *logical constant* iff for all domains $\mathfrak{D}$ c's semantic value on $\mathfrak{D}$ is a logical notion with respect to $\mathfrak{D}$.

A constant is a logical constant iff for all domains its semantic value is invariant under all permutations of that domain.[135]

---

[135] In "Logical Notions" which usually serves as the main reference point for introducing the criterion of permutation invariance, Tarski did not actually present a definition of logical *constants*, but only of logical *notions*. The definition of a logical constant only appears in the posthumously published book *A Formalization of Set Theory without Variables*. Here Tarski and Givant spell out the definition of a

To evaluate whether this is a reasonable definition, we should determine which terms are declared logical by (C). Let's look at *individual constants* first. The semantic value of an individual constant a is an element o of the domain. In a domain with at least two objects, there is always a permutation of this domain that maps o on a different object. Under this permutation p, it holds that p(o) = p*(o) ≠ o. Thus, the semantic value of an individual constant is not permutation invariant, and no individual constant is declared a logical constant. Are there any *predicate* or *relation constants* that are declared logical? According to the semantics of FL, which treats predicates and relation terms like individual constants by mapping them on an element of the domain, obviously no predicate or relation term will be declared a logical constant either. If we assume the semantics of PL, exactly those predicates that have on all domains the whole domain or the empty set as their semantic values will be declared logical.[136] Four kinds of binary

---

logical constant based on the definition of a logical notion. The original formulation in (Tarski & Givant 1987) goes as follows:

(i) Given a basic universe U, a member M of any derivative universe $\tilde{U}$ is said to be logical, or a logical object, if it is invariant under every permutation P of U. (Strictly speaking, since an object M can be a member of many derivative universes, we should use in (i) the phrase "is said to be logical, or a logical object, as a member of $\tilde{U}$.")

(ii) A symbol S of [the language L] is said to be logical, or a logical constant, if, for every given realization U of this [language L] with the universe U, S denotes a logical object in some derivative universe $\tilde{U}$. (Tarski and Givant 1987: 57)

Tarski and Givant presuppose a fixed basic universe U here. A derivate universe $\tilde{U}$ contains all objects of the same type which are in U. Thus, the class of all individuals constitutes a derivative universe, and the class of all relations of individuals constitutes another derivate universe and the class of all classes of relations yet another, etc. As my aim is systematic rather than exegetical, we need not be concerned with these peculiarities of Tarski and Givant's original definition.

[136] This might actually turn out to be problematic. Consider a necessarily empty predicate, as, e.g., the predicate "is wheen" expressing the property of being white and green (all over at the same time). Given we only consider domains with possible objects, there will not be any domain which contains objects that are wheen and thus the predicate will have a permutation invariant semantic value on every domain. Therefore, "is wheen" will qualify as a logical constant. This might not only be anti-intuitive, but it has the consequence that, e.g., the sentence "$\neg \exists x\, Fx$" (where "F" stands for the predicate "is wheen") is logically

relations turn out to be logical constants: all binary relation constants that have on each domain as their semantic value (i) the universal relation that holds between any two individuals, or (ii) the empty relation that holds between no individuals, or (iii) the identity relation that holds only between identical objects, or (iv) the diversity relation that holds exactly between the non-identical objects.[137] Similar con-

> true according to the interpretational definition of logical truth. Most philosophers will not like this consequence. McCarthy 1981 and 1987 tries to avoid it by suggesting a modification of the definition of a logical constant. He introduces the term of a 'modality', where a modality is simply a class of possible worlds, in some sense of 'possible'. Examples for modalities in McCarthy's sense are the class of physically possible worlds, the class of metaphysically possible worlds, the class of doxastically possible worlds and the class of conceptually possible worlds. A constant is then defined as a logical constant with respect to a modality M iff on all domains $\mathfrak{D}$ of the modality M the constant's semantic value is invariant under all permutations of $\mathfrak{D}$. (This is not quite correct. McCarthy actually demands invariance under all bijections between all domains of a modality M that have the same cardinality. Here we need not bother about this subtlety.) Thus, we might assume that there is a conceptually possible domain containing wheen objects (and objects that are not wheen). In such a domain, the semantic value of "is wheen" is not permutation invariant. Thus, if we choose the conceptual modality as the relevant modality for the definition of a logical constant, the predicate "is wheen" will not be declared logical. However, as Gómez-Torrente 2002: 18 ff. correctly notes, McCarthy's strategy will not exclude predicates like "is a male mother", i.e., predicates that are empty on conceptual grounds, from the logical constants, because their semantic value is invariant in all domains of the conceptual modality M. It seems that in order to also exclude this predicate we would have to demand invariance under all permutations of domains of the logical modality, making the definition viciously circular. (McCarthy acknowledges this. However, he does not take the circularity to be a serious problem because he does not aim at giving a reductive definition (see McCarthy 1987: 426)). To avoid all these complications, I strongly recommend that one employs the semantics of FL. According to this semantics, the predicates "is wheen" and "is a male mother" are mapped on an element of the domain. Therefore, they do not have a permutation invariant semantic value in any domain with at least two objects and need thus not be classified as logical constants.

[137] For the question whether mathematics is part of logic, it is particularly interesting whether the membership relation is permutation invariant. It turns out that the answer depends on the underlying set theory. The membership-relation of a theory of types, as it was used in the *Principia Mathematica*, is permutation invariant. Here, we have only entities of the lowest type, i.e., individuals, in the domain, and the membership relation is invariant under all permutations of the

siderations apply to relations of higher arity. As it should be, the truth-functional sentence connectives and the universal and the existential quantifier are declared logical constants. The same holds for all cardinality quantifiers, including generalized quantifiers as "most" or "there are infinitely many". On the other hand, quantifiers as, e.g., the quantifier "some planet" do not turn out to be logical constants.[138] To sum up, the criterion of permutation invariance seems to fare quite well. All the paradigm cases of logical constants, i.e., the truth-functional sentence connectives and the standard quantifiers, satisfy the criterion of permutation invariance. On the other hand, no individual constant satisfies it and only very special predicate and relation constants do so.

8.2 Counter Examples

It is widely agreed that the criterion of permutation invariance provides necessary conditions for a term to be a logical constant: if the semantic value of a term is not permutation invariant, then it is not a logical constant.[139] However, hopes that the criterion also provides

universe of individuals. This contrasts with a different construction of set theory, where we do not have a hierarchy of types, but only one universe of entities (may they be objects or sets or sets of sets, etc.) and understand the membership relation as a primitive two-place relation between the elements of the universe. This membership relation is not permutation invariant. (See Tarski 1986: 152 f.)

[138] Let me briefly prove that the quantifier "some planet" does not satisfy the criterion of permutation invariance. Consider the domain $\mathfrak{D} = \{a, b, c\}$. Let only the object a and the object c have the property of being a planet, and only a and b have some further property F. Let there be just one variable x in the alphabet and let the variable assignments be as follows: β_1: $x \mapsto a$, β_2: $x \mapsto b$, β_3: $x \mapsto c$. Consider the permutation p defined as follows: $a \mapsto b$, $b \mapsto c$, $c \mapsto a$. Now, consider the formula "some planet Fx" and let $*_{\text{some planet}}$ be the semantic value of the quantifier "some planet" defined in the obvious way: $*_{\text{some planet}}$ is the function mapping the set B of variable assignments that fulfill a given formula to the set of variable assignments containing all assignments in B that map x on a planet. We have: $p(*_{\text{some planet}} (\{\beta_1, \beta_2\})) = p(\{\beta_1\}) = \{\beta_2\}$. However, we also have $*_{\text{some planet}} (p(\{\beta_1, \beta_2\})) = *_{\text{some planet}} (\{\beta_2, \beta_3\}) = \{\beta_3\}$. As $\{\beta_2\} \neq \{\beta_3\}$, the quantifier "some planet" is no logical constant according to the criterion of permutation invariance.

[139] See, however, Dutilh Novaes 2014 who argues that there are logical constants that do not satisfy the criterion of permutation invariance.

sufficient conditions for a term to be a logical constant have been dashed at least since McCarthy's prominent counter example.

McCarthy introduces the one-place sentential connective 'N' characterized as follows (McCarthy 1981: 514):

$\forall s(s$ satisfies "Nφ" iff $[(\neg s$ satisfies $\varphi \wedge K) \vee (s$ satisfies $\varphi \wedge \neg K)])$.

'K' represents a certain *a posteriori* contingently true statement of the metalanguage. Of course, the above characterization does not yet define a connective, but is only a schema for the definition of a connective yielding different connectives for different values of "K". (For the sake of simplicity, I will nevertheless also speak of "the N-connective" in the following.)

The above schema is not free of ambiguities. It is particularly unfortunate that McCarthy's definition does not carefully distinguish the object language and the metalanguage, so that it is not clear from the mere definition of the N-connective whether "K" is supposed to belong to the metalanguage or to the object language. The use of the object language connectives "$\wedge$" and "$\neg$" actually suggests an object language reading of "K". But as McCarthy makes explicit in his comment, "K" has to be understood as a metalanguage sentence. To avoid ambiguities, let us thus reformulate McCarthy's schema for a definition of "N" as follows:

$\mathfrak{M} \models N\varphi$ iff ((K and $\mathfrak{M} \not\models \varphi$) or (not-K and $\mathfrak{M} \models \varphi$))

(Though "K" is a parameter, I do not put it in italics, as it belongs to the meta-language, while "φ" belongs to the object language.) McCarthy takes the parameter "K" to stand for a contingently true sentence of the meta-language. As "K" is true, "Nφ" is true in a model $\mathfrak{M}$ just in case "φ" is not true in $\mathfrak{M}$. Thus, the N-connective expresses the same operation as the classical negation connective. As the operation of negation is permutation invariant, so is the operation expressed by the N-connective. However, McCarthy argues that we should not understand it as a logical constant. His argument goes as follows:

> [I]n any counterfactual situation [...] in which 'K' is false, the sentence "N$\varphi \leftrightarrow \neg\varphi$", though a logical truth, is false. However, it seems a reasonable constraint on any theory of validity for a language L that a sentence of L that it construes as a logical truth is not possibly false in L. As the choice of 'N' as a logical constant does violence to this constraint, I suggest that

we are entitled to conclude that 'N' is not, after all, a logical constant [...]. (McCarthy 1981: 515)

Assuming that "K" is some true sentence, the sentence "N$\varphi \leftrightarrow \neg \varphi$" is true, because the N-connective expresses the same operation as the negation connective. If we treat "N" as a logical constant (and, of course, also "$\leftrightarrow$" and "$\neg$"), the sentence "N$\varphi \leftrightarrow \neg \varphi$" is logically true according to the interpretational definition. The only term that is open for reinterpretation is "φ", and "N$\varphi \leftrightarrow \neg \varphi$" remains true under all interpretations of "φ". But, as McCarthy correctly notes, the sentence is only contingently true if, as we assume, the sentence substituted for "K" is contingent. Under a circumstance where the sentence substituted for "K" is false, the sentence "N$\varphi \leftrightarrow \neg \varphi$" is false: "N$\varphi$" is then true in a model $\mathfrak{M}$ iff $\mathfrak{M} \models \varphi$. Since we do not want contingent sentences to be declared logically true, we should not classify the N-connective as a logical constant. As a result, the definition (C), proposed in the previous section, fails.

The argument against the view that the N-operator is a logical constant crucially depends on the contingency of the sentence substituted for "K". The argument does not go through if a necessarily true sentence is substituted for "K". So, can we at least classify the N-connective as a logical constant iff we restrict the admissible substitutions of "K" to necessary sentences? McCarthy argues that we should not do so. Consider that an *a posteriori*, necessary sentence is substituted for "K", e.g., the sentence "water is H$_2$O".[140] This yields the following connective "H":

$\mathfrak{M} \models$ Hφ iff ((water is H$_2$O and $\mathfrak{M} \not\models \varphi$) or ((not water is H$_2$O) and $\mathfrak{M} \models \varphi$))

The sentence "Hφ" is true in a model just in case "φ" is not true in a model. The sentence "H$\varphi \leftrightarrow \neg \varphi$" is thus true in all models. We can no longer argue that this sentence should not turn out to be a logical truth by referring to a counterfactual situation in which it is false. The sentence "H$\varphi \leftrightarrow \neg \varphi$" is necessarily true because "water is H$_2$O" is necessarily true. McCarthy argues that it should nevertheless not be declared logically true because it implies an *a posteriori* sentence:

---

[140] It is debatable whether the sentence "water is H$_2$O" is really necessary and *a posteriori*. Here I accept this assumption for the sake of McCarthy's example.

> If we make the plausible assumption that, for example, structural traits such as atomic number are necessary to the substances to which they apply, and 'K' represents a true sentence ascribing such a trait, 'K' is necessarily true. If 'N' thus interpreted were a logical constant, [...] the sentence ['H$\varphi \leftrightarrow \neg\varphi$'] would be a logical truth. However, the latter is epistemically linked to a posteriori data in an essential way: given knowledge that ['H$\varphi \leftrightarrow \neg\varphi$'] is true and of its truth condition, one can know a priori that K; and 'K', under its present interpretation, is a posteriori. (McCarthy 1981: 515 f.)[141]

As the sentence "water is H_2O" can be known only *a posteriori*, one should not be able to derive it from the fact that some logically true sentence is true. Thus, so the argument goes, we should not understand the H-connective as a logical constant. Then, "H$\varphi \leftrightarrow \neg\varphi$" is not logically true and it does not constitute a problem that an *a posteriori* truth can be inferred from it being true. Since the H-connective has on all domains a semantic value which is invariant under all permutations, it is taken to constitute a counter example to definition (C).[142]

To identify the sources of the counter examples and hence the possible ways of patching up definition (C), I will look for a simplification of McCarthy's examples. Here is, again, the definition of McCarthy's N-connective:

$\mathfrak{M} \models N\varphi$ iff ((K and $\mathfrak{M} \not\models \varphi$) or (not-K and $\mathfrak{M} \models \varphi$)).

---

[141] I slightly adapted the example to fit my discussion. See also McGee 1996: 578 for a similar line of argument (I again adapt the example): "According to orthodox metaphysics, H_2O-negation behaves extensionally like a logical connective in every possible world, since it is necessarily coextensive with ordinary negation. Yet 'H' isn't a logical connective, since, if it were, ['H$\varphi \leftrightarrow \neg\varphi$'] would be a logical truth, and ['H$\varphi \leftrightarrow \neg\varphi$'] isn't a logical truth, since it entails 'Water is H_2O,' which isn't a logical truth."

[142] Of course, this reasoning is already applicable to instances of the N-connective that are not necessary: if we substitute a true, contingent sentence of the metalanguage for "K", the sentence "K" is implied by the object language sentence "N$\varphi \leftrightarrow \neg\varphi$". The substitution of a necessary sentence for "K" only reveals that the crucial point is not that there is a counterfactual situation in which the sentence "N$\varphi \leftrightarrow \varphi$" is false, but that it implies a sentence of the metalanguage which is not logically true.

McCarthy asks us to substitute a true sentence of the metalanguage for "K". Because of the truth of "K", the second disjunct will actually not be realized in any model; thus, "Nφ" is true in a model $\mathfrak{M}$ if "$\neg\varphi$" is true in $\mathfrak{M}$. This suggests the following simpler schema for a connective that constitutes a counter example to (C):

$\mathfrak{M} \models N\varphi$ iff (K and $\mathfrak{M} \not\models \varphi$).[143]

We again assume that "K" is substituted by a true sentence of the metalanguage. Thus, "Nφ" is true in exactly those models in which "φ" is false. The simplified N-connective has the same semantic value as the original N-connective on all domains, namely the operation of negation. As the sentence substituted for "K" is actually true, the sentence "N$\varphi \leftrightarrow \neg\varphi$" is actually true. If we treat "N" as a logical constant, "N$\varphi \leftrightarrow \neg\varphi$" is true under all admissible reinterpretations and thus logically true. However, from knowledge of the fact that "N$\varphi \leftrightarrow \neg\varphi$" is true, we can infer the metalanguage sentence substituted for "K". The simplified N-connective has essentially the same features as McCarthy's original.

We can simplify the counter example even further. Consider the following connective:

(N) $\mathfrak{M} \models N\varphi$ iff K.

This version of the N-connective is of a very special character. Whether or not "Nφ" is true in a model is now totally independent of the truth value of "φ" in the model. If we substitute "K", as before, with a true sentence of the metalanguage, the N-connective has the same semantic value as the tautology connective. According to definition (C), it is thus a logical constant. Furthermore, as the sentence substituted for "K" is true, the sentence "Nφ" is true. If we treat "N" as a logical constant, the sentence "Nφ" is trivially true under all reinterpretations and thus logically true. However, from the fact that

---

[143] For an instance of this connective, see also McGee 1996: "[C]onsider H_2O-*negation*, defined as follows: H$\varphi \stackrel{\text{def}}{=} (\neg\varphi \wedge$ water is H_2O). According to orthodox metaphysics, H_2O-negation behaves extensionally like a logical connective in every possible world, since it is necessarily coextensive with ordinary negation. Yet, H_2O-negation isn't a logical connective [...]." (McGee 1996: 578) For yet other examples pulling in the same direction, see Hanson 1997 and Gómez-Torrente 2002.

"Nφ" is true, one can infer the metalanguage sentence substituted for "K" which may only be contingently true and/or *a posteriori*. Under the assumption that no sentence which is not logically true may be implied by the truth of a logical truth – an assumption which I will clarify and discuss soon – the N-connective constitutes a counter example to (C). As the example involving the simplified N-connective is less complicated than McCarthy's original example, I will discuss this connective instead of McCarthy's original one in the following.

(N) is only a schema for a connective. Different substitution instances of "K" yield different connectives. We will discuss several different instances of (N). Although McCarthy is explicit that a sentence of the metalanguage should be substituted for "K", it is instructive to see what happens if a sentence of the object language is substituted for "K". Thus, I will also consider a connective where a sentence of the object language is substituted for "K". To keep those connectives where a sentence of the metalanguage is substituted for "K" apart from those where a sentence of the object language is substituted for "K", I index the N-connectives with "M" and "O", respectively. To indicate that a substitution of K belongs to the metalanguage, I put the sentence in small capitals, and to indicate that it belongs to the object language, I put it in italics. It will be illuminating to discuss instances of the N-connective that differ with respect to whether the sentence substituted for "K" is contingently, necessarily, analytically or logically true.[144] A list of the connectives I want to discuss helps us to keep track:

(N_M) $\mathfrak{M} \vDash N_M \varphi$ iff K.

   Instances of (N_M):
(N_{MC}) $\mathfrak{M} \vDash N_{MC} \varphi$ iff PLATO IS A PHILOSOPHER.
(N_{MN}) $\mathfrak{M} \vDash N_{MN} \varphi$ iff (IF SNOW IS WHITE, SNOW IS NOT GREEN).
(N_{MA}) $\mathfrak{M} \vDash N_{MA} \varphi$ iff MOTHERS ARE FEMALE.
(N_{ML}) $\mathfrak{M} \vDash N_{ML} \varphi$ iff PLUTO IS A PLANET OR PLUTO IS NOT A PLANET.

---

[144] As I extensively argued in the former chapters, I don't think that the boundaries between these categories are sharp. I here just choose paradigm examples of sentences of the respective categories.

(N_O) $\mathfrak{M} \models N_O \varphi$ iff $\mathfrak{M} \models K$.

Instances of (N_O):
(N_{OC}) $\mathfrak{M} \models N_{OC} \varphi$ iff $\mathfrak{M} \models$ *Plato is a philosopher.*
(N_{ON}) $\mathfrak{M} \models N_{ON} \varphi$ iff $\mathfrak{M} \models$ *if snow is white, snow is not green.*
(N_{OA}) $\mathfrak{M} \models N_{OA} \varphi$ iff $\mathfrak{M} \models$ *mothers are female.*
(N_{OL}) $\mathfrak{M} \models N_{OL} \varphi$ iff $\mathfrak{M} \models$ *Pluto is a planet or Pluto is not a planet.*

I will start with discussing instances of the N_O-connective. Consider the N_{OC}-connective first. For every model $\mathfrak{M}$ it holds that either $\mathfrak{M} \models$ *Plato is a philosopher* or $\mathfrak{M} \not\models$ *Plato is a philosopher*. In models $\mathfrak{M}$ with $\mathfrak{M} \models$ *Plato is a philosopher*, it holds that $\mathfrak{M} \models N_{OC} \varphi$. In models with $\mathfrak{M} \not\models$ *Plato is a philosopher*, it holds that $\mathfrak{M} \not\models N_{OC} \varphi$. The truth value of "$N_{OC} \varphi$" in a model equals the truth value of "Plato is a philosopher" in that model. In models with $\mathfrak{M} \models$ *Plato is a philosopher*, the N_{OC}-connective works like the tautology connective. In models with $\mathfrak{M} \not\models$ *Plato is a philosopher*, the N_{OC}-connective works like the contradiction connective. This yields the following truth table for the N_{OC}-connective:

Plato is a philosopher.	$N_{OC} \varphi$
T	T
F	F

Interestingly, we do not need a column for "φ" because the truth value of "$N_{OC} \varphi$" is independent of the truth value of "φ".

The sentence "Plato is a philosopher" is actually true and thus, per definition of the notion of an intended model, true in the intended model $\mathfrak{M}^*$: $\mathfrak{M}^* \models$ *Plato is a philosopher*. By definition of the N_{OC}-connective, it thus holds that $\mathfrak{M}^* \models N_{OC} \varphi$ (for an arbitrary formula φ). On all domains, the semantic value of the N_{OC}-connective is permutation invariant: the N_{OC}-connective has the same semantic value as the tautology operator in models in which "Plato is a philosopher" is true and it has the same semantic value as the contradiction operator in models in which "Plato is a philosopher" is false. According to the definition (C) of logical constants, it therefore qualifies as a logical constant.

One might now think that it follows that the sentence "$N_{OC}\,\varphi$" is true under all interpretations and thus logically true, because the only term open for reinterpretation is φ, but the truth value of "$N_{OC}\,\varphi$" does not depend on the truth value of φ. If that were the case, the N_{OC}-connective would constitute a counter example to the criterion of permutation invariance since the sentence "$N_{OC}\,\varphi$" implies the contingent object language sentence "Plato is a philosopher". This would constitute a serious problem: there are interpretational models in which the sentence "Plato is a philosopher" is false. Let $\mathfrak{M}$ be such a model. We would then have both, $\mathfrak{M} \models N_{OC}\varphi$ (because "$N_{OC}\,\varphi$" is logically true) and $\mathfrak{M} \not\models$ *Plato is a philosopher*. As we also have $\mathfrak{M} \models N_{OC}\,\varphi$ iff $\mathfrak{M} \models$ *Plato is a philosopher* (from the definition of the N_{OC}-connective), it follows that $\mathfrak{M} \models$ *Plato is a philosopher* and $\mathfrak{M} \not\models$ *Plato is a philosopher*, which cannot be the case. Thus, one might conclude that we should not treat the N_{OC}-connective as a logical constant.

However, a closer investigation reveals an interesting flaw in this reasoning. The N_{OC}-connective is indeed a logical constant, but, contrary to the above reasoning, this does not yield the consequence that "$N_{OC}\,\varphi$" is logically true. "$N_{OC}\,\varphi$" is true in the intended model. If we treat "N_{OC}" as a logical constant, it is not open for reinterpretation. However, it does not immediately follow that "$N_{OC}\,\varphi$" is true in all interpretations! This is due to the very special character of the connective. In a model in which the object-language sentence "Plato is a philosopher" is false, the N_{OC}-connective no longer stands for the tautology connective, but for the contradiction connective. Although we keep the interpretation of the N_{OC}-connective fixed, i.e., although we do not allow any direct reinterpretation of the connective, the connective stands for different operations in different models. Thus, the fact that "$N_{OC}\,\varphi$" is true in the intended model does not imply that "$N_{OC}\,\varphi$" is logically true even if we treat the N_{OC}-connective as a logical constant. As unusual as the connective may be, there is no problem in treating it as a logical constant.

Before discussing the N_{OA}- and the N_{ON}-connectives, let us jump to the N_{OL}-connective. "$N_{OL}\,\varphi$" is true in a model if the sentence "Pluto is a planet or Pluto is not a planet" is true in the model. This sentence is, however, true in all models. In all models, the N_{OL}-connective works like the tautology operator. According to definition (C), it is thus a logical constant. Thus, "$N_{OL}\,\varphi$" is logically true. The sentence "$N_{OL}\,\varphi$" implies the object language sentence "Pluto is a planet or Pluto is not a planet". Now, we indeed have the case that a logical truth entails the substitution instance of "K". However, this is obviously unproblematic since "Pluto is a planet or Pluto is not a planet" is itself a logical truth of the object language. A logical truth may well imply a logical truth. Again, there is no problem in treating the respective instance of the N_O-connective as a logical constant.

Next, consider the more interesting case of the N_{OA}-connective. "$N_{OA}\,\varphi$" is true in a model if the sentence "mothers are female" is true in a model. As I have argued extensively in the previous chapters, whether this sentence turns out to be logically true depends on the chosen restrictions on interpretations. If one subscribes to restriction (I3*), "mothers are female" is indeed true under all admissible interpretations. In this case, the N_{OA}-connective works exactly like the N_{OL}-connective: it maps any sentence in any model on TRUE. The sentence "$N_{OA}\,\varphi$" is logically true and it implies the sentence "mothers are female". Again, this is unproblematic because we assumed that the sentence is a logical truth of the object language anyway. On the other hand, if one does not subscribe to restriction (I3*), the sentence "mothers are female" is not a logical truth of the object language. Then, the N_{OA}-connective does not work analogous to the N_{OL}-connective, but analogous to the N_{OC}-connective: it functions like the tautology operator in models in which "mothers are female" is true, and like the contradiction operator in models in which "mothers are female" is false. In this case, the same reasoning that established that "$N_{OC}\,\varphi$" is not logically true also shows that the sentence "$N_{OA}\,\varphi$" is not logically true, even if one takes the connective "N_{OA}" to be a logical constant. Either way, the N_{OA}-connective does not constitute a counter example to definition (C).

Perfectly analogous considerations apply to the N_{ON}-connective. Whether "$N_{ON}\,\varphi$" turns out to be logically true depends on the chosen restrictions on interpretations. Exactly if "if snow is white, snow is not green" is logically true, the sentence "$N_O\,\varphi$" will be logically true. This result is, as we have seen, unproblematic. We can therefore accept all the instances of the N_O-connective as logical constants. They do not provide counter examples to definition (C).

The object language versions of the N-connective do not yield any serious problems for (C). We now have to discuss the metalanguage versions, i.e., the instances of the N_M-connective. The instances of the N_M-connective are one-place connectives which map a given sentence of the object language on the truth value TRUE in a model if a certain metalanguage sentence is true. To prepare the discussion of the N_M-connective, let me introduce "⟨⟩" as a name-forming device: "⟨x⟩" is a name in the language L^{n+1} for the expression "x" of the language L^n.[145] The sentence "$\mathfrak{M}\models$ ⟨φ⟩", which stands for "⟨φ⟩ is true in $\mathfrak{M}$" (where "φ" is a formula of the object language), is a sentence of the metalanguage.

Let us now discuss the instances of the N_M-connective, beginning with the N_{MC}-connective, which results from substituting "PLATO IS A PHILOSOPHER" for "K". As already laid out in the previous section, the semantic value of the N_{MC}-connective is permutation invariant. Assume that we therefore take the connective to be a logical constant. The sentence "$N_{MC}\,\varphi$" is then logically true: the only expression open for reinterpretation is "φ", but the truth value of "$N_{MC}\,\varphi$" is, as we have seen, independent of the interpretation of "φ". Furthermore, in contrast to the N_{OC}-connective, the N_{MC}-connective stands for the same operation in all models. Thus, the sentence "$N_{MC}\,\varphi$" is a logical truth of the language L^0.

Based on this observation, McCarthy develops his objection to (C) as follows: the truth of the object language sentence "$N_{MC}\,\varphi$", together with knowledge of the definition of "N", implies that the metalanguage sentence PLATO IS A PHILOSOPHER is true. The sentence "$N_{MC}\,\varphi$" is true in an object language model iff the sentence "PLATO IS A PHILOSOPHER" is actually true. However, McCarthy objects, the sentence "$N_{MC}\,\varphi$" is a logical truth and as such the fact that it is true should not entail a sentence which is not a logical truth itself.

Let me give a closer analysis of this argument. The crucial and critical step in this argument is the claim that the truth of the sentence " "$N_{MC}\,\varphi$" is true" implies the sentence "PLATO IS A PHILOSOPHER". Let us try to reconstruct the informal reasoning step by step. Assume we know that "$\mathfrak{M}\models$ ⟨$N_{MC}\,\varphi$⟩" is true (where $\mathfrak{M}$ is an arbitrary model for

---

[145] To be precise, I should index the name-forming device "⟨⟩" to a language. For reasons of readability, I omit the index.
  We are here confronted with the intricacies of the distinction between object- and metalanguage: "x" is here used as a place-holder for an expression of the object language (but "x" is also the 24th letter of the alphabet). "⟨x⟩" must not be understood as a name of the place-holder (or even as a name of the 24th letter of the alphabet), but as a name of whatever expression the parameter stands for.

sentences of L^0). We can then directly infer from the definition of the N_{MC}-connective that the sentence "PLATO IS A PHILOSOPHER" (as a sentence of L^1) is true. We thus infer the contingent fact that Plato is a philosopher from the truth of "$\mathfrak{M} \models \langle N_{MC} \, \varphi \rangle$", i.e., we infer a contingency from a logically true sentence being true. Note, however, that we can only perform the derivation if we are familiar with the definition of the N_{MC}-connective. This is, I think, the crux of the matter! The definition of the N_{MC}-connective says that it either stands for the tautology operator or the contradiction-operator, depending on whether or not Plato is a philosopher. Thus, from the truth of "$\mathfrak{M} \models \langle N_{MC} \, \varphi \rangle$" we can infer, in a first step, that the N_{MC}-connective stands for the tautology operator. We know from the definition of the connective that it stands for the tautology operator just in case the sentence "PLATO IS A PHILOSOPHER" (as a sentence of L^1) is true. We therefore infer, in a second step, that the latter sentence is true. We thus derived the truth of the contingent fact that Plato is a philosopher not only from the truth of a logical truth, but also from the definition of the logical constant occurring in the logical truth. The following passage indicates that this is indeed how McCarthy intended his argument (however, the passage refers to McCarthy's analog to the N_{MA}-connective):

> [..G]iven knowledge that ["H$\varphi \leftrightarrow \neg \varphi$"] is true *and of its truth condition*, one can know a priori that K; and 'K', under its present interpretation, is a posteriori. (McCarthy 1981: 515 f., my emphasis)[146]

We can derive a contingency from "$N_{MC} \, \varphi$" being true only because we know that it is a contingent matter what the N_{MC}-connective stands for, i.e., whether it stands for the tautology- or the contradiction-operator.

Now, the tie between a word and its meaning is not a matter of necessity. Words get assigned their meaning via some convention or

---

[146] I again slightly adapted the example to fit my discussion. See also McGee 1996: 578 for a similar line of argument (I again adapt the example): "According to orthodox metaphysics, H$_2$O-negation behaves extensionally like a logical connective in every possible world, since it is necessarily coextensive with ordinary negation. Yet 'H' isn't a logical connective, since, if it were, [H$\varphi \leftrightarrow \neg \varphi$] would be a logical truth, and [H$\varphi \leftrightarrow \neg \varphi$] isn't a logical truth, since it entails 'Water is H$_2$O,' which isn't a logical truth."

stipulation. Of course, this also holds for the logical constants. For example, it could have been the case that we agreed to use the sign "∨" for conjunction. Knowledge of the fact that the sentence "$p \vee \neg p$" is a logical truth allows us to infer (given knowledge of the meaning of the other signs) that "∨" does not stand for conjunction. So, in some sense, also the fact that the logical truth "$p \vee \neg p$" is true implies a contingent fact, namely, e.g., the semantic fact that "∨" does not stand for conjunction.[147] As I have stressed in section 4.2., it is crucial to distinguish between the information that can be derived from the fact that a certain proposition holds, and the information that can be derived from the fact that a certain sentence, expressing this very proposition, is true. The latter fact also allows one to derive *semantic* information. The fact that the proposition p or not-p obtain does not imply anything about the semantics of "∨". The fact that the sentence "$p \vee \neg p$" is (logically) true, however, does. Analogously, we can derive from the logical truth of "$N_{MC}\, \varphi$" and the definition of "N_{MC}" that the N_{MC}-connective stands for the tautology operator. As such, this is unproblematic. Problems are caused only by the very peculiar definition of the N_{MC}-connective. This connective is defined such that its meaning depends on some non-semantic contingent fact, namely on whether Plato is a philosopher. This is why we can even infer a non-semantic contingency from the truth of "$N_{MC}\, \varphi$".

Obviously, analogous reasoning establishes perfectly parallel results for the further sample instances of the N_M-connective. As the respective metalanguage substitutions of "K" are all true, the N_{MN}-, N_{MA}- and N_{ML}-connectives all stand for the tautology operator and are thereby logical constants according to definition (C). Thus, "$N_{MN}\, \varphi$", "$N_{MA}\, \varphi$" and "$N_{ML}\, \varphi$" will be declared logically true by the interpretational definition. "$N_{MN}\, \varphi$" being logically true will imply "IF SNOW IS WHITE IT IS NOT GREEN", "$N_{MA}\, \varphi$" being logically true will imply "IF GAIA IS A MOTHER, GAIA IS FEMALE", and, finally, "$N_{ML}\, \varphi$" being logically true will imply "PLUTO IS A PLANET OR PLUTO IS NOT A PLANET". The last implication will probably not cause any worries. It is logically true that Pluto is a planet or not, and logical truths are implied by everything. Whether the two former implications cause any

---

[147] For a similar argument with regard to McCarthy's original connective, see Sagi 2015. For a discussion, see also Woods 2017.

troubles depends on the status one assigns to the implied sentences. If they are merely necessary or analytically true, they must not be implied by a logical truth being true. As I argued extensively in the former chapters, the status of these sentences depends on the chosen restrictions on interpretations.

The fact that a certain logically true object language sentence is true must not imply a metalanguage sentence that is not logically true. If "N_{MC}" is a logical constant, then "$N_{MC}\,\varphi$" is a logical truth, and "$N_{MC}\,\varphi$" being true entails a non-logically true metalanguage sentence. It follows McCarthy's claim that the N_{MC}-connective, and the further relevant instances of the N_M-connective, cannot be logical constants.

We will now bring these observations together and provide an amendment of the definition of a logical constant that can cope with McCarthy's challenge. As this will involve a discussion of the general relation between object- and metalanguage, we will use the next chapter to do so.

9 Logic, Language and Metalanguage

In this chapter, I will amend the definition of a logical constant such that it escapes McCarthy's objection. The reformulated definition, presented in the first section, will raise intricate questions about the role of the distinction between object- and metalanguage in model theory. I will therefore make some, rather programmatic, remarks on this distinction, and on the relation between the logical constants of the metalanguage and the logical constants of the object language, in the second section.

9.1 Permutation Invariance Reinterpreted

Instances of the N_M-connective only yield problematic results if "K" is replaced by some sentence of the metalanguage that does not constitute a logical truth or a logical falsehood.[148] We should therefore exclude these instances of the N_M-connective from the logical constants.

Definition (C) only takes into account whether or not a constant has (on each domain) a permutation invariant semantic value. If we want to classify some instances of "N_M" as logical constants while classifying other instances as non-logical constants, we cannot let the semantic value of a term decide whether or not it is a logical constant: all instances of the N_M-connective have the same semantic value as long as a true sentence is substituted for "K". McCarthy therefore suggests that we should also take into account how the term is introduced:

> The general point suggested by these observations is that the logical status of an expression is not settled by the functions it introduces, independently of how those functions are specified. (McCarthy 1981: 516)

McCarthy does not elaborate on this idea, so let us try to do so.

We define a metalanguage sentence as *invariant under all admissible interpretations* iff it has the same truth value under all admissible inter-

---

[148] The previous chapter identified the problems that arise when "K" is substituted by a logical *truth*. If we substitute "K" by a logical *falsehood*, the respective instance of "$N_M \varphi$" implies the falsity of the substituted sentence. This is problematic iff the implied sentence is not logically false.

pretations of the metalanguage. If one subscribes to the interpretational definitions of logical truth and logical falsity with respect to sentences of the metalanguage, a sentence is invariant under all admissible interpretations iff it is a logical truth or a logical falsehood of the metalanguage. By means of the notion of invariance under interpretations, we can modify definition (C) of logical constants as follows:

DEFINITION (C*): A constant c of the language L^n is logical iff
(i) for all domains $\mathfrak{D}$ c's semantic value on $\mathfrak{D}$ is a logical notion with respect to $\mathfrak{D}$, and
(ii) c's semantic clause is invariant under all admissible interpretations of the terms of the improper metalanguage L^{n+1}.

Let the *improper metalanguage* of L^n be given by those expressions of L^{n+1} that are translations of expressions of L^n. The *proper metalanguage* L^{n+1} consists of those expressions that are names for the expressions of L^n and of the terms needed to talk about the syntactic or semantic properties of L^n (e.g., the truth-predicate of L^{n+1}). The *semantic clause* of an n-ary connective or quantifier "∗" is the expression stating its truth conditions. For example, the truth conditions for the connective "∧" are usually spelled out as follows: $\mathfrak{M} \models \langle \varphi \wedge \psi$ iff $\mathfrak{M} \models \langle \varphi$ and $\mathfrak{M} \models \langle \psi$" (where "$\varphi$" and "$\psi$" are arbitrary formulas of the object language). Thus, the semantic clause of the connective "∧" is "$\mathfrak{M} \models \langle \varphi$ and $\mathfrak{M} \models \langle \psi$". The truth conditions of the N_{MC}-connective are given as follows: $\mathfrak{M} \models N_{MC} \varphi$ iff PLATO IS A PHILOSOPHER. The semantic clause of the N_{MC}-connective is just "PLATO IS A PHILOSOPHER". "$N_{MC} \varphi$" is true in a model just in case Plato is a philosopher.

Let's see which terms are classified as logical constants by the modified definition (C*). Obviously, (C*) agrees with the original definition (C) in the classification of individual terms and predicates. These constants do not have a semantic clause in the relevant sense and thus the second condition is trivially fulfilled. The connectives and quantifiers provide more interesting cases. The instances of the N_O-connective are logical constants by definition (C*): their semantic value is permutation invariant, and their semantic clause is trivially interpretation invariant as it does not contain expressions of the improper metalanguage. As we have already established, this is an unproblematic result. I will therefore focus on the different versions of the N_M-connective, beginning with the N_{MC}-connective.

Although this connective meets the first condition for logical constants, it fails to fulfill the second. The semantic clause of the connective is given by the sentence "PLATO IS A PHILOSOPHER". Under any reasonable choice of restrictions on interpretations of the metalanguage, this sentence is not invariant under all interpretations of the improper part of the metalanguage. There is an admissible interpretation in the metalanguage that makes "PLATO IS A PHILOSOPHER" false. Thus, the N_{MC}-connective is excluded from the logical constants by the above definition. This is the intended result.

Second, consider the N_{MA}-connective. As the N_{MA}-connective has a semantic value that is invariant under all permutations, it is a logical constant iff its semantic clause, i.e., the sentence "MOTHERS ARE FEMALE" is interpretation invariant in the metalanguage. Whether this is the case depends on the chosen restrictions on interpretations of the metalanguage. If one subscribes to the metalanguage version of restriction (I3*), the sentence is indeed true under all admissible interpretations and the N_{MA}-connective is a logical constant. However, this has no negative consequences. It is utterly unproblematic that the sentence "MOTHERS ARE FEMALE" is implied by "$N_{MA}\ \varphi$" being true, if "MOTHERS ARE FEMALE" is itself considered a logical truth of the metalanguage. If however, the metalanguage version of (I3*) is not accepted, we obtain the then desired result that the N_{MA}-connective is not a logical constant.

Analogous considerations apply to the N_{MN}-connective. The connective is a logical constant just in case the sentence "IF SNOW IS WHITE, SNOW IS NOT GREEN" is invariant under all admissible interpretations of the improper part of the metalanguage. This in turn depends on the chosen restrictions on interpretations of the metalanguage. Only if the sentence is true under all admissible interpretations of the metalanguage, the N_{MN}-connective is a logical constant and the sentence "IF SNOW IS WHITE, SNOW IS NOT GREEN" is implied by the fact that a certain logical truth of the object language is true.

Finally, the N_{ML}-connective obviously comes out as a logical constant. Not only does it fulfill the first criterion of the definition, but also the second: its semantic clause is invariant under all interpretations of the improper part of the metalanguage (again assuming a reasonable choice of restriction on interpretations of the metalanguage). Yet this is the desired result as "PLUTO IS A PLANET OR PLUTO

IS NOT A PLANET" is a logical truth of the metalanguage and thus implied by everything.

With regard to the various instances of the N_M-connective, (C*) yields the intended results. So McCarthy's objection can be sidestepped for the N_M-connective. Note, however, that I introduced this connective as a bare-bone version of McCarthy's original example. Let me now also discuss McCarthy's more complicated original version. The relevant instance of McCarthy's N_M-connective, the H-connective, goes as follows:

$\mathfrak{M} \vDash \langle H\varphi \rangle$ iff (WATER IS H_2O and $\mathfrak{M} \nvDash \langle \varphi \rangle$) or ((not WATER IS H_2O) and $\mathfrak{M} \vDash \langle \varphi \rangle$).

We have already seen that the semantic value of the H-connective is permutation invariant; on all domains it has the same semantic value as the negation connective. Thus, the operator is a logical constant iff "(WATER IS H_2O and $\mathfrak{M} \nvDash \langle \varphi \rangle$) or ((not WATER IS H_2O) and $\mathfrak{M} \vDash \langle \varphi \rangle$)" is invariant under all admissible interpretations of the improper metalanguage, i.e., under all interpretations of "WATER IS H_2O".[149] If there is no admissible interpretation of the metalanguage which makes "WATER IS H_2O" false, the semantic clause of the connective is indeed invariant under the admissible interpretations of the improper metalanguage and the connective turns out to be a logical constant. However, it is then also unproblematic that the sentence "WATER IS H_2O" is implied by a sentence being logically true, as it is considered to be a logical truth itself.

However, it seems reasonable to assume that there is an admissible interpretation of the metalanguage that makes this sentence false. For example, we could reinterpret "WATER" as referring to, say, grass. As the sentence "WATER IS H_2O" is false under this interpretation (given the intended interpretation of the other terms), it is not a logical truth of the metalanguage. To evaluate whether the semantic clause is invariant under all interpretations, we must now distinguish between two cases: the case in which "$\mathfrak{M} \nvDash \langle \varphi \rangle$" holds and the case in which "$\mathfrak{M} \vDash \langle \varphi \rangle$" holds. In order for "H" to be a logical constant, the semantic clause "(WATER IS H_2O and $\mathfrak{M} \nvDash \langle \varphi \rangle$) or ((not WATER IS

---

[149] Here I implicitly assume that "and", "or" and "not" are logical constants of the metalanguage and may not be reinterpreted. See below for a discussion.

H₂O) and $\mathfrak{M}\models \langle\varphi\rangle$)" must be interpretation invariant in both cases. (Importantly, we do not consider cases in which the expressions "$\mathfrak{M}\not\models \langle\varphi\rangle$" or "$\mathfrak{M}\models \langle\varphi\rangle$" are reinterpreted. As these expressions belong to the proper metalanguage, they are held fixed. However, we must, of course, check whether the semantic clause is permutation invariant for both cases, the case in which "$\mathfrak{M}\not\models \langle\varphi\rangle$" is true and the case in which "$\mathfrak{M}\models\langle\varphi\rangle$" is true.) Consider the first case first: assume that $\mathfrak{M}\not\models \langle\varphi\rangle$. As "WATER IS H₂O" is true, it thus holds that the whole semantic clause is true. However, we assumed that there is an interpretation of the metalanguage under which the sentence "WATER IS H₂O" is false. With respect to this interpretation of the metalanguage the expression "(WATER IS H₂O and $\mathfrak{M}\not\models \langle\varphi\rangle$) or ((not WATER IS H₂O) and $\mathfrak{M}\models \langle\varphi\rangle$)" is false (under the assumption that "$\mathfrak{M}\not\models \langle\varphi\rangle$" is true and thus "$\mathfrak{M}\models \langle\varphi\rangle$" is false). Therefore, the expression is not true under all admissible interpretations and thus not invariant under all interpretations. This suffices to exclude McCarthy's operator from the logical constants. However, it is obvious that the semantic clause of the operator is also not interpretation invariant in the second case, i.e., if it holds that $\mathfrak{M}\models \langle\varphi\rangle$. In this case, the whole expression is false. Yet, there is an admissible interpretation of the metalanguage under which "WATER IS H₂O" is false. With respect to this interpretation, the semantic clause is true and thus, again, it is not interpretation invariant.[150]

---

[150] Let me also quickly discuss McGee's example of H₂O-negation introduced in Section 8.2. The operator "H" is here defined as follows: $\mathfrak{M}\models \langle H\varphi\rangle$ iff (WATER IS H₂O and $\mathfrak{M}\not\models \langle\varphi\rangle$). The semantic value of this operator is permutation invariant; thus, it is a logical constant iff its semantic clause "(WATER IS H₂O and $\mathfrak{M}\not\models \langle\varphi\rangle$)" is invariant under all admissible interpretations of the improper metalanguage. We again have to distinguish the case in which "$\mathfrak{M}\not\models \langle\varphi\rangle$" is true and the case in which "$\mathfrak{M}\not\models \langle\varphi\rangle$" is false. In order for H₂O-negation to be a logical constant, its semantic clause must be invariant under all interpretations in both cases. Consider first the case in which "$\mathfrak{M}\not\models \langle\varphi\rangle$" is false. In this case, "(WATER IS H₂O and $\mathfrak{M}\not\models \langle\varphi\rangle$)" will be false no matter how we interpret "WATER IS H₂O", and thus the semantic clause of H₂O-negation is indeed interpretation invariant. However, consider the second case, i.e., the case in which "$\mathfrak{M}\not\models \langle\varphi\rangle$" is true. In this case, the semantic clause "(WATER IS H₂O and $\mathfrak{M}\not\models \langle\varphi\rangle$)" is true. Since there is an interpretation under which "WATER IS H₂O" is false and thus an interpretation under which the conjunction is false, the semantic clause of the H₂O-operator is not interpretation invariant in all cases. Thus, McGee's H₂O-negation is not a

So far, the modified definition of logical constants yields very intuitive results. We still have to show, however, that the paradigm cases of logical constants, i.e., the truth-functional connectives and the standard quantifiers, satisfy the modified condition. Here is, exemplarily, the satisfaction condition for conjunction: $\mathfrak{M} \vDash \langle \varphi \wedge \psi \rangle$ iff $\mathfrak{M} \vDash \langle \varphi \rangle$ and $\mathfrak{M} \vDash \langle \psi \rangle$ (where "φ" and "ψ" are arbitrary formulas of the language L^0). The conjunction operation is, as we have already seen, permutation invariant; consequently, the first condition of the modified definition is satisfied. Whether the second condition is fulfilled depends on whether "$\mathfrak{M} \vDash \langle \varphi \rangle$ and $\mathfrak{M} \vDash \langle \psi \rangle$" is interpretation invariant. First note that the "and", which belongs to the metalanguage language L^1, has to be understood as a pure truth-functional connective here. It must not be understood as having any additional, e.g., temporal or causal, meaning. Otherwise, the clause would not yield the truth conditions of our purely truth-functional object language connective "$\wedge$". To indicate this, we symbolize it with "$\wedge$". The question to be answered is thus whether "$\mathfrak{M} \vDash \langle \varphi \rangle \wedge \mathfrak{M} \vDash \langle \psi \rangle$" is interpretation invariant.

"$\mathfrak{M} \vDash \langle \varphi \rangle$" and "$\mathfrak{M} \vDash \langle \psi \rangle$" are expressions of the proper metalanguage and thus not open for reinterpretation. The only critical expression is "$\wedge$". If we treat it as a logical constant of the metalanguage, it is not open for reinterpretation and the expression "$\mathfrak{M} \vDash \langle \varphi \rangle \wedge \mathfrak{M} \vDash \langle \psi \rangle$" is trivially interpretation invariant. If we do not treat it as a logical constant, it is open for reinterpretation. We can then reinterpret "$\wedge$" as, e.g., expressing the operation of disjunction. In a model $\mathfrak{M}$ with $\mathfrak{M} \vDash \langle \varphi \rangle$ and $\mathfrak{M} \nvDash \langle \psi \rangle$, the sentence "$\mathfrak{M} \vDash \langle \varphi \rangle \wedge \mathfrak{M} \vDash \langle \psi \rangle$" is then false according to the intended interpretation, i.e., according to the interpretation that interprets "$\wedge$" as conjunction, and the sentence is true in an interpretation that interprets "$\wedge$" as disjunction. Thus, the semantic clause of the object language connective of conjunction would not be interpretation invariant and, therefore, the conjunction term of the object language, "$\wedge$", would not qualify as a logical constant. To sum up: whether or not the conjunction term of the object language, i.e., "$\wedge$", is a logical constant,

logical constant according to (C*). The modified definition of logical constants disarms McGee's counter example to (C).

depends on whether the conjunction term of the metalanguage, i.e., "∧", is a logical constant.

Let me illustrate the situation with a further paradigm case of a logical constant, the universal quantifier, which is defined as follows: $\mathfrak{M} \models \langle \forall x \varphi \rangle$ iff $⋀a\ \mathfrak{M}a/x \models \langle \varphi \rangle$ (where "⋀" is the universal quantifier of the metalanguage). The universal quantifier, of course, satisfies the first condition for logical constants: its semantic value is permutation invariant. Whether it also satisfies the second condition depends on whether the expression "$⋀a\ \mathfrak{M}a/x \models \langle \varphi \rangle$" is interpretation invariant. "$\mathfrak{M}a/x \models \langle \varphi \rangle$" belongs to the proper metalanguage and is thus not open for reinterpretation. ("a" is bound by the universal quantifier of the metalanguage and thus its semantic value is irrelevant for the truth value of "$⋀a\ \mathfrak{M}a/x \models \langle \varphi \rangle$" anyhow.) The crucial expression is "⋀", i.e., the universal quantifier of the metalanguage. Only if it is a logical constant of the metalanguage L^1, the semantic clause of the universal quantifier of the object language is interpretation invariant. Thus, whether the universal quantifier of the object language is a logical constant depends on whether the universal quantifier of the metalanguage is a logical constant: either both are, or neither is.

To determine whether the object-language connectives and quantifiers are logical constants of the object language, we first have to determine whether the respective connectives and quantifiers of the metalanguage are logical constants of the metalanguage. So, do the metalanguage connectives and quantifiers fulfill the two conditions specified by (C*)? They obviously have a permutation invariant semantic value and thus fulfill the first criterion on logical constants. Do they also fulfill the second condition, i.e., are their respective semantic clauses interpretation invariant? The semantic clause of, say, the conjunction term of the metalanguage is given in the meta-metalanguage L^2. Whether the semantic clause of the conjunction term of the metalanguage is interpretation invariant depends on whether the conjunction term of the meta-metalanguage is a logical constant. We are entering into a regress here. To determine whether the conjunction term of language L^n is a logical constant, we already have to presuppose a demarcation of the logical from the non-logical terms of the language L^{n+1}.[151]

As we have already seen in the last chapter, however, we can make an even more general observation. To determine the logical constants of the language L^n, we must not only presuppose a demarcation of the constants of L^{n+1} into logical and non-logical ones, but we have to presuppose a demarcation of the admissible from the inadmissible interpretations of language L^{n+1}. Only by presupposing such a demarcation can we decide whether, e.g., the different instances of the N_M-connective are logical constants. For example, the N_{MA}-connective is a logical constants only if we assume a restriction along the lines of (I4*) with regard to the admissible interpretations of the metalanguage. Again, the problem of demarcating the logical from the non-logical constants is only a particularly interesting instance of a more general demarcation problem.

Let us bring this all together. The interpretational definition of logical truth presupposes a demarcation of the admissible from the inadmissible interpretations. This line of demarcation partly rests on the demarcation of the logical from the non-logical constants of the object language. As I argued in this chapter, we have to presuppose a demarcation of the admissible from the inadmissible interpretations of the metalanguage to demarcate the logical from the non-logical constants of the object language. It follows that the demarcation of the admissible interpretations of the object language is dependent on the demarcation of the admissible interpretations of the metalanguage. The logic of the object language is grounded in the logic of its metalanguage. Although object- and metalanguage have to be careful-

---

[151] One might argue that this regress only arises if we assume that the language L^{n+1} contains only a translation of the object language, not the object language itself. Indeed, we can also construct the hierarchy of languages such that the language L^{n+1} literally contains the language L^n. (See the next section for more on this.) Under this conception, there are not two conjunction terms, "∧" and "∧", of which the first belongs to the language L^0 and the second to the language L^1, but those terms are identified: there is just one conjunction term which is contained in all languages of the hierarchy. The postulated regress does not get off the ground. However, this does not yield any relief because we are now faced with a circularity problem. Whether or not "∧" is a logical constant now depends on whether or not "∧" is a logical constant, where "∧" and "∧" are identical. The definition of a logical constant is no longer well-founded.

ly kept apart in order to make sense of model theory, they live in an intimate relationship. Let's try to better understand it.

9.2 Metalanguage

In the preceding section, we strictly distinguished between languages of different levels. According to this view on language, we do not have one truth-predicate or one notion of 'truth in a model', but infinitely many, arranged in a hierarchy. Furthermore, the improper metalanguage L^{n+1} was given by translations of the expressions of L^n. We distinguished the sentence "Plato is a philosopher" as a sentence of the language L^0, from its translation in the language L^1, given by "PLATO IS A PHILOSOPHER". Analogously, we distinguished the conjunction term of the language L^0 ("∧") from its translation, i.e., the connective "∧" of the language L^1.

It has been argued that such an approach in terms of a hierarchy does not provide an adequate account of natural language.[152] When one utters "'snow is white' is true' is true", one does not seem to be using two different truth-predicates. There is just one expression "is true" in natural language, not an infinite number of different truth-predicates. Kripke is prominent for putting forward this line of critique in his "Outline of a Theory of Truth":[153]

> Philosophers have been suspicious of the orthodox approach as an analysis of our intuitions. Surely our language contains just one word 'true,' not a sequence of distinct phrases 'true$_n$,' applying to sentences of higher and higher levels. (Kripke 1975: 694 f.)

---

[152] Tarski himself, of course, is the first to agree. As already mentioned, he explicitly restricts his investigation to formal languages exactly for the reason that natural language seems to contain its own truth-predicate.

[153] In his attempt to define the notion of truth, Kripke 1975 also distinguishes truth-predicates of different levels, each applying only to sentences of a lower level. However, Kripke extends the hierarchy of languages to the transfinite and introduces languages of level ω, ω+1, etc. He argues that there is a fixed point in the hierarchy, i.e., there is a language that contains its own truth-predicate. Kripke seems to think that we can understand natural language as that very language. I will not evaluate Kripke's argument here.

Kripke suggests that natural language only contains one truth-predicate, rather than an infinite number of different, hierarchically ordered truth-predicates.[154]

This view might appear even more plausible with respect to the terms of what we called the "improper metalanguage". The improper metalanguage L^{n+1} is given by translations of the expressions of L^n. The sentence "PLATO IS A PHILOSOPHER" belongs to the improper metalanguage L^1, because it is a translation of the sentence "Plato is a philosopher" of the language L^0. As it might seem awkward to say that natural language contains an infinite number of truth-predicates of different levels, so it seems strange to say that natural language contains an infinite number of sentences all saying that Plato is a philosopher, one being the translation of the other. As far as natural language is concerned, the distinction between the object-language sensentence "Plato is a philosopher" from its metalanguage translation seems at least highly artificial. Or to say it with Hilary Putnam's words:

> [W]hat we call a language (a "mother tongue") is, from a Tarskian point of view, an infinite series of formalized languages [...]. English is an object-language (E), plus a metalanguage (meta-E), plus a metametalanguage (Meta-meta-E), and so forth. [...] Still, when one is speaking a natural language, one treats a sentence as the same sentence whether it occurs in what a logician might view as the metalanguage or in what a logician might view as the object-language. (Putnam 1985: 68 f.)

Putnam surely has a point here. However, at least at first view, there seems to be a straightforward way to accommodate Putnam's view without giving up the core idea of the hierarchical approach. We can grant that there is just one truth-predicate in natural language, and also that the sentences "Plato is a philosopher" and "PLATO IS A PHILOSOPHER" are not really two different sentences, if we only insist

---

[154] One also runs into a technical problem with the claim that natural language fragments into a denumerable infinite number of metalanguages. This claim cannot be made in natural language itself: for example, the sentence "for all n, the truth-predicate applying to sentences of L^n is of L^{n+1} (with $n \in \mathbb{N}$)" is not expressible in any language L^k ($k \in \mathbb{N}$), but only in a language at a transfinite level.

that the terms can be used in an object-language way, in a metalanguage way, in a meta-metalanguage way, etc.: "truth$_n$" and "truth$_m$" need not be taken to be two different terms, but they can be understood as one term which is used in different roles. Analogously, we can claim that one and the same sentence, "Plato is a philosopher", can be used, say, in the role of an object-language sentence and in the role of a metalanguage sentence. We need not talk of different languages, structured in a hierarchy, as it suffices to distinguish between different roles of a term or sentence.

This reaction, however, fails to address the real worry. Those that are sceptic to the classical hierarchical approach will also doubt that it makes sense to speak of 'different roles' of the sentences of a language. The distinction between object- and metalanguage roles seems as foreign to natural language as the claim that natural language fragments into different languages ordered in a hierarchy. In assuming that there is a metalanguage role for sentences, we are – in some sense – transgressing the boundary of natural language. And this is, I think, the source of the scepticism concerning the hierarchical view. I will try to tentatively address this intuition in the remaining part of this section.

Opponents of the hierarchical approach seem to worry about the fragmentation of language into languages of different order, because they deny the very possibility of meaningful statements in the metalanguage.[155] Importantly, however, this possibility is presupposed by the whole model-theoretic approach to language. The notion of 'truth in a model' rests on the possibility of speaking in a metalanguage meaningfully about the truth or the interpretation of sentences of the object language. Model theory requires us to transcend the object language. The opponents of the model-theoretic view take this to be impossible at least for 'interesting' languages, i.e., languages akin to

---

[155] I already distinguished between two different roles of the metalanguage in the former chapter. There are sentences in the metalanguage about the signs of the object language (as in " 'true' has four letters"), and about the semantic properties of the sentences of the object language (as in " "snow" refers to snow", or in " 'snow is white' is true"). I merely want to expound the problems of the second role of the metalanguage. The first role seems innocent to me. Furthermore, I did not intend to provide an exhaustive characterization of the roles of the metalanguage.

natural language. Natural language is, so it is said, 'universal': there is no language beyond natural language in which one could talk about natural language.

Two fundamentally different views on logic and language seem to collide here, one that stresses the universal character of language and the impossibility of stepping outside it, while the other tradition approaches languages from a meta-logical viewpoint, spelling out its syntactical and semantical properties in a metalanguage. Jaakko Hintikka distinguishes and discusses these two traditions under the labels "universalist tradition" and "model-theoretic tradition" (see Hintikka 1988, 1997).[156] With the universalist tradition, Hintikka associates Frege, Russell, and Wittgenstein, while Boole, Schröder, Löwenheim, and Gödel are said to belong to the model-theoretic tradition.[157] From a universalist viewpoint, there is just one fully interpreted and universal language. It does not make sense to consider different interpretations of a language or different domains of discourse. Because of its universality, it is, in a strict sense, impossible to talk about the language and its properties. This contrasts with the view of the model-theoretic tradition whose members reject the idea that there is just one universal language coming with a fixed interpretation. Rather, they consider different interpretations of a language, assume various

---

[156] Hintikka refers to van Heijenoort 1967[b] for this distinction. Van Heijenoort contrasts the view of logic as a *lingua characterica*, from the view of logic as a *calculus ratiocinator*. Van Heijenoort refers to Frege, who used these expressions to characterize the enterprise of his *Begriffsschrift* as providing a *lingua characterica* in opposition to the Boolean works trying to develop a *calculus ratiocinator*. (See Frege 1880/81, 1882 and 1883.) Frege's reference point is, in turn, Gottfried W. Leibniz. Here I cannot discuss whether Hintikka's distinction between the universalist and the model-theoretic tradition coincides with Frege's distinction between a *lingua characterica* and a *calculus ratiocinator*. Furthermore, it is far beyond the scope of this work to decide whether Frege's characterization of a *lingua characterica* and a *calculus ratiocinator* adequately captures the original Leibnizian distinction. For these reasons, I want to stick to Hintikka's characterization of the two views detached from their relations to van Heijenoort's, Frege's and Leibniz' distinctions between a *lingua characterica* and a *calculus ratiocinator*.

[157] It is difficult to locate Tarski in this picture. As the founding father of model theory, he of course understood language to be reinterpretable. And of course, he himself properly defined the notion of 'truth in a model'. However, Tarski only allowed the reinterpretability of formal languages and famously stressed the universality of natural language.

domains of discourse, and investigate the meta-logical notions. Hintikka gives the following vivid characterization of the two traditions:

> [According to the universalist tradition] we cannot "reach" the world linguistically except by means of our actual language. We are, in this sense, prisoners of our own language. If we are to believe in the universalist dogma, this prison is a maximum-security one from which there is no hope of an escape. According to the other, competing idea of language [the model-theoretic tradition – A. Z.] we are not tied to our language. Our language is our servant, we are its masters. (Hintikka 1997: 22)

One driving idea of the universalist view seems to be as follows: in speaking meaningfully, we must already presuppose that our language properly relates to the world, i.e., we must already presuppose a semantics. Therefore, we cannot talk about the semantics in a meaningful, non-tautological way in that very language. Everything we say is already presupposed by the meaningfulness of what we say. The semantics is transcendental to and presupposed by language. We cannot talk about the semantic properties of a language in a non-tautological way in that very language because the semantic properties are already presupposed by the meaningfulness of the utterance. That seems to be an important insight. However, we must be very careful not to draw any illegitimate consequences from this observation.[158] Assume that the metalanguage sentence "Φ" says that the object language sentence "φ" has certain semantic properties (e.g., "Φ" says what "φ" means or whether "φ" is true in a given model). What exactly is presupposed by the meaningfulness of "Φ"? Obviously, the semantic properties, or some semantic properties, of "Φ" are presupposed, not the semantic properties of "φ". We can meaningfully talk about the properties of "φ" using the sentence "Φ", because, in using the sentence "Φ", we must only presuppose the meaningfulness of "Φ", not the meaningfulness of "φ". Thus, the above argument does not imply that the semantic properties of "φ" are ineffable. The argument only shows that we cannot express the semantics of *all* sentences of a language in that very language. We cannot meaningfully talk about the meanings of all sentences of a language because the meaningfulness

---

[158] For the following argument, see also Hintikka 1997: 34f.

of some expressions must already be presupposed. The argument of the universalist is correct, but its scope must not be overestimated.

My characterization of the universalist viewpoint and its critique of the model-theoretic approach is, of course, hardly sufficient. Nevertheless, I am convinced that the model-theoretic approach can be defended from many worries of the universalist. We must be careful not to give it up too hastily; its fruits are too colorful and tasty. It seems possible to meaningfully talk about the semantic properties of a sentence in a model because only the meaningfulness of the metalanguage expressions we are using to do so is thereby presupposed, not the meaningfulness of the sentence of the object language. Nevertheless, we must admit that in order to meaningfully use a metalanguage sentence to talk about the meaning of an object-language sentence, the meaningfulness of the metalanguage sentence must be presupposed. Notably, the regress diagnosed in the preceding section shows something very similar: in order to determine whether or not a certain sentence of the object language is logically true, one has to assume the logic of the metalanguage, i.e., one already has to assume the classification of the metalanguage sentences into those that are logically true and those that are not. Which sentence of the object language is declared logically true depends, as we have seen, on the logical truths of the metalanguage.

To spell out the logical properties of a language we have to presuppose the logics of the language in which we do so. In particular, we cannot define the notion of logical truth for the object language without already presupposing it for the metalanguage. This indicates the impossibility of a self-contained definition of logical consequence. The attempt to define the notions of logical truth and logical consequence is thereby not doomed to fail, or uninteresting, useless or unfruitful. However, we must acknowledge that the definitions of logical truth and of logical consequence for the object language rely on a notion of logical truth and logical consequence in the metalanguage.

This is, of course, no new insight. The relation between object language and metalanguage and the status of the definitions of central logical concepts governed large parts of the analytical tradition of the last century. We still do not have a clear view on these questions. To better understand the model-theoretic definitions of logical truth and logical consequence we must dive yet deeper into the mysteries of language.

Concluding Remarks

Tarski intended his model-theoretic definitions to capture our common concepts of logical truth and logical consequence. Whether they succeed in doing so depends on what models model. At bottom, there are two ways of understanding models. The one focuses on the semantic meaning of terms and results in the interpretational definition of logical truth. A sentence is logically true iff it is true under all variations of meaning. The other emphasizes the role of facts and yields the representational definition of logical truth. A sentence is logically true iff it is true under all variations of facts. While the two readings are not clearly distinguishable within the standard semantics of first-order predicate logic, they are properly kept apart with respect to form-logical semantics. In this new semantic framework, we can formulate the two definitions of logical truth as follows (where $\mathfrak{I}^*$ and $\mathfrak{S}^*$ are the intended interpretation and state, respectively):

Interpretational definition of logical truth:
(IT*)   A sentence φ is logically true iff $(\mathfrak{D}, \mathfrak{I}, \mathfrak{S}^*) \models \varphi$ for all admissible $\mathfrak{I}$ and all $\mathfrak{D}$.

Representational definition of logical truth:
(RT*)   A sentence φ is logically true iff $(\mathfrak{D}, \mathfrak{I}^*, \mathfrak{S}) \models \varphi$ for all admissible $\mathfrak{S}$ and all $\mathfrak{D}$.

Definitions (IT*) and (RT*) make explicit what is only implicit in the definition of logical truth as 'truth in all models': the quantifier must be restricted. A literal reading of the definition of logical truth as truth in *all* models whatsoever would have the consequence that no sentence will turn out to be logically true. The quantifier must be understood to range over all *admissible* interpretations and states, respectively.

Which sentences are declared logically true depends on the chosen demarcation of admissible from inadmissible interpretations or states. Focusing on the interpretational definition, I claimed that we already implicitly assume some restrictions on interpretations, in particular the grammatical restriction and the identity restriction, and argued that these restrictions naturally generalize to further restrictions on interpretations. The new restrictions would yield the result that paradigm cases of structural truths or analytic truths are declared logically true. I also showed that the interpretational definition, just like the representational definition, is not 'free of metaphysics', and, furthermore, that if the metaphysical assumptions are made explicit in the form of restrictions on interpretations, paradigm cases of allegedly merely necessary sentences turn out to be logically true. Defining these sentences logically true, however, would not violate the 'formality of logic', as the boundary between formally true and not formally true sentences shifts together with the boundary between admissible and inadmissible interpretations.

'Admissibility' can be determined in such a way for both the interpretational and the representational definition such that they hold the same sentences to be logically true. Both definitions are extensionally equivalent under analogous restrictions. These findings suggest that the central task of the philosophy of logic is to provide a non-trivial distinction between the admissible and the inadmissible models, independently of whether models are read interpretationally or representationally. To properly spell out these restrictions, we have to engage with intricate questions concerning grammatical and ontological categories, word-identity, the notion of a logical constant, etc. As the discussion of the division of terms into logical and non-logical terms should have exemplified, we still have to pave our paths here. However, let me sketch what I take to be the desired destination.

In the introduction, we identified two desiderata on logical consequence: logically valid arguments must be necessarily truth-preserving and formal. As the desideratum of formality turned out to be insubstantial in the current context, we are left with the sole criterion of necessary truth-preservation. This indicates that we should restrict the admissible models such that exactly the necessarily truth-preserving arguments are declared logically valid. The restrictions I tentatively suggested may succeed in doing so. Exactly those arguments are then picked out as logically valid in which the transmission from premises to conclusion is perfectly 'safe'. I think that this is, in the end, the essence of deductive validity. In an adequate formal system, logical and metaphysical modalities are happily married.

My primary aim in this book was not, however, to redefine the extension of the notions of logical truth and logical consequence. My aim was to explicate what it would take to justify the chosen extension. I hope to have shown that one would have to dive deep into semantics and metaphysics. It was once suggested that logic should take the place of metaphysics. It can do so, but only insofar as it becomes metaphysics.

Bibliography

ABELARD, Petrus: *Dialectica*. Transl. by L. M. De Rijk 1956. Van Gorcum: Assen.

ALMOG, Joseph and Paolo Leonardi (eds.) 2009: *The Philosophy of David Kaplan*. Oxford: Oxford University Press.

ANDERSON, R. Lanier 2004: It Adds Up After All: Kant's Philosophy of Arithmetic in Light of the Traditional Logic. *Philosophy and Phenomenological Research* 69: 501–540.

— 2005: The Wolffian Paradigm and its Discontents: Kant's Containment Definition of Analyticity in Historical Context. *Archiv für Geschichte der Philosophie* 87: 22–74.

ARMSTRONG, David 1978: *A Theory of Universals*. Cambridge: Cambridge University Press.

— 1997: *A World of States of Affairs*. Cambridge: Cambridge University Press.

BALCERAK-JACKSON, Brendan 2017: Structural Entailment and Semantic Natural Kinds. *Linguistics and Philosophy*: 207-237.

BARRETT, Robert 1965: Quine, Synonymy, and Logical Truth. *Philosophy of Science* 23: 361–367.

BAYS, Timothy 2001: On Tarski on Models. *Journal of Symbolic Logic* 66, 1701–1726.

BEALER, George 1982: *Quality and Concept*. Oxford: Clarendon Press.

— and U. Mönnich 1989: Property Theories. *Handbook of Philosophical Logic*, Vol. 10: 133–251.

BELNAP, Nuel 1962: Tonk, Plonk, and Plink. *Analysis* 22: 30–34.

BOLZANO, Bernard 1837: *Theory of Science*. Transl. by J. Berg 1973. Dordrecht: Reidel.

BONNAY, Denis 2008: Logicality and Invariance. *Bulletin of Symbolic Logic* 14: 29–68.

— and van Benthem 2008: Modal Logic and Invariance. *Journal of Applied Non-Classical Logics* 18: 153–173.

BRANDOM, Robert B. 1994: *Making it Explicit*. Harvard: Harvard University Press.

BRUN, Georg 2003: *Die richtige Formel*. Frankfurt a.M.: Hänsel-Hohenhausen.

CARET, Colin R. and O.T. Hjortland (eds.) 2015: *Foundations of Logical Consequence*. Oxford: Oxford University Press.

CARNAP, Rudolph 1937: *The Logical Syntax of Language*. Transl. by A. Smeaton. London: Routledge & Kegan Paul.

— 1947: *Meaning and Necessity*. Chicago: The University of Chicago Press.

— 1952: Meaning Postulates. *Philosophical Studies* 3: 65–73.

CHOMSKY, Noam 1957: *Syntactic Structures*. Paris: Mouton.

COOPER, John M. 1997: Plato: *Complete Works*. Indianapolis: Hackett.

CORCORAN, John and J. M. Sagüillo 2011: The Absence of Multiple Universes of Discourse in the 1936 Tarski Consequence-Definition Paper. *History and Philosophy of Logic* 32: 356–374.

CRESSWELL, Max J. 1976: The Semantics of Degree. In: B. Partee (ed.): *Montague Grammar*. 261–292.

DAVIDSON, Donald and G. Harman (eds.) 1975: *The Logic of Grammar*. California: Dickenson Pub.

DE JONG, Willem R. 1995: Kant's Analytic Judgment and the Traditional Theory of Concepts. *Journal of the History of Philosophy* 33: 613–641.

DUMMETT, Michael 1973: *Frege: Philosophy of Language*. London: Duckworth.

— 1991: *The Logical Basis of Metaphysics*. London: Duckworth.

DUTILH NOVAES, Catarina 2011: The Different Ways in which Logic is (said to be) Formal. *History and Philosophy of Logic* 32: 303–332.

— 2012: Reassessing Logical Hylomorphism and the Demarcation of Logical Constants. *Synthese* 185: 387–410.

— 2014: The Undergeneration of Permutation Invariance as a Criterion for Logicality. *Erkenntnis* 79: 81–97.

ECKARDT, Regine 1998: *Adverbs, Events and Other Things: Issues in the Semantics of Manner Adverbs*. Tübingen: Max Niemeyer Verlag.

ETCHEMENDY, John 1988[a]: Models, Semantics, and Logical Truth. *Linguistics and Philosophy* 11: 91–106.

— 1988[b]: Tarski on Truth and Logical Consequence. *The Journal of Symbolic Logic* 53: 51–79.

- 1990: *The Concept of Logical Consequence.* Cambridge, MA: Harvard University Press.
- 2008: *Reflections on Consequence.* In D. Patterson (ed.) 2008: 263–300.

EVANS, Gareth 1985: *Collected Papers.* Oxford: Oxford University Press.

FEFERMAN, Solomon 1999: Logic, Logics, and Logicism. *Notre Dame Journal of Formal Logic* 40: 31–54.

- 2010: Set-Theoretic Invariance Criteria for Logicality. *Notre Dame Journal of Formal Logic* 51: 3–20.

FIENGO, Robert and Robert May 2006: *Di Lingua Belief.* Cambridge: MIT.

FINE, Kit 2011: An Abstract Characterization of the Determinate/Determinable Distinction. *Philosophical Perspectives* 25: 161–187.

FREGE, Gottlob 1879: *Concept Script.* Transl. by S. Bauer-Mengelberg. In J. van Heijenoort (ed.) 1967[a]: 1–83.

- 1880/81: Boole's Logical Calculus and the Concept-Script. Transl. by P. Long and R. White. In Frege 1979: 9–46.
- 1882: Boole's Logical Formula Language and my Concept-Script. Transl. by P. Long and R. White. In Frege 1979: 47–52.
- 1883: On the Scientific Justification of a Concept-Script. Transl. by J. M. Bartlett. In *Mind* 73, 1964: 155–160.
- 1892: On Sense and Reference. In P. Geach and M. Black (eds.) 1980. Oxford: Blackwell: 56–79.
- 1979: *Posthumous Writings.* H. Hermes, F. Kambartel, F. Kaulbach (eds.), transl. by P. Long and R. White. Oxford: Blackwell.

FREITAG, Wolfgang 2009: *Form and Philosophy. A Topology of Possibility and Representation.* Heidelberg: Synchron.

- and A. Zinke 2012: The Theory of Form Logic. *Logic and Logical Philosophy* 21: 363–389.

GEACH, Peter and M. Black (eds.) 1980: *Translations from the Philosophical Writings of Gottlob Frege.* Oxford: Blackwell.

GLEZAKOS, Stavroula 2009: Can Frege pose Frege's Puzzle? in J. Almog and P. Leonardi (eds.) 2009: 202–208.

GÖDEL, Kurt 1931: On Formally Undecidable Propositions of *Principia Mathematica* and Related Systems I. In Gödel 1986: 144–195.

— 1986: *Collected Works. I: Publications 1929–1936*. S. Feferman, S. Kleene, G. Moore, R. Solovay, and J. van Heijenoort (eds.). Oxford: Oxford University Press.

GÓMEZ-TORRENTE, Mario 1996: Tarski on Logical Consequence. *Notre Dame Journal of Formal Logic* 37, 125–151.

— 1998: On a Fallacy Attributed to Tarski. *History and Philosophy of Logic* 19: 227–234.

— 2002: The Problem of Logical Constants. *Bulletin of Symbolic Logic* 8: 1–37.

— 2009: Rereading Tarski on Logical Consequence. *Review of Symbolic Logic* 2: 249–297.

GOODMAN, Nelson 1972: Seven Strictures on Similarity. In Goodman: *Problems and Projects*. Indianapolis: Bobs-Merril.

GRICE, Paul 1991: *Studies in the Way of Words*. Harvard: Harvard University Press.

HANSON, William H. 1997: The Concept of Logical Consequence. *The Philosophical Review* 106: 365–409.

HAWTHORNE, John and Ernest Lepore 2011: On Words. *Journal of Philosophy* 108: 447–485.

HIGGINBOTHAM, James 1985: On Semantics. *Linguistic Inquiry* 16: 547–593.

HINTIKKA, Jaakko 1988: On the Development of the Model-Theoretic Viewpoint in Logical Theory. *Synthese* 77: 1–36.

— 1997: *Lingua Universalis vs. Calculus Ratiocinator*. Dordrecht: Kluwer.

HODGES, Wilfrid 1986: Truth in a Structure. *Proceedings of the Aristotelian Society*: 135–151.

HOSSACK, Keith 2007: *The Metaphysics of Knowledge*. Oxford: Oxford University Press.

JOHANSSON, Ingvar 2000: Determinables are Universals. *The Monist* 83: 101–121.

IAU 2006: *General Assembly: Resolutions 5 and 6*. 2006-08-24.

JANÉ, Ignacio 2006: What is Tarski's *Common* Concept of Consequence? *Bulletin of Symbolic Logic* 12: 1–42.

JOHNSON, William E. 1921: *Logic*, Part I. New York: Dover.

KANT, Immanuel 1781: *Critique of Pure Reason*. Transl. by P. Guyer and A. Wood 1998. Cambridge: Cambridge University Press.

KAPLAN, David 1990: Words. *Proceedings of the Aristotelian Society* 64: 93–119.

KATZ, Jerrold J. 1986, *Cogitations*. Oxford: Oxford University Press.

KATZ, Graham 2003: Event Arguments, Adverb Selection, and the Static Adverb Gap. In: E. Lang, C. Maienborn & C. Fabricius-Hansen (eds.), *Modifying Adjuncts*. Berlin: Mouton de Gruyter.

KLEIN, Felix 1893: A Comparative Review of Recent Researches in Geometry. *New York Mathematical Society Bulletin* 2: 215–249.

KRIPKE, Saul 1975: Outline of a Theory of Truth. *Journal of Philosophy* 72: 690–716.

LEWIS, David 1986[a]: *On the Plurality of Worlds*. Oxford: Blackwell.

— 1986[b]: Against Structural Universals. *Australasian Journal of Philosophy* 64: 25–46.

LINDENBAUM, Adolf and A. Tarski 1936: On the Limitations of the Means of Expression of Deductive Theories. In Tarski 1969: 384–392.

MAUTNER, F. I. 1946: An Extension of Klein's Erlanger Program: Logic as Invariant-theory. *American Journal of Mathematics* 68: 345–384.

MCBRIDE, Fraser 2011: Extreme Metaphysics: Hossack on Logical Objects, Facts, Propositions and Universals. *Dialectica* 65: 87–101.

MCCARTHY, Timothy 1981: The Idea of a Logical Constant. *Journal of Philosophy* 78: 499–523.

— 1987: Modality, Invariance, and Logical Truth. *Journal of Philosophical Logic* 16: 423–443.

MCCONNELL-GINET, Sally 1982: Adverbs and logical Form: A Linguistically Realistic Theory. *Language* 58: 144–184.

MCFARLANE, John 2000: What Does it Mean to say that Logic is Formal? PhD dissertation, University of Pittsburgh.

— 2009: Logical Constants. *The Stanford Encyclopedia of Philosophy*, Edward N. Zalta (ed.). http://plato.stanford.edu/archives/fall2009/entries/logical-constants/.

— (unpublished): What is Modelled by Truth in All Models?

MCGEE, Vann 1996: Logical Operations. *Journal of Philosophical Logic* 25: 567–580.

MENZEL, Christopher 1990: Actualism, Ontological Commitment, and Possible World Semantics. *Synthese* 85: 355–389.

MONTAGUE, Richard 1970[a]: English as a Formal Language. In Thomason (ed.) 1974: 188–221.

— Richard 1970[b]: Universal Grammar. In Thomason (ed.) 1974: 222–246.

MOSTOWSKI, Andrzej 1957: On a Generalization of Quantifiers. *Fundamenta Mathematicae* 44: 12–35.

PARSONS, Terence 1990: *Events in the Semantics of English: A Study in Subatomic Semantics*. Cambridge: MIT Press.

PARTEE, Barbara (ed.) 1976: *Montague Grammar*. New York: Academic Press.

PATTERSON, Douglas 2008: *New Essays on Tarski and Philosophy*. Oxford: Oxford University Press.

PLATO: *Euthydemus*. Cited from John M. Cooper (ed.) 1997.

POLLOCK, John L. 1984: *The Foundations of Philosophical Semantics*. Princeton: Princeton University Press.

POPPER, Karl R. 1955: A Note on Tarski's Definition of Truth. *Mind* 64: 388–391.

— 1965: *The Logic of Scientific Discovery*. London: Hutchinson & Co.

PRIEST, Graham 1995: Etchemendy and Logical Consequence. *Canadian Journal of Philosophy* 25: 283–292.

PRIOR, Arthur 1960: The Runabout Inference-Ticket. *Analysis* 21: 38–39.

PUTNAM, Hilary 1985: A Comparison of Something with Something Else. *New Literary History* 17: 61–79.

QUINE, Willard V. O. 1951: Two Dogmas of Empiricism. *The Philosophical Review* 60: 20–43.

— 1970: *Philosophy of Logic*. Harvard: Harvard University Press.

RAMSEY, Frank P. 1927: Facts and Propositions. *Proceedings of the Aristotelian Society* 7: 153–170.

RAY, Greg 1996: Logical Consequence. A Defense of Tarski. *Journal of Philosophical Logic* 25: 617–677.

RAYO, Agustín and G. Uzquiano 2006: *Absolute Generality*. Oxford: OUP.

READ, Stephen 1994: Formal and Material Consequence. *Journal of Philosophical Logic* 23: 247–265.

RUSSELL, Bertrand 1912: *The Problems of Philosophy*. London: Williams and Norgate; New York: Henry Holt and Company.

— 1913: *Theory of Knowledge*. London: Allen & Unwin.

— 1914: *Our Knowledge of the External World*. Chicago and London: The Open Court Publishing.

— 1918: *The Philosophy of Logical Atomism*. London and New York: Routledge.

— 1938: *The Principles of Mathematics*. 2nd ed. Cambridge: Cambridge University Press.

SAGI, Gil 2014: Formality in Logic: From Logical Terms to Semantic Constraints. *Logique et Analyse* 227: 259–276.

— 2015: The Modal and Epistemic Arguments against the Invariance Criterion for Logical Terms. *Journal of Philosophy* 112: 159–167.

SAINSBURY, Mark 1991: *Logical Forms*. Malden: Blackwell.

SALMON, Nathan 1986: *Frege's Puzzle*. Cambridge, MA: MIT Press.

SCHAFFER, Jonathan 2004: Two Conceptions of Sparse Properties. *Pacific Philosophical Quarterly* 85: 92–102.

SCHIRN, G. (ed.) 1998: *The Philosophy of Mathematics Today*. Oxford: Oxford University Press.

SEARLE, John 1967: Determinables and Determinates. *The Encyclopedia of Philosophy*, vol. II. P. Edwards (ed.). New York: Macmillan: 357–359.

SHAPIRO, Steward 1998: Logical Consequence: Models and Modality. In G. Schirn (ed.) 1998: 131–156.

SHER, Gila 1991: *The Bounds of Logic*. Cambridge, MA: MIT Press.

— 1996: Did Tarski Commit 'Tarski's Fallacy'? *Journal of Symbolic Logic* 61: 653–686.

— 2008: Tarski's Thesis. In D. Patterson (ed.) 2008: 300–339.

SOAMES, Scott 1987: Direct Reference, Propositional Attitudes, and Semantic Content. *Philosophical Topics* 15: 47–87.

STRAWSON, Peter 1952: *Introduction to Logical Theory*. London: Methuen.

— 1957: Propositions, Concepts, and Logical Truths. In Strawson 1971: 116–113.

— 1971: *Logico-Linguistic Papers*. Suffolk: Methuen & Co.

TARSKI, Alfred 1933: Some Observations on the Concepts of ω-Consistency and ω-Completeness. In Tarski 1969: 279–296.

— 1935: The Concept of Truth in Formalized Languages. In Tarski 1969: 152–268.

— 1936: On the Concept of Logical Consequence in Tarski 1969: 409–421.

— 1941: *Introduction to Logic and the Methodology of Deductive Sciences*. Transl. by O. Helmer. Oxford: Oxford University Press.

— and R. Vaught 1956: Arithmetical Extensions of Relational Systems. *Compositione Mathematica* 13: 81–102.

— 1960: Truth and Proof. *Scientific American* 220: 63–77.

— 1969: *Logic, Semantics, Metamathematics*. Transl. by J. H. Woodger. Oxford: Oxford University Press.

— 1986: What are Logical Notions? *History and Philosophy of Logic* 7: 143–154.

— and S. Givant 1987: *A Formalization of Set Theory without Variables*. Providence: American Mathematical Society.

THOMASON, Richmond H. (ed.) 1974: *Formal Philosophy. Selected Papers of Richard Montague*. New Haven and London: Yale University Press.

— and R. C. Stalnaker 1973: A Semantic Theory of Adverbs. *Linguistic Inquiry* 4: 195–220.

VAN BENTHEM, Johan 1989. Logical Constants Across Varying Types. *Notre Dame Journal of Formal Logic* 30: 315–342.

VAN HEIJENOORT, Jean (ed.) 1967[a]: *From Frege to Gödel: A Source Book in Mathematical Logic, 1879–1931*. Cambridge, MA: Harvard University Press.

— 1967[b]: Logic as Calculus and Logic as Language. *Synthese* 17: 324–330.

WILLIAMSON, Timothy 2007: *The Philosophy of Philosophy*. Malden: Blackwell.

WITTGENSTEIN, Ludwig 1922: *Tractatus Logico-Philosophicus*. Transl. by C. K. Ogden. London: Keagan and Paul.

— 1929: Some Remarks on Logical Form. *Philosophical Occasions 1912–1951*. J. Klagge and A. Nordmann (eds.). Hackett Publishing Company 1993: 2–35.

WOODS, Jack 2017: Characterizing Invariance. *Ergo* 3/30: 778–807.

Index of Names

Abelard, Petrus 23
Anderson, R. Lanier 73
Aristotle 134
Armstrong, David 73 f., 83

Balcerak-Jackson, Brendan 57
Barrett, Robert 64
Bays, Timothy 19
Bealer, George 38
Belnap, Nuel 136
Bolzano, Bernard 22 ff., 51, 132
Bonnay, Denis 136
Boole, George 168
Brandom, Robert B. 15
Brun, Georg 9

Carnap, Rudolph 53, 75.
Chomsky, Noam 55
Corcoran, John 88
Cresswell, Max J. 57

Davidson, Donald 18
de Jong, Willem R. 73
Dummett, Michael 29, 135
Dutilh Novaes, Catarina 101, 134 f., 144

Eckardt, Regine 57
Etchemendy, John 4 f., 16, 18 ff., 27 ff., 31, 51, 54, 60, 76, 79., 85 ff., 117
Evans, Gareth 56

Feferman, Solomon 136
Fiengo, Robert 61
Frege, Gottlob 65 ff., 70, 119., 168
Freitag, Wolfang 37 ,39, 70, 110

Givant, Steven 141 f.
Glezakos, Stavroula 70 f.
Gödel, Kurt 19, 168
Gómez-Torrente, Mario 19, 28, 85, 88, 143, 148
Goodman, Nelson 65
Grice, Paul 133

Hanson, William H. 46, 85, 148
Harman, Gilbert 18
Hawthorne, John 61
Higginbotham, James 57
Hintikka, Jaako 168 f.
Hodges, Wilfrid 87
Hossack, Keith 120 f.

Jané, Ignacio 19
Johnson, William E. 94 f., 97

Kant, Immanuel 72 f.
Kaplan, David 18, 61
Katz, Graham 57
Katz, Jerrold J. 73, 75 f.
Klein, Felix 136
Kripke, Saul 28, 165 f.

Lepore, Ernest 61
Lewis, David 23, 39, 74, 118
Lindenbaum, Adolf 136
Löwenheim, Leopold 88, 168

Mautner, Friedrich I. 136
May, Robert 61
McBride, Fraser 119
McCarthy, Timothy 139, 143, 145 ff., 153 ff., 157, 160 f.
McConnell-Ginet, Sally 57
McFarlane, John 46, 101, 107, 136 f., 117 f.

McGee, Vann 136, 147 f., 145, 161 f.
Menzel, Christopher 34
Mönnich, Uwe 38
Mostowski, Andrzej 136
Montague, Richard 10, 37, 45, 57

Parsons, Terrence 57
Patterson, Douglas 85
Plato 11
Pollock, John L. 123
Popper, Karl R. 24, 117
Priest, Graham 85, 92 f.
Prior, Arthur 135
Putnam, Hilary 166

Quine, Willard V. O. 15, 53, 63 f.

Ramsey, Frank P. 133 f.
Ray, Greg 19, 28, 85, 88
Rayo, Agustin 88
Read, Stephen 16, 71 f.
Russell, Bertrand 38, 40 f., 44, 50, 67, 80, 83, 118 ff., 125 ff., 129, 139, 168

Sagi, Gil 47, 106, 155
Sagüillo, José M. 88
Sainsbury, Mark 54
Salmon, Nathan 68 f.
Schaffer, Jonathan 39
Schröder, Ernst 168
Searle, John 95
Shapiro, Steward 46
Sher, Gila 19, 28, 85, 88, 120, 136
Soames, Scott 40
Stalnaker, Robert C. 57
Strawson, Peter 11, 62 ff.

Swift, Jonathan 23
Tarski, Alfred 6, 11., 18 ff., 42 ff., 50 f., 53, 61 f., 85 f., 88 f. 93, 99, 131 f., 136, 141 f., 144, 165 f., 171, 168
Thomason, Richmond 57

Uzquiano, Gabriel 88

van Benthem, Johan 136, 139
van Heijenoort, Jean 168
Vaught, Robert 18, 44

Williamson, Timothy 2
Wittgenstein, Ludwig 17, 82 f., 118 f., 123, 168
Woods, Jack 155

Zinke, Alexandra 37, 39, 110